D1487125

THE HUDNUT YEARS
IN INDIANAPOLIS

The
HUDNUT
YEARS
in
Indianapolis
1976-1991

William H. Hudnut III

WITH CONTRIBUTIONS BY
Mark S. Rosentraub and Others

INDIANA UNIVERSITY PRESS

BLOOMINGTON AND INDIANAPOLIS

The paper used in this publication meets the minimum requirements of
American National Standard for Information Sciences—Permanence of
Paper for Printed Library Materials, ANSI Z39.48-1984.

Manufactured in the United States of America

Library of Congress Cataloging-in-Publication Data

Hudnut, William H., date.
The Hudnut years in Indianapolis, 1976–1991 / William H. Hudnut
III, with contributions by Mark S. Rosentraub and others.
p. cm.
ISBN 0-253-32829-2
1. Hudnut, William H., date. 2. Indianapolis (Ind.)—Politics
and government. I. Title.
F534.I353H833   1995
977.2′52043′092—dc20   94-37239

1   2   3   4   5   00   99   98   97   96   95

With sincere gratitude
to the members of the mayor's staff and cabinet
January 1, 1976, through December 31, 1991
Indianapolis, Indiana

Contents

❦ PART ONE. **FROM INDIA-NO-PLACE TO INDIA-SHOW-PLACE**
           William H. Hudnut III

Illustrations follow p. 132

❦ PART TWO. **ACADEMIC CRITICS**

❧ PART THREE. CITIZEN CRITICS

FOREWORD:

URBAN AMERICA IN THE

HUDNUT YEARS

Peter A. Harkness

Governing American cities in the late 20th century has been hazardous duty, requiring guts, ingenuity, flexibility and resolve. To a great extent, how you fared depended on where you were and when. A touch of affluence did wonders for your ability to provide good government. An eroding tax base and mounting social problems were close to impossible to overcome—a quagmire many mayors understood all too well.

Starting in the late 1960s, the decline of American manufacturing began to change the urban equation. A whole population of people dependent on the traditional supremacy of the United States in steel, autos, glass, rubber, and other basic industries for dignified and meaningful work were suddenly either out of work or were giving back pay and benefits. The career path veered to the lower-skill service-sector jobs that paid less and carried few benefits.

Urban unemployment soared. By 1985, unemployment in many inner cities in the Northeast left two of three working-age black men without jobs. The employment disaster left communities ripe for the invasion of new illegal drugs, including the cheap and powerful crack cocaine that swept through the country in the 1980s.

The Reagan era saw a boom in sectors of the economy that, though they benefited the nation generally, were of little direct help to most inhabitants of inner cities. The finance, real estate, and retail sectors in particular did well. And certainly the overall buoyancy of the economy helped the larger cities, particularly those on the two coasts and in metropolitan areas that were sufficiently diversified to absorb the shock of lost manufacturing.

Boston became the locomotive pulling all of New England. New York, buoyed by an infusion of foreign cash, rose from the indignity of its brush with bankruptcy in the mid-1970s to become the new mecca for the legions of ambitious financial whiz kids who orchestrated the leveraged buyouts and rode the red-hot equity markets that made them overnight millionaires, the kind of people so vividly described in Tom Wolfe's *Bonfire of the Vanities.* Los Angeles prospered as its aerospace and defense industries surged, banking and finance expanded, and its port capitalized on trade with Asia. Seattle also enjoyed the uplift in aerospace and interest in Asia, as well as positioning itself as the capital of the Pacific Northwest. The Atlanta metropolitan area strengthened its position as the economic hub of the New South, attracting capital and business not only from the northern United States but also from Europe. Almost all the Florida cities—Miami, Orlando, Tampa–St. Petersburg, and others—grew like topsy.

That was the upside. The expanding economy helped soften the blow of the downside—another trend in the Reagan era—the abolishment or cutback in urban and social programs. In fact, the pinch started a couple of years earlier, in 1978, when the Carter Administration, worried about the budget deficit and under pressure to increase defense expenditures in the face of new Soviet aggressiveness, began pulling back the throttle on aid to cities. In the same year, angry California voters passed Proposition 13, slashing local property taxes by half and hooking the state on a frenetic economic development jag to expand the necessary revenues to meet demand.

But it was in the early years of the Reagan Administration that Washington put on the brakes. The most significant cuts in urban aid were in three central programs: the Comprehensive Employment and Training Act of 1973, or CETA, which was expensive and politically controversial but had helped poorer citizens make it through the crippling recession of 1981–82; the Urban Development Action Grants, which were more popular and in many places effective in revitalizing downtowns; and revenue sharing, President Nixon's program for returning federal revenues to localities without strings attached. Community Development Block Grants also were reorganized and reduced. Transfer payments to individuals generally were unaffected and in fact grew during the 1980s, but the aid to governmental entities was reduced substantially.

Overall, federal aid to cities was cut almost in half in the 1980s. The direct line city governments had established to Washington, circumventing the states, was severed. Like it or not, cities were forced to depend less on the federal government and more on their state legislatures, which traditionally had not been sympathetic to their needs.

The other phenomenon of the Reagan era, one that was beyond the control of any local political leader, was the wave of mergers and acquisitions of large companies—some friendly, others hostile, but almost all of them resulting in economic dislocations, substantial layoffs, and sometimes the end of hometown control over major community institutions: large private employers, financial institutions, the local newspaper or television station, the regional airline. Ownership slipped out of town with the signing of documents written by high-priced lawyers in faraway boardrooms. Local leadership was replaced by executives on temporary assignment representing an "absentocracy" that saw particular cities not as home but as one of many assets in its far-flung organizations. The trend became so widespread that some state legislatures desperately drew up plans to protect home-state companies. But it was hard to control. It left local elected officials with a well-warranted feeling of powerlessness. They in fact could exert less and less control over national and international economic forces that could have immediate and significant impact on their cities, for better or for worse.

So, for the cities, the economic good times bore mixed results. While the overall economy was strong, corporate restructuring took its toll at the same time that aid from Washington was reduced and employment in manufacturing continued to contract.

Though often reluctantly, most cities did their best to adjust to the new political equation, and began establishing relationships with their state governments. By the end of the 1980s, direct aid from states had to a great extent replaced or reduced federal aid. Local governments began to change the tenor of the relationship with their business communities from adversarial to cooperative and even, in some cases, downright chummy. In many areas, local political leaders and officials from the chambers of commerce worked together to market their communities, improve their workforces and create an atmosphere conducive to economic development.

Whether by intention or not, the Reagan White House helped out. The administration had altered federal tax law in such a way that

Ronald Reagan might well go down in history as the greatest urban architectural preservationist ever to occupy the White House. The tax break for preserving historic structures that went into effect in 1981 was so generous that whole downtown redevelopments were centered on restoration projects that probably never would have been economically feasible otherwise.

A common pattern developed, with downtown redevelopment anchored by an old marketplace, a train station, or a former working harbor converted to a "festival" mall. In some cities it worked, most notably in Boston with its Quincy Market, Baltimore with its inner harbor, Seattle with its Pike Street Market, Atlanta with its rejuvenated underground, and Washington with its train station. But it could be a risky business, and many failed: Flint, Toledo, and Richmond, among others. The Indianapolis experience is related and critiqued in this volume.

Another anchor was convention centers, high-priced ventures that often had dubious direct payback. As with the marketplaces, in some cities they attracted enough new commerce to justify themselves. But most lost money. The question was whether the commerce they attracted to the surrounding hotels, restaurants, and nightclubs made it worth it. As more cities built centers, even while the convention business remained flat, the proposition became dicier. The same could be said for many of the public-sector counterparts, entrepreneurs in their own right, who cut deals with the private developers, offering city land, development rights, and tax abatements in return for a remaking of downtowns in their own vision.

Real growth in the nation's metropolitan areas was happening. By the end of the 1980s, more than half of the country's citizens lived in metropolitan areas with populations of one million or more. One quarter of them lived in the seven largest such areas.

The question was where most of the growth occurred and who benefited from it. For central city mayors, the underlying numbers were not good. Despite the downtown boom, most of the jobs, the housing, and the accompanying commercial activity were moving to the suburbs. And despite the glitter and polish of downtown business districts, they increasingly were becoming islands of affluence in a sea of decaying and isolated neighborhoods populated mostly by minorities and recent immigrants.

Most of the millions of new jobs created in the 1980s did not wind up in center cities. More and more companies shifted their operations to further-out suburban areas, seeking cheaper rents, transportation, and labor. Even the prestigious downtown law and accounting firms, financial institutions, and corporate headquarters moved their back-shop operations out of the city. It was the continuation of a movement that had started in the 1950s and accelerated during every decade since, facilitated in large part by the creation and maintenance of accessible highway systems and by a federally guaranteed program of home finance.

As the companies and the jobs and the housing and the attendant services moved farther and farther out from the core cities, political power followed. Documented by the 1990 census and mandated by the subsequent redistricting of political boundaries, the suburbs and exurbs were poised to exert newly discovered political power, largely at the expense of inner cities. Forty years ago, as the migration to the suburbs was just beginning, almost one-third of the nation's population was classified as urban, less than a quarter suburban, and nearly one-half rural. By 1990 more than half the population lived in the suburbs and exurbs, with the cities and rural areas splitting the remainder. The census showed that the closer-in ring of suburbs hardly grew during the 1980s, and many began to assume the same demographic characteristics of the cities they surrounded. The explosive growth of the decade was in the outer suburbs. It was in these areas that the new political muscle was being flexed as state legislatures and the U.S. Congress were rearranged, with the cities, especially of the Northeast and the Midwest, relinquishing seats to the burgeoning suburbs and exurbs.

And there might have been more to it than that. "Big cities are becoming a code name for a lot of things," Cleveland's mayor Michael White complained, "for minorities, for crumbling neighborhoods, for crime, for everything that America has moved away from."

In any case, even the most generous states soon found that they could no longer afford to support their cities, because by 1990 the commercial real estate bubble had burst, and it was clear that the bloom was off the economy. In fact there had been a recession rolling around the country for years, starting in the states of the industrial Midwest in the early 1980s; spreading on down to the states of Texas, Oklahoma, and Louisiana, as well as Colorado and Wyoming; moving up through the agricultural heartland; and then—finally—to the two coasts. At that point, the whole nation was affected. As the real estate pyramid began to crumble, a compromised savings and loan industry unraveled, triggering what, in terms of real damage to the public, was the most significant financial scandal in U.S. history, calculated at $500 billion in losses. The high-rolling developers went bust, and many of their lenders followed right behind. Taxpayers were left to pick up the tab.

For inner cities, the collapse was a calamity. Frantic developers tried to unload properties at fire-sale prices. Rents plummeted. Tenants began maneuvering to cut costs either by moving into new buildings at cut-rate prices or threatening to do so, thereby depressing rents in established buildings. As city assessments caught up with the reality of the market, property taxes went into a nosedive. Consumer spending fell, so state sales tax revenues suffered. For the two preceding decades, at least, cities had been expanding their services, particularly to the disadvantaged. Now the twin pincers of recession—increased demand generated by the downturn coupled with depressed revenues—put urban governments in a serious squeeze.

Hard times demanded a new kind of leader, one less concerned with building and developing and more with managing. As noted, how well you fared depended, to a great extent, on where you were. Tight budgets focused attention on expenses, and particularly on levels of public employment. In the largest cities, especially in the Northeast, the statistics were disturbing. In a number of cities, public employment continued to increase during the same years that the urban population declined. More than half of local payrolls were eaten up by salaries. The American Federation of State, County, and Municipal Employees figured that during the decade of the 1980s, middle-management positions increased twice as fast as the positions they were managing. The disparity seemed most pronounced in school systems, where the number of administrators, as opposed to teachers, emerged as an issue nationwide.

"There's a little bit of good in austerity in that it makes it possible to do hard things that you can't do in good times," noted Richard Nathan, an eminent urban scholar and head of the public affairs school at the State University of New York in Albany. "This is a good time to attack the management issues, politics being what they are."

Unquestionably, politics as they are had changed. Budgets had tightened. Money for cities—either from the feds or from the states— no longer was a given. The private sector had endured significant restructuring throughout the 1980s and on into the 1990s, leaving a lot of taxpayers impatient with governments that were unwilling to do the same. In some cities, political leaders simply cut expenses across the board, without much attempt to make hard decisions about what services might be jettisoned altogether. As it became clear that hard times were not going to disappear anytime soon, though, more governments began a process of "rightsizing," or prioritizing which services the city must deliver and which it could drop. That was a lot easier in some places than others.

In general during the early 1990s, every city in the nation had to raise more revenue, cut services, or both. How much depended on how deeply the recession had cut into the local economy. How difficult it was depended on the political climate and history. What might be relatively easy to achieve in Phoenix, Charlotte, Orlando, or Portland could turn tense and ugly in New York, Cleveland, Philadelphia, or Washington. How fast and how far the older cities moved depended on how hard they were pushed.

The economic slowdown at the turn of the decade may have marked a turning point for most cities. Their support from Washington had been disrupted by the Reagan Administration and the deficit. Their reliance on their states had been shaken by severe cost-cutting. There was a growing reality that they were—to a great extent—on their own.

One would think, given all these circumstances, that the near-term future for cities was completely bleak, but that was not entirely true. There were at least five reasons.

The first reason involves a definition of terms. The worst conditions in urban America were concentrated in a comparative handful of cities. There were many others, particularly in the South and West and particularly those of middle size, that—though they had problems—were far better off. The 1990 census showed that about the same number of citizens lived in cities with populations of 100,000 or less as lived in the larger, core cities of 100,000 or more. Many of these smaller cities had grown up in the suburbs of the larger metropolitan areas, where most growth has occurred. By and large, they were far better off than the inner cities.

Second, there were early signs that urban reform and renewal might well come from the bottom up rather than the top down. In some of the nation's worst-off areas, public, nonprofit, and private leadership in communities was beginning to enjoy some small successes in attracting new business, renovating and building housing, improving some schools, and providing some jobs. What was common to efforts in these and other cities was that they all germinated in the communities themselves, not at some higher level or authority. They therefore were far more reflective of what people in the neighborhoods actually saw as their own needs, rather than what someone from the outside prescribed for them. That homegrown genesis meant that citizens in the affected areas had ownership in the programs, most of which were nurtured and administered by local nonprofit community development organizations.

Third, many cities and their suburbs were reexamining their relationship with one another. Suburban leaders were beginning to understand that for their region as a whole to prosper, the relative health of the inner core was relevant, since many potential investors and businesses tended to identify a region by the reputation of its center city. The result has been a lessening of the adversarial relationship between city and suburban leaders and more attempts at cooperation on issues involving economic development. Even in cities like Detroit, where city-suburban relationships traditionally have been contentious, officials realize that a further deterioration of the inner city serves no one's interest except those of competitive regions. In Indianapolis, a consolidation of city and county government and services, called Unigov, centralized government services under a mayor elected countywide and a city-county council. Unigov broadened the tax base by incorporating suburbs into the city and created a more unified approach to development.

Now Detroit's mayor, Coleman Young, and the leaders of four surrounding counties have formed an ad hoc group to work on regional problems involving the region's image, infrastructure, and the siting of future development. They also decided that any future stadium for the Detroit Tigers must be located in the city—a sharp departure from what happened to the football franchise, which now plays in a dome located in neighboring Pontiac. Indiana's Hoosier (now RCA) Dome too was built in the center of downtown to counter the forces that so often pulled development and citizens to the surrounding suburbs. Regionalism could work because leaders of both government and business perceived a conjunction of interests. Economic development in the region meant a healthier overall economy, which translated into higher tax revenues.

Fourth, not everyone who fled the cities for the jobs and quality of life in the suburbs was white. Beginning in about the mid-1970s, middle-class black families also migrated from inner cities either to more stable neighborhoods within the city or to closer-in suburban areas, reestablishing a pattern seen before in urban history. These newly populated neighborhoods, where black, Hispanic, and Asian families moved, were identified and described by Richard Nathan and other political and social scientists as "zones of emergence." The movement to them is reminiscent of past migrations of the Irish, Italian, Jewish, German, and other ethnic groups that escaped the squalor of one neighborhood and bought their own homes in a better area to raise their children and live their lives. It appeared to be happening again.

Finally, many state and local government leaders realized both that there no longer was anyone from above willing or able to help them work through problems and that their own governments were not capable of doing it themselves without significant reform. Public managers stood at the same precipice as their colleagues in the private sector a few years earlier. Just as those companies that were smaller, more flexible and less rule-bound had adapted faster than the behemoths of heavy industry, the same was true in government.

To some extent, the book *Reinventing Government: How the Entrepreneurial Spirit Is Transforming the Public Sector,* simply chronicled what already was going on in different governments around the country. But the book, merely by staying on the *New York Times* best-seller list for two months, underlined the changes that were taking place and gave them some coherence. Elected officials, in particular, were attracted to many of the principles outlined in the book; city managers and other professionals tended to be more skeptical about achieving some of the shifts in thinking and behavior the authors called for. In effect, the "r-word" movement—to remake, reinvent, reengineer or rightsize government—was a call to make public organizations behave more like those in the private sector. The authors, journalist David Osborne and former city manager Ted Gaebler, understood the differences between public and private organizations, but were still convinced that the top-down, inflexible, rule-and-regulation-ridden management systems developed during the Progressive Era to protect governments from the big-city political machines had outlived their usefulness. They argued that many of the wrenching changes made in private companies—flattening the bureaucracy, pushing decision-making lower, emphasizing results, providing incentives—would help make government work better, too.

A less ebullient economy and tighter budgets changed the tenor of the times. Through much of the country the emphasis seemed to be shifting from concern over the interests of the individual that had dominated since the 1970s to those of the community. A new sense of reality dictated that those who sought help from government must accept some personal responsibility as a quid pro quo.

The quality and brand of leadership was an important part of the mixture. Some mayors were a lot tougher than others. When the economy had been robust and downtowns were enjoying the development boom, mayors who could forge coalitions with their business communities, market their cities, and direct the course of development fared well.

Andy Young, a former ambassador to the United Nations, positioned Atlanta as an international city; Bill Frederick managed to have Orlando keep pace with the dizzying development in his region, as did Pete Wilson in San Diego; in Indianapolis, Bill Hudnut focused resources and community pride on an "amateur sports capital"; in Baltimore, William Donald Schaefer and his successor, Kurt Schmoke, and in Cleveland, George Voinovich and his successor, Mike White, all had success in holding together the business base in their older industrial cities while slowly but effectively rejuvenating their downtowns.

Some mayors were known as boosters (Ed Koch in New York), others as superbly competent and forward thinking (Charles Royer and his successor, Norm Rice, in Seattle; Terry Goddard in Phoenix; Kathy Whitmire in Houston; Dick Riley in Charleston), some as master politicians able to please disparate constituencies (both Richard Daleys in Chicago, Ray Flynn in Boston), and some managed to survive politically for long stretches against great odds (Bill Morris in Shelby County/ Memphis, Tom Bradley in Los Angeles, Coleman Young in Detroit, Don Fraser in Minneapolis, and Hudnut in Indianapolis).

Ed Rendell gained quick national recognition as the mayor who saved Philadelphia from financial ruin, mostly by renegotiating union contracts. In Chicago, "Richie" Daley launched an extensive program of privatizing public services, in effect challenging the public employee unions that had been such an integral part of his father's political machine of decades earlier.

Given that mayors could not affect the great political, social, and economic trends that shaped their regions, the quality of the leadership they exerted with the cards they were dealt looks impressive across the sweep of the past three decades. And that is true in a time when there was great concern about lack of leadership at other levels of government and elsewhere.

This book contains the story of governing in one Midwestern city during the ebullient and the tough times. Indianapolis is known among urbanologists nationally as a success for a number of reasons: its Unigov system of consolidated government, its successful economic development efforts, and its defiance of the trends in its region. As much as anything, though, it is the story of good, visionary leadership over an extended period. For anyone looking forward to the challenge facing urban America in the next decade, it is a story worth studying.

Peter A. Harkness is the Editor and Publisher of Governing *magazine, which he founded in 1987. It reports on state and local government issues and is published by Congressional Quarterly.*

PREFACE AND
ACKNOWLEDGMENTS

"Fellow citizens of this 'no mean city,'" I began many speeches during my tenure as mayor of Indianapolis. This Biblical phrase appears on the cornerstone of the old City Hall (now the Indiana State Museum) at Ohio and Alabama in downtown Indianapolis. I liked it and used it often during my sixteen years in office to signify the high and affectionate regard in which I held the city I felt privileged and honored to serve.

So when, toward the end of my time in office, Mark Rosentraub, associate dean of the School of Public and Environmental Affairs at Indiana University and director of its Center for Urban Policy and the Environment, started talking with me about writing a book on Indianapolis to describe the years I served as mayor, I was interested. I thought it would give me a chance to summarize those "Hudnut years" and pay a final tribute to the people who worked with me in building a better city and to the citizens of Indianapolis themselves.

A city is people. Its most important asset is the pride, the will, the strength of spirit, of its people. And Indianapolis, "where the sun always shines, the grass is always green, the flowers always bloom, the chuckholes are always filled, the snow is always plowed, the trash is always picked up, and the Colts and Pacers always win" (again, as I said often, with a touch of hyperbole, in welcoming remarks to conventioneers come to town for meetings and fun) is blessed with such people.

In addition to my own thoughts, I believed it might be useful, interesting, and helpful in placing these sixteen years in a more objective and responsible perspective if I invited others to participate. I did not want these pages to be viewed as a self-serving encomium. So I asked a number of academic colleagues and friendly critics if they would like to join in, and they all responded enthusiastically. The foreword is intended to establish the context of urban America for the Indianapolis story that follows. The academic pieces, analyzing what happened in Indianapolis during the Hudnut years from the vantage point of professorial expertise, appear in the middle part of the book, along with a group of critical essays by citizens of our city who view the events of these years from perspectives that differ from mine. I hope that the collection of these observations brings balance and spice to the book, and I express my sincerest appreciation to all the contributors.

One thing I did not do was respond to the critics, where I thought their points were unfair or inaccurate. That struck me as quibbling. I did not read their pieces before I wrote my sections of the book and decided that it would be best to let theirs and mine stand, without engaging in rebuttals. I leave it to the reader to consider the merits of each case, with only the observation that truth usually lies between opposing viewpoints.

Toward the end of my time in office, I wrote a number of former mayoral colleagues around the country whom I had known, worked with, and come to respect, asking them if they would share with me their thoughts about what they had learned during their experiences in public life, to the end of including some of their observations in this book. I want to thank them, too, for their responses, and have endeavored to include most of them.

I trust that it is not too immodest to hope that this book can serve as a case study in urban management and leadership at a critical juncture in American urban history as well as a readable account of the years in which Indianapolis emerged as a major American city. Cities are the laboratories in which the experiment in American democracy is being conducted. There is no guarantee that the experiment will succeed. But in some instances it has worked fairly well, as I believe it has in Indianapolis. Experiences we had here, lessons we learned, problems we coped with, initiatives we undertook, may be useful to others who are interested in problems of governance in urban America, and possibly this narrative can serve as a useful recapitulation of the events and issues that dominated the Indianapolis scene in the 1970s and '80s. That, certainly, is my hope.

In addition to the contributors, I would like to thank Teresa A. Bennett of Indiana University's School of Public and Environmental Affairs for her substantial contributions to the editing process, and John Gallman, director of Indiana University Press, who made invaluable suggestions all along the way as the book developed. My colleagues at the Kennedy School of Government's Institute of Politics at Harvard, where I began this work after leaving the mayor's office, and at the Hudson Institute in Indianapolis, where I finished it, provided me with the intellectual stimulation and freedom to work on this project, for which I am most grateful. Thanks to Cindy Higbee, Sam Karnick, and Anita Selig of the Hudson Institute, who spent many hours working on drafts of the manuscript, and the photo librarian at the *Indianapolis Star* and *News,* Charlotte Means, who helped assemble the photographs. I also appreciate critiques offered by former colleagues in City Hall: Deputy Mayors John Krauss and Dave Frick, Directors of Metropolitan Development Dave Carley and Mike Higbee, Controller Fred Armstrong, and Press Secretary Dave Arland. Needless to say, errors of fact or interpretation are mine, no one else's. And for her input as well as her steadfast and loving encouragement, I owe a special debt of gratitude to my wife, Beverly.

In truth, there's no such thing as a self-made man or woman. I am acutely aware that the growth of our city in the 1970s and '80s represented the fruits of a team effort and was not a solo performance. Consequently, I also want to thank the workers in City Hall— trash collection crews with whom I used to pick up and put down the garbage, engineers, landscape architects, accountants, secretaries, planners, administrators, police officers, firefighters, and a whole host of others—who performed the often unsung jobs that provided the public with those services that made Indianapolis a "city that works." Additionally, since government could not accomplish its goals by itself, I want to pay tribute to those who helped from the private sector: men and women, civic leaders all, whether heralded or unknown, CEOs or rank-and-file, in the business and professional community, in organized labor and the philanthropic and social-service organizations, in neighborhood organizations and political offices, who served their city without pay in various volunteer capacities, forming essential components of the public-private partnership that orchestrated the emergence of Indianapolis as a major American city. And finally, above all, to the men and women who were members of the mayor's staff and cabinet from January 1, 1976, to January 1, 1992, with whom I worked, without whom I could have accomplished nothing, and to whom I dedicate this volume, I express a deep and heartfelt thanks.

WILLIAM H. HUDNUT III
Hudson Institute
Indianapolis
July 15, 1994

WHAT WOULD YOU DO?

William H. Hudnut III

In classes I have taught on urban politics, I have asked students to pretend that they were the mayor of Indianapolis and to think through what they might do in various situations. In this exercise I present a dozen or so real-life situations I faced during my 16 years as mayor and ask students to conjecture about how they would respond to each challenge. The chart lists the situations on the left and my own responses on the right. In every case, I had to decide on the best course of action and then proceed, recognizing that not everyone would agree with my decisions. What would you have done if you had been in my shoes? Possibly you might have chosen other paths.

Some of these situations will be described in greater detail in the following pages. For now let me observe that three themes seem to emerge as I reflect on how my colleagues and I addressed these 12 challenges.

The first theme is that there are not necessarily any right answers in matters of urban governance and leadership. For example, we were severely criticized by elements of the African-American community for our handling of the shooting of Michael Taylor in 1987 (situation number 10 in the chart). On a radio program where I took calls from the public, the Police Department was accused of executing the young man, and many callers wondered why the police officers involved in the incident were not fired on the spot. Critics called the disciplinary actions ultimately taken against the officers too lenient. The city was scolded for engaging in a cover-up of essential facts.

Here's another example. A lot of folks have second-guessed our efforts to promote downtown revitalization. They suggest that we

IF YOU WERE MAYOR, WHAT WOULD YOU DO IF . . .

WHEN I WAS MAYOR, HERE'S WHAT WE DID . . .

1. The city was called Naptown, India-no-place, or Brickyard in a Cornfield and had a decaying downtown?

1. We began working at improving our city's image. We hoped that through a proactive approach utilizing amateur sports to promote our city and a conscious public policy aimed at reversing downtown deterioration by generating new development, jobs, amenities, and housing, we could turn our city's image around. We were not completely successful, but we made a start.

2. You had an opportunity to build a 60,000-seat domed stadium but had no National Football League team to put in it?

2. We built the stadium anyway and got in the hunt for an NFL franchise.

3. AT&T told you on a Tuesday afternoon that the next morning it was going to announce the closing of your city's Western Electric plant, which employed 8,700 persons?

3. With Indiana's governor and lieutenant governor, I journeyed to the New York headquarters of AT&T to protest the decision, but to no avail. So I appointed a task force to discover new uses for the 1.8-million-square-foot building and set our employment and training people to the task of working with the employees who were laid off.

4. You became aware that even though your city had not been invited to join the competition, 92 other cities were vying for a United Airlines maintenance facility that would employ 6,500 persons at an average annual salary of $45,000, and it would probably

4. We became the 93rd city in the hunt and ended up first.

cost about $300 million to close a deal with UAL?

5. You had made a decision to terminate a police take-home car program because the expense was too great, and while you were away on vacation, you received a call from the deputy mayor advising you that the police were picketing the City-County Building in protest?

5. I came home from vacation early with my family. By the time we reached Indianapolis, the sirens and emergency blinker lights had been turned off on the police cars that had encircled the City-County Building, the keys thrown in a big basket had been unscrambled, and the city had returned to normal. I held firm on my decision to end the take-home car program because I honestly believed the city could not afford it any longer.

6. The city was running out of landfill and you still had the responsibility of picking up and disposing of 2,200 tons of trash a day?

6. We found an alternative to landfill to dispose of the trash.

7. The Children's Defense Fund announced out of the blue that your city had the highest big-city infant-mortality rate in the nation, worse than some "third world" countries?

7. I publicly stated my concern, brought the issue to a public forum in the Greater Indianapolis Progress Committee, put together a consortium of public- and private-sector interests to bring resources to bear on solving the problem of infant mortality, and squeezed an allocation of $3 million into the city budget, with the support of a City-County Council committee that had been holding simultaneous hearings on the subject.

8. As the United States Congress was planning to terminate general revenue sharing ($12 million for

8. Even though the decision involved considerable political risk and it would have been easy to

your city) you discovered that within 15 years the police and fire pension funds would have a deficit of more than $90 million?

pretend the problem did not exist, we enacted a local income tax to cover the shortfall and plan for avoiding the rainy day.

9. The federal Justice Department filed a suit to force you to dismantle an affirmative-action program that had been in place for nearly ten years, working, it appeared, to everyone's satisfaction?

9. We fought 'em, tooth and nail!

10. An African-American teenager, after being arrested by police, given a pat-down search, and handcuffed and placed in the back seat of a police car, ended up dead, shot in the head when a police officer came around the car to let him out at the Juvenile Detention Center?

10. We referred the killing to the appropriate authorities outside the Police Department—the FBI, the U.S. Justice Department, the coroner, and the prosecutor—for investigation and appropriate action, as well as to the Firearms Review Board and other disciplinary units within our public safety framework. The police chief also held an unprecedented news conference detailing the facts of the shooting as openly and forthrightly as he could. Ultimately we appointed a Human Relations Task Force to provide a citywide public forum where citizens could express their views on this highly controversial matter, and we forwarded recommendations from the task force to the Police Department and City-County Council for implementation.

11. A group of African-American clergymen, upset over police-action shootings, held a news conference on the steps of City Hall demanding that the police chief and mayor resign?

11. I did not resign nor ask the police chief to do so.

12. You felt that far too many high school students were dropping out?

12. We set up a program called Invest Indianapolis, an effort to forge a compact with students stating that in return for staying in school and graduating with acceptable grades, local businesses would give them first preference in hiring if they were not going on to college.

should have kept the government out of the picture altogether, or that we failed in what we wanted to accomplish because the projects we put together are not generating a positive cash flow, or that we provided too many incentives to private developers. These are all valid points of view, I think, but they are not ours. We did the best we could with the options and facts before us and must let it go at that.

Or again, consider the matter of the Colts football franchise moving to Indianapolis from Baltimore in 1984. The mayor of Baltimore and his constituents obviously had another point of view about it. They expressed their view very effectively in lawsuits accusing me of being a conspirator to deprive them of their rights and property, even though I had called the mayor two months before the event occurred to tell him that Indianapolis was entering the competition for the Colts franchise along with several other cities, to which he responded, "Fine, no problem. Good luck. May the best city win." There also were pros and cons to consider on the home front. I took a day to weigh the positives and negatives. In the end, was I right to conduct the negotiations with the Colts and enable the Baltimore franchise to move here? I believe so, even though not everyone agreed. As I recollect it, on the day we announced that the Colts were coming, Judson Haggarty, a local Democratic party leader, held a news conference complaining about the money we had put into the Hoosier Dome and the Colts deal, opining that it would have been better spent on filling potholes and building low-income housing.

Lincoln said it best: "The true rule in determining to embrace or reject anything, is not whether it has any evil in it, but whether it has more of evil than of good. There are few things wholly evil or wholly good. Almost everything, especially of government policy, is an inseparable compound of the two; so that our best judgment of the preponderance between them is continually demanded." Indeed, if we cannot act on a project until all possible objections are removed, nothing will ever be accomplished.

The second theme that arises from our handling of the 12 challenges is this: stand firm; don't back down; trust yourself. Do the best thinking you can, make your decision, and stand by it. Don't be a weathervane; be a gyroscope. Don't be a wet-finger-in-the-air politician whose every action and statement is conditioned by the latest poll. Do what you think is right, and let the chips fall where they will. Thus we resisted when our city was sued by the federal Justice Department to abandon our commitment to equal opportunity through affirmative action. I did not yield to pressure to resign or to change my decision on the take-home car program. We instituted new taxes to build the Hoosier Dome and to fund the police and fire pension programs.

In matters of governance, people need a clear decisive word. Most citizens are not concerned about the nuances of policy. Academics may counsel finessed, fine-tuned solutions. But the people need to hear yes or no, go or no go. They deserve leadership, not pusillanimous poll reading, from their elected officials.

Occasionally, of course, reversing the field and admitting a mistake is prudent. We did that, for example, in our efforts to rebuild an old downtown public-housing project. In the late 1970s, when we were trying to develop a plan for the renovation of Lockefield Gardens on Indiana Avenue deep in the heart of the African-American community in downtown Indianapolis, one idea I embraced was to raze all the buildings and start fresh with new construction. The place had fallen into acute disrepair since the last tenant had moved out years earlier. When I journeyed to Washington with others to testify in behalf of demolition (federal dollars were involved), I was astounded at the reaction in our African-American community. I realized how wrong I had been. I had tremendously underestimated the affection for this particular space among local residents. It was part of their heritage. We were considering destroying their roots, and they did not like it. Their objections to our plan were cogent, so we changed our minds, backed off, and found a compromise: tear some of the buildings down, rehabilitate others, and build some new ones.

Leadership for the most part stands firm, however. Near the end of my time in office I asked several mayoral colleagues what they had learned during their terms as mayor. Ed Koch of New York replied, "The lesson that I learned from my experience as mayor is to have confidence in yourself. . . . And once you make a decision, unless the facts or your conclusions have changed, stick with it!" Ray Flynn of Boston responded, "I have learned that there are times when you have to move forward with a mayoral decision, even if that decision is highly unpopular." And Mayor Jerry Abramson of Louisville, who was faced with clearing land and displacing 4,000 persons from their neighborhoods to build an up-to-date airport, said that the greatest lesson he learned was that "someone must be willing to step forward, develop a plan, put it on the table, and stand behind it. It is the only way to make a difference."

I like the phrase "make a difference." That's the third theme to be found in our responses to the 12 challenges: making positive things happen. A mayor sees the positive possibilities in events and looks upon crises as opportunities. So we have high infant-mortality rates in our city? Let's start a Campaign for Healthy Babies and change the statistics. So AT&T is abandoning its huge plant on the east side of town? Let's help those workers in their various transitions and then find a new use for the building. So kids aren't finishing high school? Let's get the business community involved in a compact with them to provide the skills and motivation they need to graduate and then find meaningful work.

The most important political event during my terms of office does not appear on the list of challenges, but it was a challenge nonetheless. The blizzard of 1978 left our city absolutely paralyzed. If we had floundered in our attack on the snowdrifts, cabin fever would have turned to outrage, and the perception that I could not handle the management job in a big city would have gained a strong foothold in the body politic. But it did not turn out that way. Through almost hourly appearances on radio and TV and ceaseless efforts out in the field with the work crews, I was able to convey a feeling to our community that we were going to overcome this problem. A challenge became an opportunity.

In 1994 I received a letter from someone who recalled the events of another severe snowstorm that paralyzed our city, in January 1982. "I was at the State House that day doing a bit of lobbying for the Library Association when snow started falling," the letter read. "Literally within minutes it developed into a deluge, leaving the city no opportunity to get ready for it. By 4 P.M. I was gridlocked in the biggest traffic mess I ever experienced. Then Mayor Hudnut came over WIBC telling the folks that we were under attack. 'This is war,' he said, 'and we are going to win it.'" Concluded the writer: "that, to me, is what leadership is all about. Insofar as your mayoral service is concerned, I think its capstone was its ability to inspire the community toward many high and lofty goals, all the time keeping its eyes on the prize down the road."

Leadership is a job, not a post. One is not magically endowed with it because one assumes a position; one has to work at it, develop it, earn it. Really good mayors possess an ability to lift their community's sights above the mundane and transitory to a vision of what their city can become. They inspire people to come together, believe in themselves, and cooperate for the common good. Such leaders know the value of preaching a vision and continually reaffirming it. They bring enthusiasm, energy, commitment, and pride to their work and thus persuade people to embrace their goals, somewhat as Lincoln did when the renewal of America's vision of freedom and equality expressed in his speeches reinforced the American spirit in dark times. Vision distinguishes true leaders from mere managers. Ultimately, for the mayor, the governor, the president, and the corporation head, the role of manager is less important than the role of leader, articulating a vision and direction and appointing good managers to work on making it real.

I had had no special education for the mayor's job. Professionally, I had received my training as a clergyman, and after having served for 15 years in churches in Buffalo, Annapolis, and Indianapolis, I had run for the United States Congress in 1972 and been elected. Two years later, in the backlash against Republicans over Watergate, I discovered that so many people missed me back in Indiana's old 11th Congressional District that 51 percent of them voted for me to come home. In other words, I lost. I ran for mayor in 1975 and was fortunate enough to be elected, then reelected to three succeeding terms in 1979, 1983, and 1987. In 1991 I decided that 16 years was enough, that I needed new challenges and the city needed new leadership. As the venerable Charlie Halleck, one of Indiana's best-known congressmen, once remarked, there are three ways to leave office, and two of them aren't any good. I left the good way—voluntarily.

Serving as mayor of the nation's 12th-largest city was extraordinarily satisfying. The mayor sits where the action is, in the midst of a turbulent flow of events that is exciting and challenging. Having been a clergyman, I entered politics viewing public office in terms of service. I occupied the mayor's office to address human need and help people solve their problems. My goal was to make life better in the community where our citizens lived and worked, providing them the infrastructure of services, such as trash pickup and snow removal, streets and sewers, zoning and parks, within the context of which their lives would flourish. I always tried to be people-oriented and customer-sensitive and wanted our City Hall workers to be the same. As I frequently reminded our staff over the years, "We never get complaints, just opportunities for service

. . . and lots of them!" One of the first things I suggested after coming into the office on the 25th floor of the City-County Building was to change the words on one of the doors from "Neighborhood Complaint Division" to "Neighborhood Services Division."

My aim was always to make positive things happen. I had a proactive philosophy of government, not a caretaker one. I believed that it was not always true that that government is best which governs least. Of course, this aphorism applies to the regulatory and tax burdens government places on individuals and businesses, but I believe that a position of leadership in an executive branch of government provides a person with ample opportunity not to sit back and merely avoid mistakes or risks but to make good things happen for the community.

I wanted Indianapolis to become a greater city as a result of my stewardship of the office of mayor. I wanted to develop a public policy that would assist our city in attracting business and creating jobs, holding the downtown core, improving neighborhoods, and sensitizing our citizens to the special problems minorities face. Such policies would help counteract the forces of deterioration that lurk in the shadows of urban America. I could have watched passively as nature took its course. But in my heart and mind I believed that I was not elected to run an administration averse to taking risks. It is my hope that a fair assessment of the Hudnut years would conclude that many positive things happened in Indianapolis and that the revitalized city became a better place, with an enhanced national reputation.

George Latimer, the former mayor of Saint Paul, believes that a city can be viewed in four ways and that a mayor serves a different role for each, although all four are obviously entwined. The mayor is the "chief economist" for the city as economy, a place where jobs are generated, investments stimulated, and tax base hopefully widened; the "celebrator, and sometimes the mourner," to the city as community; the "architect" of the city as space or place, that is, as a known, defined environment; and the CEO in the city as corporation. Latimer, in an unpublished paper, suggests, quite correctly, that the view of the city as community "comes closest to the deepest sense of what a city is at its heart," because it has to do with a sense of interdependence or connectedness, of all being in one boat together. What is a city if not a set of connections that, by choice or by chance, govern, bless, and occasionally cripple our lives?

One of the kindest compliments I ever received came from a Democratic mayor when she introduced me for a speech after I had left office. Said Margaret McGovern, mayor of Greenwood, Indiana: "Bill Hudnut made it look easy, and he made it look fun." It is true in sports and the arts that the better the player, the easier he or she makes it look, and I am grateful for Margaret's words. I loved the job, the city, and the people, and during my 16 years in office I discovered the truth of the old saws about management being the art of getting things done through people. I discovered that the mayor is not so much at the peak of a pyramid as at the center of intersecting circles, an insight originally offered by Robert A. Dahl in his book *Who Governs?* about governance in New Haven, Connecticut (Yale University Press, 1961).

Whatever the final assessment, I enjoyed it all—putting deals together, touching bases to build consensus, forming strategic alliances, working with members of the City-County Council and the state legislature, riding on a snowplow during a blizzard, pitching trash with the solid-waste collectors, parading on Saint Patrick's Day in a green leprechaun outfit, cooling off at a sprinkler on a torrid summer day with neighborhood kids, preparing the annual budget, presiding over planning that would affect the city's built environment, giving speeches about Indianapolis around the country and indeed the world, eating lunch with senior citizens or workers in a plant cafeteria, clipping ribbons, filling chuckholes, turning shovels of earth at groundbreakings, reading to children in the local libraries, resolving concerns at a neighborhood association meeting, reconciling differences of opinion, establishing a stronger commitment to diversity, holding receptions in the mayor's office for young people who had made significant achievements, bridging gaps of misunderstanding between the Police Department and the community in one tense meeting after another, discussing plans with department heads on a weekly basis, saving the Indiana Pacers, welcoming the Colts, attending concerts, conducting the Indianapolis Symphony, touring local theaters and art galleries, going on four radio stations each month to talk with the people, visiting fairs and festivals, holding news conferences, cutting airline spots for TV, power brokering, reviewing plans and designs that would change the face of the city, campaigning in the bowling alleys, knocking on doors. Being at all those places day after day was hard work, to be sure, but the inner satisfaction of working with people to advance goals and build a better place in which to live and work and raise a family was very satisfying and enjoyable. I wept when I let go of it after 16 years.

PART
ONE

FROM

INDIA-NO-PLACE

TO

INDIA-SHOW-PLACE

William H. Hudnut III

Indianapolis,
Now and Then

Into the life of every city there comes an occasional vintage year. For Indianapolis, 1991 was such a year.

It began with the city hosting the National Collegiate Athletic Association's Final Four, men's basketball championship. Sixty thousand visitors poured into the "bannered and blooming" city in early April. Only three-quarters of them could actually attend the games in Indianapolis's new stadium known as the Hoosier Dome (rechristened the RCA Dome in 1994), but there was much to do outside the facility for those who could not get in—such as shooting baskets in a nearby street roped off for that purpose. Events that travel with the Final Four—parties, lunches, dinners, receptions of all kinds—spread good cheer through the assembled throng. The weekend had an economic impact in the neighborhood of $39 million, but its boost to the city's civic pride and enhancement of its national reputation were more significant in the long run.

The year also brought to Indianapolis the World Gymnastics Championships, another successful event, thanks to the meticulous hard work of the local organizing committee and hundreds of volunteers. World-class athletes from more than 50 countries participated, and the event generated positive publicity in all those countries for the host city.

At approximately the same time the United States Postal Service announced its selection of the city for a new $62-million mail-sorting facility, confirming that Indianapolis could compete successfully for economic development projects as well as athletic events. The city had already landed a Federal Express sorting facility for the Indianapolis airport, making it a secondary hub to Memphis, and USAir had built a large reservations-booking facility on the site. The project would provide 750 new Postal Service jobs for the Indianapolis area, using 100 empty acres at the airport that had been landbanked across the years for just such an opportunity.

In mid-October, builders poured concrete to begin foundation work for a downtown retail mall to be known as Circle Centre. A controversial and frustrating project, the mall had taken too long to pull together, and people were becoming impatient. The timing was difficult because a general business restructuring and an economic downturn in commercial real estate—coupled with a credit crunch—had made investors skittish and financing more difficult to obtain. The mall required $150 million of front-end investment by the city to assemble the land for the site and prepare it, a process of razing several empty buildings that left eyesore holes in their wake. These holes became objects of ridicule, complaint, and politicization. But the signing of an agreement between the city and the development partnership made further progress possible. The start of work on the foundations suggested forward movement; in time the mall would become a reality.

Then, within days, the governor of Indiana and I joined with the chairman of United Airlines to announce that UAL, one of America's strongest airlines, had picked Indianapolis as the site for a new billion-dollar facility to maintain its expanding fleet of Boeing 737s. UAL promised to build a three-million-square-foot complex at Indianapolis International Airport that would produce 6,300 permanent new jobs within 12 years at an average annual wage and benefit package of $45,000. The project would also generate an estimated 12,000 temporary construction jobs and some 18,000 to 20,000 spin-off jobs, providing a ten-year economic impact of more than $1 billion.

Not since 1984, when the Baltimore Colts and the Hudson Institute moved to Indianapolis and the Pan American Sports Organization selected Indianapolis to host the 1987 Pan American Games, had so much excitement and drama been packed into a 12-month period in the city. People around the country must have scratched their heads in amazement. Indianapolis? Naptown? That sleepy midwestern brickyard in a cornfield? How could it be?

Accolades poured in from the media after the Final Four in early April. "Indianapolis is in a league of its own," one sportswriter said. By their own admission, sportswriters tend to be a jaundiced lot, but they waxed uncharacteristically poetic about the Circle City. Some even suggested that Indianapolis, along with New Orleans, should become a permanent site in the rotation for the Final Four. They "oohhed" and "aahhed" over the Hoosier hospitality and organizing skills; the handsome, accessible venues; and the clean downtown. "One of the best setups I've ever seen." "Perfect." "India-no-place is a great place." "There's not another complex in the country that can match the convenience of Indianapolis with its hotels, the Dome and the convention center." And a local sportswriter concluded: "The Final Four goes away and life goes on. But it is my belief that our city and many of its citizens from all walks of life have been enriched by the event in ways that have nothing to do with economic impact. Like many of us, I remember what Indy was like in the old days. I would challenge anyone who says our overall quality of life hasn't improved significantly. And the ability to stage events such as the Final Four is part of the reason."

After the announcement of the United Airlines decision, similar comments about Indianapolis appeared in newspapers around the country. The *New York Times* labeled the decision "a victory for the city and Indiana." In Oklahoma City—one of the four finalists, along with Denver and Louisville—the headline read: "Can-Do Attitude Credited for Indianapolis Successes." One Denver newspaper called the UAL project "one of the nation's biggest economic development prizes," and another wrote, "This isn't the first time others have underestimated the city that was once known only for auto racing or dismissed as 'the neon cornfield.' Indeed, Indianapolis has established a reputation as an economic development pit bull." A local paper's headline read, "United deal strikes development experts as savvy work," and the *Washington Post* spoke of the city's "renaissance." A survey of top executives judged Indianapolis "the tenth best city in the United States in which to do business."

In 1985 *Newsweek* wrote about Indianapolis as "the Cinderella of the Rust Belt."[1] The city had been transformed from "India-no-place" to "India-show-place." When a new mayor, Stephen Goldsmith, replaced me in 1992, he said, "In the past decade, Indianapolis had become a role model for cities throughout the United States. It is a magnet for amateur sports, for economic development, and for a burgeoning cultural scene."[2] Indianapolis had developed a positive image around the country. For generations the city's problem had been lack of any image whatsoever. Not that it had a negative one; it was just neutral, neither bad nor good, just mayonnaise on white bread.

Looking back, old-timers said that Indianapolis had come a long way. Founded in 1821 "in a vast mud-hole," as one pioneer girl wrote in her diary, Indianapolis became an important link in the nation's highway, canal, and railway systems, adopting "The Crossroads of America" as its motto. To this day, transportation has played a crucial role in the city's development. The New York Central Railroad built "the world's largest locomotive hospital" in Beech Grove. At one time, Indianapolis was "the interurban capital of the world" and housed the world's largest traction (electric trolley) terminal. The city developed as a warehousing and distribution center and began growing hometown industries such as Eli Lilly and Company, which opened its doors as a small pharmaceutical business in 1876.

By the turn of the century Indianapolis had become "the first capital of the early auto industry" as carriage makers, millwrights, and bicycle makers became auto manufacturers.[3] Their plants turned out more than 60 kinds of cars, including some of America's most famous, such as the Marmon, Stutz, Duesenberg, and Chevrolet. In 1913 Indianapolis ranked second in auto production, but it disappeared from the list of the top ten cities by 1920 owing to competition, high business mortality, and what historian Edward A. Leary called the city's industrial "hardening of the arteries."[4] The city's love affair with the automobile had started, however, and has yet to end. Indeed, mass transportation never caught on very well in Indianapolis because people loved their cars too much. In 1911 the first Indianapolis 500-Mile Race was held, and the city has been known ever since as the home of the 500, "the greatest spectacle in sport."

The golden days of the city's history were the 50 years between 1871 and 1921. Then, giants strode across the stage—distinguished persons such as President Benjamin Harrison and his wife, Caroline; famous men of letters such as Booth Tarkington and James Whitcomb Riley; the great industrialist Colonel Eli Lilly; the founder of the *Indianapolis News,* William Fortune; the automotive geniuses Carl Fisher and James Allison; the Hoosier School painter T. C. Steele; Madame C. J. Walker, the nation's first black female millionaire; and Vice-President Charles Warren Fairbanks.

Those days, however, mellowed into twilight. The auto industry moved to Detroit. International labor unions moved to Washington. (John L. Lewis had set up his United Mine Workers office originally in Indianapolis.) During World War II, the city was known as "Toolmaker to the Nation."[5] Many local firms were merged or sold to become divisions or subsidiaries of national corporations.[6]

The outside world looked on Indianapolis as a sleepy, stolid, blue-collar manufacturing town. It was a smoky, grimy city. In *Inside USA,* published in 1947, John Gunther described Indianapolis as "an unkempt city, unswept, raw, a terrific place for basketball and auto racing, a former pivot of the Ku-Kluxers." He condemned Indianapolis as the "dirtiest" city in the United States. In its politics the city was decidedly conservative, and Gunther spoke of its "trenchantly conservative labor leaders."[7] Leary, the city's unofficial historian, who wrote a history of the city for the 150th anniversary in 1971, pointed out that "perhaps nowhere in America were the social and economic reforms of the New Deal fought more bitterly."[8] The city exhibited a definite bias against federal aid until the late 1960s (the city's public schools in those years even refused to accept surplus federal agricultural commodities for school lunch programs), and the John Birch Society was founded in the Indiana capital in 1958. The city is home to the American Legion, with its beautiful mall of greenspace in the heart of downtown, and the people love the flag and are strongly patriotic.

Some have called Indianapolis the "most southern" of all the northern cities, and they are embarrassed by the fact that the Ku Klux Klan achieved great power in the state during the 1920s. The city was racially segregated. Oscar Robertson's famous state champion basketball teams of the late 1950s played out of Crispus Attucks, a segregated high school. When the Presbyterian Church held its annual national General Assembly in Indianapolis in 1959, the delegates were appalled to find places where African-Americans were not welcome, and when I moved to Indianapolis in 1963 as a 30-year-old Presbyterian minister to assume the pastorate of one of the city's largest and most influential parishes, one of the first things I heard about was the snubs that blacks received in that meeting. A national race-relations survey conducted in 1965 had Indianapolis worse than the South in racial segregation.

Meanwhile the demographic trends that characterized post–World War II America—analyzed so capably by Dennis R. Judd in *The Politics of American Cities*—affected Indianapolis.[9] Growing suburbanization began to tighten a noose around the midwestern industrial city by limiting its spatial growth and bleeding off a disproportionate share of the affluent population. The population inside the noose was becoming increasingly composed of minorities and poor people. This process set up the dichotomy that most older cities faced as the 1960s unfolded: between suburbs and inner city, which is to say, between white and black, rich and poor. Fragmented political jurisdictions were juxtaposed to one another without many cohesive forces to hold them together.

As the drama of an evolving city unfolded in the mid-1960s, Indianapolis was ripe for positive change and new leadership. Attitudes and positions were shifting subtly. A transformation was beginning, and it would soon touch every facet of the city's life. As Leary writes, "The city that had moved so reluctantly from small town to big town, the city once described as a place of 'dynamic nostalgia,' the city where visitors were advised to turn back their calendars to the nineteenth century, appeared to have cut its umbilical cord to the past."[10] Indianapolis was poised on the threshold of a new stage in life, during which it would come of age and emerge as a major American city.

Laying the
Foundations of
a Renaissance

A description of Indianapolis's transition from no-place to show-place has to begin with two important events that occurred in the 1960s and early '70s: the formation of the Greater Indianapolis Progress Committee under Mayor John Barton (1964–67) and the establishment of Unigov (unified government) under Mayor Richard Lugar (1968–75). Anyone who accomplishes anything stands on the shoulders of those who went before. Acknowledging indebtedness is a form of maturity that sometimes escapes elected officials, who tend to want all the credit for themselves and consequently ignore the contributions of their predecessors, publicly bragging that all their accomplishments are brand new and that they started from scratch. So it must be said publicly and gratefully that the Indianapolis renaissance referred to by the media in 1991 had its roots in these two initiatives. They laid the transforming foundations on which the modern city has been built.

The first initiative was the founding of GIPC by Mayor Barton and two private-sector leaders: Eugene S. Pulliam, publisher of the *Indianapolis Star* and *News,* and Frank McKinney, Sr., chairman of the American Fletcher National Bank. They perceived that for Indianapolis to grow and progress in the last third of the 20th century, the city would need a forum in which to discuss ideas relating to its needs and problems. The founders of GIPC had three significant insights: (1) the future is now, (2) cooperation can often achieve more progress than confrontation, and (3) the dialogue in a democracy is more important than the specific agenda item being discussed. Therefore, they asked, why not pull together a group of concerned citizens from the private sector to advise the mayor and serve as a sounding board? The only ground rule was to be that the Progress Committee would not be politicized. Partisan politics would be kept at bay. Political operatives would not be hired as its executive directors. Its membership would include identifiable Democrats and Republicans, public figures, but also private citizens whose motivation was solely the betterment of the city in which they lived, not their personal political aggrandizement.

The organization of GIPC marked the beginning of the public- and private-sector partnership for which Indianapolis became well known during the next quarter century. Starting small, with movers and shakers meeting around a table, GIPC grew from an elitist organization into a broader-based one that included leaders from neighborhoods and organized labor, representatives of different constituent groups such as the Jaycees and the League of Women Voters, and state and local elected officials, while business and professional leaders always constituted the dominant numbers. GIPC membership was fluid, and its meetings were open to the public.

In telling the Indianapolis story around the country, I have discovered that many cities do not have such a forum for communication, in which local leaders and decision makers can gather around one table to address an urgent issue—but they would like to have one. In community after community there is a real yearning for such an expression of partnership, but it will never materialize unless the chief local elected official has the inclination and the ability to bring people together.

In Indianapolis, whatever was on the city's agenda was grist for GIPC's mill. In the late '60s it might be housing or drugs; in the '70s, neighborhood or downtown revitalization; in the '80s, clean air, infant mortality, or minority business. We invited the committee to discuss plans for our city in sports, transportation, and medical technology as areas for economic development. The media frequently covered these discussions. Deliberations often led to positive actions. The Greater Indianapolis Housing Development Corporation was a child of GIPC, as were the Clean City Committee, a downtown revitalization plan known as Indianapolis 2000, the Campaign for Healthy Babies, the Community Desegregation Advisory Council, the Community Addiction Services Agency, and a plan for the development of Eagle Creek Park and Reservoir, the second largest municipal park in the country.

GIPC helped provide public information about the work of the

Government Reorganization Task Force, which led to Unigov. It prepared the applications that resulted in two All-America City awards from the National Civic League. Its Waterways Task Force was instrumental in the modernization of the old Indianapolis Water Company Canal to make it a beautiful downtown amenity. It held public hearings on issues of importance to the city, such as whether an interstate highway should be built to connect downtown with the suburbs and the development of a state park in downtown greenspace. The Central Indiana Council on Aging would never have come into being without initial work by the Progress Committee, nor would the Lockefield Gardens housing project in the downtown area have been renovated.

One example of the Progress Committee at its best came in the late '70s, when the community was troubled by the issue of court-ordered busing for racial balance in the public schools. While serving in Congress (1973–74), I had taken a strong stand against busing in favor of neighborhood schools. But as the chief executive officer of the city, I believed that we should comply peacefully and responsibly with the federal judge's order that 5,500 minority students be bused to suburban schools in the outlying townships, regardless of whether or not we agreed with the court's decision. After all, we are "a government of laws, and not of men," as the original draft of the Massachusetts Constitution phrased it so well in 1779. Therefore I asked GIPC to address the problem, hoping to resolve a potential conflict before it arose by bringing different constituencies together to discuss the issues and formulate a game plan.

The result was a task force known by its acronym, PRIDE—Peaceful Response in Indianapolis to Desegregated Education. The chairman of GIPC and I had many meetings with school officials, and the task force pulled together law-enforcement officials, clergy, media, parents, educators, and concerned citizens to map a strategy for compliance that would avoid the confrontations cities such as Boston had experienced.

The task force formed subcommittees to deal with such issues as how to escort and, if necessary, protect the children in the buses, how the media should be encouraged to cover the issue, how messages from pulpits would be given, how the receiving schools would react, and how to support parents of the children who were bused. As a result, the desegregation process occurred without uproar. After the busing began, when problems were identified at certain schools, they were dealt with within the schools, although sometimes there would be a meeting or rally involving leaders from the broader community—such as the mayor, a local pastor, a representative of the NAACP, or well-known sports figures. Following the initial developments, the Community Desegregation Advisory Council was put in place to provide continued counseling and technical assistance to schools and pupils involved in the desegregation process.

Although there is a difference between desegregation and true integration, Indianapolis was spared much of the pain other communities experienced in the process of implementing court-ordered busing. The Progress Committee deserves much of the credit.

Throughout its more than a quarter century of existence, the Progress Committee has rendered an important public service by facilitating discussion of a large number of public issues. Open, honest exchanges among concerned citizens about what a city's problems are and where it is going are vital to any community. The work of GIPC has been to air opinions, face problems directly rather than pretending they do not exist, bring troublesome matters up for public focus, bring leaders together to talk and deal with difficult questions, decide on constructive courses of action to meet community needs, and develop consensus. GIPC has served the city well.

Working with the Progress Committee revealed what I understand to be one of the primary functions of the mayor of a large city. The mayor is like an orchestra leader, trying to bring harmony out of the potential for urban cacophony. There are many different parts to play, many different lines and notes, and the mayor's job is to reconcile it all into a musical whole. Not everyone will always agree, but the mayor must bring people together rather than drive them apart. The mayor is a consensus builder. It takes considerable time and quiet work behind the scenes, but such work eventually pays off.

The second initiative that helped lay a firm foundation for the emergence of modern Indianapolis was the consolidation of city and county government in Indianapolis and Marion County, known as Unigov. Without Unigov, Indianapolis would still be Naptown. The revitalization and entrepreneurial development of the past 20 years would not have been possible. When this consolidation of city and county government occurred, Indianapolis became the 12th-largest city in the United States overnight, jumping from a population of 525,000 to a number half again as large. Unigov came into being on January 1, 1970, after the Indiana General Assembly passed the authorizing bill and the governor signed it into law.

No crisis prompted the formation of Unigov. It was precipitated by reformist zeal for better services at lower cost. Its chief cause was "the frustrations of the fractionated pre-Unigov system," as one observer put it. Ironically, no documented needs assessment or comprehensive outside study preceded the effort, much less a formal commission to look into the matter. According to C. James Owen of Indiana University, the motive for the change boiled down to a growing frustration over problems presented by a divided city-county relationship.[11] Mayor Lugar phrased the problem in a rhetorical question: "Why are eight different authorities responsible for drainage, five for transportation, and so many for the development of the four thousand acre Eagle Creek Park, that the whole lake is becoming a quagmire of frustration and not a park?"[12] The solution seemed clear: make the mayor the chief executive officer of both city and county by consolidating 47 previously separate boards, agencies, and commissions into a strong mayor system with a cabinet style of management in which a few large departments operate the city's business.

To be sure, supporters of Unigov had to overcome formidable obstacles to make their vision a reality. After community leaders made their initial assessment of the situation, they had to build a social consensus and allay substantial anxiety among voters. People feared that their taxes would rise if Unigov caused local government to become "bigger." They also supposed that fire and police protection would decrease if these agencies had larger areas to cover. They worried about local school systems and small political entities being homogenized into one huge monolith. There was also a rush to protect turf—a natural human tendency. Some citizens expressed concerns that the inclusion of predominantly white suburbs would drastically dilute minority participation in local affairs. Supporters had to reckon with apathy, self-interest, and resistance to change. Nevertheless, during the late 1960s they formulated a game plan, generated support, enlisted political leadership, and engaged in public discussion. The proposal was ultimately carried.

The Unigov system centralized local government services under a mayor elected countywide. Six departments—Public Safety, Metropolitan Development, Parks and Recreation, Transportation, Public Works, and Administration—would report to the mayor and were given the responsibility for handling the nuts and bolts of city operations and maintenance. The plan established a 29-member City-County Council (probably, in retrospect, too large), with 25 single-member districts and four at-large delegates. Thought was given to the creation of "minigov" units in neighborhoods to decentralize authority and responsibility and lodge it in the hands of citizens serving on "minicouncils." These minigovs would help decide how tax dollars would be spent in their districts on city services and economic development. The idea, however, was never given formal structure, and as the '70s unfolded, most grassroots involvement was confined to ad hoc task forces set up to deal with specific issues. "Minigov" still lies on the back shelf awaiting implementation.

Unigov established independent municipal corporations to run the bus company, airport, health and hospital apparatuses, libraries, and certain municipal buildings such as the Convention Center, if they did not already exist, as well as a series of municipal and superior courts. The legislation, operating on the assumption that a division of power prevents any one branch of government from becoming too powerful, divided appointive responsibility for boards and agencies among the circuit court judge, the City-County Council, the county commissioners (the treasurer, auditor, and assessor, most of whose powers were eliminated under Unigov), and the mayor. Nine elected constitutional county offices—treasurer, clerk, recorder, coroner, auditor, sheriff, prosecutor, assessor, and surveyor—remained intact.

Unigov did not consolidate the schools, public safety, or taxes, and it protected the independence of a few cities and towns within the boundaries of Marion County—Speedway, Lawrence, Beech Grove, and Southport—as well as county and township offices. Politics is the art of the possible, and to attempt a complete consolidation of all units of government in Marion County would have doomed Unigov to failure before it started. People wanted to retain their grassroots organizations, their volunteer fire departments, and their schools.

As it was, the benefits of this partial consolidation soon became evident. First, it streamlined government and made the delivery of services more efficient by eliminating overlapping jurisdictions and centralizing accountability. One Department of Transportation was better than eight; a single authority to decide the best depth for Eagle Creek Reservoir was better than a multiplicity. Unigov gave each department enough scope and authority to move the city quickly in the direction it wanted to go. City management was put on a par with the private sector so that the two could become working partners.

Second, Unigov reduced costs by effecting economies of scale and by setting in place the basic principle that you don't pay for services you don't receive. One student of Unigov, a Pulliam Fellow working for the

Indianapolis News, collected information to the effect that "Indianapolis officials claim to have saved $600,000 the first year by simplifying governmental machinery, $150,000 a year by streamlining city and county insurance contracts, $84,000 a year by purchasing in bulk, and $123,000 by pooling legal assistance. They also claim to have increased the city's interest yield sixfold by centralizing investments."[13]

Third, Unigov broadened the tax base by incorporating the suburbs into the city, which provided a stronger, more stable financial grounding. Although it is impossible to trace a precise correlation between Unigov and the favorable (Aaa) bond rating Indianapolis has enjoyed for two decades, there is an indubitable connection. And this is important, because a high rating for a municipality's bonds means that when the city floats them for capital improvements, the taxpayers pay less because the interest rate charged is lower.

Fourth, Unigov created a wider sense of community. Structures attract individuals, and Unigov made service in local government a more attractive option for bright, talented people. It also helped people who lived on the periphery of the city to identify with what was going on downtown. It provided a more united front for the development of an aggressive marketing strategy for the city. With less political infighting between city and suburbs, we could market the city better. And contrary to what some people had feared, Unigov did not dilute the role of minorities in local government. Although the advent of Unigov undoubtedly made it more difficult for an African-American to be elected mayor, the new City-County Council reflected the same percentage of minorities as the expanded city did. Unigov also created a base upon which new metro initiatives could be launched, such as the late-1980s effort to establish a countywide emergency communications agency to deliver emergency services to the citizenry efficiently, utilizing the latest technology available.

Finally, the reformist spirit generated a good deal of civic pride. People's enthusiasm for the initiative—and the self-confidence that resulted from accomplishing such a major undertaking—enlarged people's expectations about what like-minded individuals could accomplish in a community if they set their energies to work. A progressive spirit took hold, which had as much influence on subsequent successes as the actual reform itself. Professor Owen wrote of an "infectious success image" in Indianapolis, and he quoted a former Democratic state official and civic leader, Larry Conrad, as saying in 1984, after the Colts arrived and the city began planning for the 1987 Pan Am Games, "No place in the country can boast about having so many people moving in the same direction regardless of race, sex, creed or political affiliation. Whether you talk about sports, the arts, education or something else, there is just a feeling here that we can do damn near anything we want to."[14]

Of course, Unigov had its critics. They advanced several arguments against the proposal. Some Democrats said—and continue to say to this day—that the consolidation was a blatant political power grab by Republicans, a claim that the powerful Marion County Republican chairman of the time, L. Keith Bulen, did not dispute. Other critics complained that a bigger government is always worse, never better. According to this view, a larger, more centralized, consolidated government mutes the voices of citizens, destroys grassroots independence, leads to higher taxes, and diminishes the role of minorities. Some opponents argued that Unigov created de jure segregation and that the at-large council positions were unconstitutional. They filed lawsuits, and in a sense some of these suits remain pending, because the whole question of school desegregation is still under federal court supervision and legal questions about the at-large council positions have yet to be decided.

With regard to these criticisms, it is important to recognize that advocates of Unigov did not expect it to be perfect. Nonetheless it represented a significant governmental reform. Reformation or redefinition of governmental structures always requires vision, courage, and an entrepreneurial spirit. Those who created Unigov possessed these qualities, which I tried to sustain when Mayor Lugar passed the mantle to me at the end of 1975.

Unigov produced a wider integration of functions and services at the local level of government in Indianapolis and Marion County. It met the service-delivery needs of an enlarged population base in areas such as trash pickup, sewage treatment, street and bridge maintenance, parks and recreation, zoning, and economic development. In other metropolitan areas, as the delivery of city services becomes more costly, populations shift, and old boundary lines between cities and suburbs become obsolete, the idea of consolidation will become more common.

In the past 25 years there have been fewer than a dozen attempts to create metro government around the country. Others are thinking about it, however, because as we move toward the 21st century, it seems highly imprudent for governments to remain saddled with archaic 19th-century jurisdictions for service delivery. Wichita and Sedgwick County in Kansas have counted 47 different entities in their community responsible for transportation-related services, for example, and are convinced they can do better. The Denver metro area has struggled to find a middle ground between the undesirable (doing nothing about problems of regional service delivery) and the unfeasible (complete consolidation of the city with its suburbs). Such communities look to Indianapolis as a leader and exemplar in these matters, often attributing to the city a greater degree of consolidation than actually occurred but wanting to learn from our experiences.

The simple fact, as officials at the National Association of Counties have observed, is that as financially pinched local governments scrounge for efficiencies and cost savings, the popularity of consolidation may increase dramatically. Metro government is being considered more widely as an intelligent form of governance for large urban areas, with Indianapolis serving as a model to consider.

GIPC and Unigov together made it possible for modern Indianapolis to emerge. A sleepy midwestern town could be transformed into a dynamic urban center. The Progress Committee supplied the commitment to dialogue in partnership; Unigov provided the governmental mechanism for bringing people together from throughout the county; and both attracted new young talent: bright, energetic, reform-minded men and women who would seek opportunities for public service because they cared about their community and wanted to make a positive difference. Their motto would be Ben Franklin's, as inscribed on the Curtis Publishing Company's boardroom wall in downtown Indianapolis: "We can make these times better if we bestir ourselves."

Forging the
Partnership

When the Lugar years yielded to the Hudnut Administration on January 1, 1976, the seeds of the new Indianapolis had already been planted. They required nurturing to bring them to full flower, and our team made every effort to have a smooth transition that would declare our intention to build on the strengths of my predecessor. Evolution would be better than revolution. We had to keep going in what seemed to me an essentially sound and good direction.

My vision for Indianapolis—easier to perceive in retrospect than prospect—was the development of a city in which people would work together to become competitive with other American cities and would be compassionate in their relationships with one another. A cooperative, compassionate, competitive city—that was my dream.

An essential element in achieving that dream was to engage the private sector and its resources in cooperative responses to the city's problems. If we could broaden the base of participation in the city's decision-making process and forge a partnership between the public and private sectors, both its nonprofit and for-profit components, we would replace the historic mindset of local officials—always looking to the federal government for more money to help solve our problems—with a local approach to problem solving. The cities had been driven to Washington by the Great Depression, but by the 1980s the trend had begun to reverse.

In many ways, government can and should be run like a business, but there are important differences. One difference is the necessity for building consensus. Business is much more oriented toward the chief executive officer than government is. When a public-sector CEO—a mayor, a governor, a president—wants to accomplish something, the board (a city council, a state legislature, a congress) or the stockholders (the public) will not necessarily comply with his or her desires. The public-sector CEO does not carry the aura of authority enjoyed by the private-sector counterpart. Therefore urban leaders should cultivate a participatory philosophy that strives to include many people in the life and work of the city. The hallmarks of an urban leader are coalition building, inclusiveness, sensitivity to people and their concerns, a commitment to serving the citizen-customers as faithfully and responsively as possible, and an effort to pull citizens into the life of the city. Committees and task forces cannot create a spirit of cooperation; that must come from top-down leadership.

In Indianapolis in 1976 it seemed important to give people a sense of ownership and empower them as participants in guiding the life of the city. The time had come to outgrow traditional decision-making patterns in which a small elite handed policy down from the top and everyone else acquiesced, however reluctantly. It was clear that a few white males could no longer dominate the city with benevolent paternalism as they had in the '50s and '60s. The times required the active involvement of many players in government, business, labor unions, civic groups, neighborhood associations, volunteer and educational organizations, and the like to form the kind of working coalition that gets things done.

My colleagues and I took a number of steps to implement this concept of partnership. Our goal was to create an atmosphere of interdependence that would transcend some of the traditional adversarial attitudes among elements of a local community. We believed we could accomplish more by cooperation than by confrontation.

Accordingly we set up a Mayor's Labor Advisory Council, which met with the mayor every month. Its members were union leaders from around the county (mostly from the UAW, AFL-CIO, and Teamsters), and they discussed matters of mutual concern and interest. The only proscriptions were on politics and city union problems—these were rarely mentioned. We gave strong support to a unique program called Operation Top Notch. Indianapolis unions joined management in agreeing to settle interjurisdictional disputes between individual unions before they led to work stoppages on major construction projects. The program worked successfully for 16 years.

We created a Mayor's Handicapped Advisory Council to bring together representatives of persons with disabilities to discuss ways to attend to the needs of this special element in our population. When we built the Hoosier Dome, for example, we paid careful attention to accessibility for handicapped persons.

For several years the mayor and department heads met with neighborhood leaders on a regular basis to obtain their input while making decisions on streets, parks, sewers, and zoning. We called it the Mayor's Neighborhood Advisory Council, and when interest in it began to lag, we embarked on other initiatives to accomplish the same goal of bridge building between City Hall and neighborhoods. With members of his official family, the mayor attended annual meetings of neighborhood and community-based organizations, such as the Nora and Irvington community councils. In 1986 we conducted a series of neighborhood forums, one in each township, where citizens could come and discuss plans and needs for their neighborhoods. These meetings were constructive exercises in town hall democracy that elicited positive responses from local government—millions of dollars of bond issues for sewers and sidewalks, more aggressive action against X-rated business establishments, modifications in road-building plans, zoning changes, chuckholes filled and street signs put up, dead trees taken down, and the like.

We began to formulate plans for a long-range look at our future as a city under a program called Indianapolis 2000. (Many other cities had similar programs, such as the Goals for Dallas program in Texas.) We opened an office on the Circle, in the heart of our downtown, where we could hold public meetings, invite people in to review plans that were taking shape, and share citizens' thoughts and observations with our planners. We installed computer terminals to provide citizens an opportunity for comment; the comments would be duly noted and considered by the planners, and we were pleased that by the end of the process we had received input from more than 2,000 citizens who walked in off the street to provide their ideas about the direction our downtown revitalization efforts should take during the 1980s and 1990s.

With the helpful guidance of Harvey Jacobs of the *Indianapolis News*, we established a Concerned Neighbors Crime Watch, with a coordinator loaned to us from Eli Lilly and Company. Eventually this program became part of the Public Safety Department, with a full-time staff and more than 1,000 block clubs throughout the city. Each block club involved its participants in a dialogue with law-enforcement officials, who used them as extra pairs of eyes and ears in detecting crime. The clubs were also helpful in educating children and adults on the importance of precautionary measures in the fight against neighborhood crime. This was another effort to "pull ownership out of the bureaucracy into the community," as David Osborne and Ted Gaebler describe it in *Reinventing Government.*[15]

Before the city controller and the mayor decided to proceed with a bond issue, we met with business leaders—bankers, bond and securities dealers, bond attorneys, and Chamber of Commerce representatives—to determine how much indebtedness they thought the city could prudently contract. These meetings helped us make important decisions that had a fundamental impact on fiscal policy for our city. With their expertise in financial matters, these individuals relieved us of concerns about whether we should issue debt. After looking at the numbers and analyzing our position, they encouraged us to be bold. We concluded that issuing general-obligation bonds in judicious fashion would not be fiscally irresponsible, and we felt encouraged to proceed along this path. We knew that such bonds would have an effect on the property-tax rate through the sinking funds, but we also understood that we were not just contracting new debt, because simultaneously we would be paying off old debt each year as well. These meetings convinced us that it was not improper or imprudent for a growing city to issue debt if it could be retired in a timely fashion.

In keeping with our goal of promoting greater involvement in the decision-making process and stronger feelings of partnership, we inaugurated a practice of meeting regularly with members of the City-County Council, individually and in small groups, anywhere we could, in their offices or ours, over breakfast or lunch, always with the intention of building bridges of understanding and trust to provide these councillors with a sense of ownership in our programs and instill a desire to move forward. Even though primary responsibility for governing the city lay with the full-time members of the executive branch rather than the part-time legislators, we wanted to create feelings of team spirit with them. We did not want them to feel that we were ignoring them or taking them for granted. We wanted them to consider themselves partners in the exciting enterprise we were involved in— bringing Indianapolis into the modern era, so to speak, by mounting an aggressive economic development program, managing City Hall better, and providing the best possible service at the least possible cost.

We performed much of this consensus building in private, not because we wanted to keep secrets but because we knew how important it was to explain to people what we were doing, to try to get them quietly on board, and to give them a chance for input. Coalition building was the name of our game; developing a cooperative feeling of partnership in our city was our goal; base touching was our strategy for achieving it.

Some radio stations began providing the mayor with opportunities for dialogue with citizens over the airwaves, and I readily accepted these invitations as another way of staying in touch. Over the years, literally thousands of citizens not only had chances for input on a regular monthly basis on four local radio stations but also got action, because our staff assiduously followed up on these calls to make sure that each matter was handled as constructively as possible. We also set up monthly visits to factories, plant cafeterias, and luncheon sites where senior citizens were gathered, to talk with people and find out what was on their minds. Our motto was "Since you can't get to City Hall, we'll bring City Hall to you." We wanted people to feel cared about and involved. We knew that Miami citizens had rioted because they felt cut off from the power brokers. We did not want that to happen in Indianapolis.

We created new organizations to further the public-private partnership. The Corporate Community Council gave private business leaders a place to convene and discuss the best ways to allocate their community resources. Our original motive was to avoid duplicate funding of worthy causes and programs, but members of this council (with the governor, the mayor, and the presidents of Indiana and Purdue universities, who were ex-officio members) gradually moved into discussions of far-reaching topics, such as whether to build a domed stadium and what should be the future of our city.

We started the Indianapolis Project, originally called the Image Project, to work on improving our city's image nationwide. The Chamber of Commerce had commissioned a study by the Fantus Corporation in the early 1970s that had concluded that Indianapolis suffered from a "plain vanilla" image. Near the end of the decade we began to try to establish a positive national image for our city. We hired the New York public relations firm of Jack Raymond & Associates to help us place favorable stories about Indianapolis in the national press. By the early 1980s we were generating much positive coverage on our own, thanks to achievements such as the National Sports Festival (1982). We kept this effort going, however, because it was meeting a growing need for our city to respond to the myriad inquiries we were receiving from media all over the country, and indeed the world, about the Indianapolis revival.

As the notion of becoming the amateur sports capital of the country began to form, we established an organization to help attract sporting events and festivals, the Indiana Sports Corporation. Probably no single organization in Indianapolis was more directly responsible for enhancing and extending the city's national and international reputation. With its fine staff and a board of young movers and shakers, it began promoting Indianapolis as a site for a host of competitions ranging from single events such as the Final Four basketball tournament to multisport extravaganzas such as the Pan American Games. I was often asked whether Indianapolis would bid for the Olympics. My answer was "No, we have a pretty full plate, and I don't think we are big enough to host the Olympic Games." A city has to be what it is and live up to its potential, not try to be something it is not. Indianapolis is not Atlanta or Los Angeles. We do not have the capacity, the housing, or the financial resources to host an event of Olympic proportions.

Another organization we put into place was the Indianapolis Economic Development Corporation. We established it as a point of contact between the city, the state, and the Indianapolis Chamber of Commerce to market our city and pursue new business opportunities for Indianapolis. Upon recommendation of a Progress Committee task force and with the help of the Indianapolis Power & Light Company, we undertook a national search for someone to head this effort, one person working out of the mayor's office. The mayor's office should not run programs, however, and soon this small operation spun off into an independent existence of its own, with a large staff and a quarter-million-dollar budget funded by the city, the state, and the private sector. A board of local business and political leaders supervised its work. The corporation contributed to our efforts to retain local businesses that were thinking about moving out and to assist in expansion of local businesses wherever possible, because local growth provided probably 80 percent of our city's increase in jobs. As an indication of its successful efforts across the years, the corporation prepared a summary of its activities from 1987 to 1991. The report included these figures: jobs retained—29,763; jobs created—16,918; and dollars invested—$2.46 billion.

As the building of a sense of ownership in our city proceeded, legitimate criticisms began to surface. Essentially they boiled down to the notion of too little too late. Not enough. Not enough inclusion, not enough empowerment.

Some critics believed that too many decisions were being made in private. The local newspapers filed a lawsuit to prevent the majority caucus of the City-County Council from making critical budget decisions in closed caucus—and won. A group known as the City Committee, which met informally from time to time to talk about the future of Indianapolis, was criticized for not being open to the public. In a speech to the Corporate Community Council in April 1991, a noted observer of America's urban scene, Neal R. Peirce, said, "The City Committee of the '70s and '80s, for all its brilliance in remaking the downtown, excluded women and in fact reached momentous decisions for your city with less public discussion than any parallel group I've been able to track in any other city."

That statement may have credited the City Committee with more influence than it actually had. Moreover, it glossed over the fact that any city should be happy to have a group of young business and professional leaders getting together because they cared about their community and wanted to help it move forward, not by making decisions about the direction it should take but by brainstorming the subject and sharing ideas with others. Nevertheless Peirce's general thesis that Indianapolis has "a culture of very closely-held decision making, a history of caucuses rather than primaries, a tradition of secrecy," is worth taking seriously. An excessively cynical view, as voiced by one local newspaper columnist, that "an elite club rules [this] city without any of the inconveniences of democracy—accountability, accessibility or the maintenance of an adequate quality of public life," may be extreme, but it does indicate a need for a more open style.[16]

A number of things show progress in that direction. First, many citizens had regular opportunities to make important decisions affecting the life of the city through statutory boards to which they were appointed—merit boards to supervise personnel practices in the Fire and Police departments, Unigov boards to approve departmental contracts, zoning boards to decide on thorny issues that pit developers against neighborhoods, and municipal corporation boards to oversee the programs and operations of the airport authority, the Convention Center, public health, and the libraries. Although the mayor made many appointments to these boards, it was my practice never to tell appointees how to vote on a matter. I wanted to affirm their independence and integrity by not interfering with their decisions or politicizing the process.

Second, we did seek broader citizen participation. We wanted to be as inclusive as possible. People need to feel wanted. Giving them a proprietary feeling about their city—whether they make the actual decisions that affect public policy or simply influence the decisions others make—contributes to their sense of well-being and their self-confidence. We did not want them to feel shut out. If you counted them all up, the number of citizens involved in the local governmental process in Indianapolis would run into the hundreds (the mayor alone appoints about three hundred), not including many part-time elected officials, giving their time, talent, and effort to make Indianapolis a better place.

Third, citizens were given chances to deal with specific problems along the way and recommend solutions. The Tanselle/Adams Commission in the early 1980s (named after its two chairs, a banker and a dentist) and the Task Force on Human Relations in the later years of that decade dealt with police-action shootings and made recommendations to improve relations between the Police Department and the community, many of which led to positive changes in City Hall operations.

The Tanselle/Adams Commission advised changes in police training procedures that were enacted by the department. After the Human Relations Task Force concluded its deliberations, a special ordinance was introduced and ultimately passed by the council and signed into law by the mayor, to establish a Citizen's Complaint Review Board to review and process citizen complaints against the Police Department. It had subpoena powers and could recommend to the police chief disciplinary actions to take against officers found guilty of abusive treatment of citizens or misuse of police powers. It did not have as much authority as some people in the community wanted (for example, it had no power to review police-action shootings that ended in fatalities, because those were to be considered by a grand jury; nor was it a civilian review board), but it provided more citizen involvement in a highly important area, and more citizen power to create change.

Unfortunately, opponents did not give the board a fair chance to succeed. One of its members—a preacher specifically appointed to give representation to African-American clergy who had protested so vociferously against the Police Department—called the board "a dodo bird" that had wings but could not fly. The local chapter of the American Civil Liberties Union opined that it did not "make the grade." The press discounted its potential. Some city councillors even objected to our creating it. Therefore it got off to a rocky start and has a precarious future.

This experience raises an interesting question about empowerment. What if government gives citizens the power to make decisions
and they refuse to accept the responsibility? If the idea was good in the
first place, the answer lies not in taking the power away again but in
fine-tuning the mechanism until it works.

In retrospect, I think we did not involve community groups sufficiently in the work of these task forces. To be sure, the latter represented a goodly cross section of the community, held their meetings in
open forums all around town, and issued tangible recommendations
that were subsequently implemented. But we were never able to
develop an effective working relationship of trust and respect across the
lines that divided blacks from whites and police from community. We
created some short-term goals to allow for some modest successes, but
neither the community nor the press nor the Police Department ever
really took them to heart. Consequently those elements of the minority
community that were disaffected with the Police Department remained
so after the task force's work was completed. Cynicism and suspicion
continued, to erupt another day.

This problem is not unique to Indianapolis. Police-community
relations in urban America are always prickly. There are no easy
answers. I feel sure, however, that part of the solution lies in open, credible dialogue with broad-based participation. That is why, for years, I
met regularly with the African-American clergy in our city. But more
should have and could have been done.

Fourth, contrary to the argument that democracy in Indianapolis
was insufficiently inclusive or open, we made no important public-
policy decisions without holding public hearings. This process is standard operating procedure. Whether the subject was a zoning board
decision or the adoption of a new tax or user fee, the siting of a landfill
(which was abandoned because the opposition at public hearings was so
vigorous), the construction of a downtown retail mall, the coming of
the Colts, or the landing of United Airlines, the public was not only
informed before final votes were taken but also customarily provided an
opportunity for review and comment. Sometimes, as with the Circle
Centre project and the United Airlines deal, the council's Metropolitan
Development Committee held public hearings when it was not legally
required to and no decisions were going to be made. They just wanted
to keep the public abreast of events.

Finally, the process of building consensus and becoming more
inclusive represented steps toward a more distant goal of community

empowerment. In the late 1970s the city and state faced a difficult decision: whether to extend an interstate through a heavily populated part of the city to connect to the downtown loop. We used the Progress Committee to conduct technical studies and public hearings. No preconceived notion about a "right" answer was in anyone's head. High-income suburbanites who drove downtown to work wanted the project, but people living in the neighborhoods that would be affected—primarily black and poor—did not. The group recommended to the mayor that we should not build the extension and should instead use interstate substitution monies to upgrade existing interstates and intersections in Marion County. The main reason it gave was displacement of people, but two other factors entered: the inordinate cost and the probability that construction of the highway would accelerate an exodus from Marion County to the bedroom communities beyond our borders. The mayor bought the arguments, and so did the governor. This victory was a genuine outcome of community empowerment.

That raises a couple of important public-policy questions. Did we opt for a short-term gain at the price of long-term pain, which is always a tendency in making political decisions? And if the decision was short-sighted, focusing only on the near-term advantages of peace rather than uproar and less cost rather than more, what is the proper role of a city's leadership? Should it develop consensus around what is popular at the moment or move beyond it to the long-term good? One critic of the decision—former Metropolitan Development director David E. Carley—believes that "history will show that this decision did more to encourage jobs to move to the suburbs than anything else." That was the exact opposite of what we expected to accomplish. This unintended consequence may well have occurred, although jobs move out of the central city for a number of reasons. The demographic makeup of the particular workforce is a consideration. High taxes can be a reason: wealth tends to pursue lower tax rates to the periphery of a political jurisdiction and beyond. Crime, transportation, urban deterioration, and available amenities all play roles.

In sorting through the conflicting values, no easy answers had appeared. On the one hand, building the extension would have reinforced downtown development and assisted in holding the job base in the central city by making it easier for commuters to travel there. On the other, it would have displaced thousands of residents, most of whom were black or poor. We opted to favor the latter consideration, because it struck us as a higher value. Commuters still had interstate access to downtown; it was just not as direct. But many poor people and minorities who had already been uprooted for other interstate highways going through our downtown (Indianapolis has more intersecting interstates than any other city) would have experienced another upheaval, and this would undoubtedly have compounded feelings of abandonment and exploitation that already existed. So we made the tough choice: jettison the project.

Few answers in governance are clear-cut, and few solutions to problems are wholly right or wholly wrong. In analyzing an issue, one can usually find good arguments on both sides. Ultimately, however, a decision must tilt one way or the other, and once made it must be kept. Waffling does not serve the cause of governance well. Neither does ducking hard choices and trying to shift the responsibility to someone else. At any rate, the process through which we took the community on the interstate decision exemplifies an environment in which people are viewed not as clients of the bureaucracy but as valued citizen decision makers in their own right.

Things did not always work smoothly, and recommendations were not always implemented easily. The Task Force on Human Relations is a good case in point. But these efforts were moving us in the right direction—toward a city in which citizens feel they are helping to create their own community rather than being dependent on others. Cities need to make the effort, even if it may not turn out to be entirely successful.

We also attempted to harness the volunteer spirit, which seemed remarkably alive and well in Indianapolis. It is a "roll-up-your-sleeves-and-get-with-it" spirit of civic pride and Hoosier hospitality that enlists the resources of the community to put on events in grand style. Indianapolis, wrote Edward Leary in 1971, "is a city that probably boasts more dedicated professional and volunteer workers than any city in America. It is this public-spiritedness, this civic pride, which is destined to carry Indianapolis to new greatness in the decades and centuries ahead."[17] In the 1980s we benefited from the acceleration of a national trend that began emphasizing grassroots initiatives as the federal government withdrew from local programs for the cities, coupled with an increasing willingness on the part of local officials to work with nonprofit and volunteer groups.

People wanted to become involved in the execution of the plan for the Pan Am Games in 1987, a true high-water mark for Indianapolis. When all was said and done, some 40,000 persons had become involved—including people from all over Indiana and beyond. These volunteers took vacation time and personal time to host at different venues, assist with the transportation and feeding of 6,000 athletes from all over the Western Hemisphere, work with the media, help with ticket and program sales, coordinate schedules, serve as ushers, act on stage in the opening and closing ceremonies, and in general contribute mightily to the success of the event.

This spirit of voluntarism has characterized the way in which numerous other events—parades, festivals, conventions, athletic competitions, circuses, automobile shows—have been put on in our city, and it has won us widespread praise for our ability to do these things well. Some visitors from North Carolina remarked on the spirit of "selflessness" in our city, "supported by a strong sense of partnership between the public and private sectors, which have formulated an array of cooperative thrusts to accomplish a vision of Indianapolis that began more than 30 years ago."[18]

A look at the development of our domed stadium project will illustrate the cooperative spirit so essential to the building of a better city. Feelings of partnership had to prevail over feelings of selfish concern about who would get the credit.

Many people in Indianapolis strongly wanted the city to have a major league football team. Timing makes a great difference, however, and two early initiatives brought nothing. In 1978 or so, two leaders in the private sector and I paid a quiet visit to Robert Irsay in Skokie, Illinois. Irsay owned the NFL franchise in Baltimore, and we wanted to ascertain whether he might have an interest in relocating it. He did not at that time. Then, during public discussions in 1979 about the future of White River Park, the possibility of building a stadium along the banks of the White River in downtown Indianapolis was considered—and rejected.

By late 1979, however, after a successful mayoral reelection campaign, the time seemed more auspicious. In February 1980 Deputy Mayor David Frick and I, knowing that the first step would be to analyze the feasibility and desirability of building a domed stadium, asked the Chamber of Commerce Executive Committee for help. Chairman Alex Carroll appointed a three-member ad hoc committee to work with us. We had several meetings, even flying to New York to talk with NFL officials, before deciding on a course of action. We got together with leaders in the City-County Council and the Indiana General Assembly, as well as the governor. We contacted local philanthropies to solicit their views. We discussed the idea with business leaders and representatives of organized labor. We asked both Democrats and Republicans for their support, because we did not want the stadium to become a political football.

Robert Welch, a prominent local businessman who had run against me for mayor in 1975, joined ranks with us to show a united front. He was hoping to land a franchise himself, and even though it did not work out for him, his involvement in the effort to build the stadium was a key ingredient in avoiding the intrusion of partisan politics. The support garnered from leading Democrats such as Welch and Frank McKinney, Jr. (president and CEO of American Fletcher National Bank), was critical in depoliticizing the issue. If Democrats had lined up on one side of the issue and Republicans on the other, the dream would never have been realized. As it was, there was good bipartisan support for the initiative.

When we finished our plans—some six to eight months after we had started the process of seeking guidance from many different elements in the community—we felt we were dealing from strength. So many people had joined the effort that we were fairly certain of success. Our coalition building was paying off, and we found an opportunity. The idea was to expand the Indiana Convention Center by building an $80-million addition, a multipurpose facility with meeting halls and exhibit space as well as a 60,000-seat auditorium with an inflated soft top over it. We would not build a freestanding facility somewhere just for football. And we would build it in the heart of downtown, to counteract the centrifugal forces that were pulling our city, like many others, apart. A domed stadium would draw people downtown and reinforce the core.

The $80-million project would be financed by gifts from the Lilly Endowment ($25 million) and the Krannert Charitable Trust ($5 million) in our city, the purchase of suites by private companies and individuals (roughly $3 million), and a $47.5-million city revenue bond issue, the debt on which would be financed by a 1 percent tax on food and beverage served in Marion County. No property tax money or federal dollars would be used. A provision in the legislation would provide that after the debt was paid off, the tax would disappear.

We held public hearings in the early 1980s and listened to opposing points of view. Democrats and Republicans stood shoulder to shoulder in testifying in support of the project; the General Assembly passed a bill, which the governor signed, giving the city permission to enact the food and beverage tax; the City-County Council passed the ordinance; the mayor signed it; and the city began work on the Hoosier Dome (even though a rather frivolous lawsuit was filed against the project by political opponents). The gratifying aspect of this process was the way people worked together to accomplish something that practically everyone agreed would be good for Indianapolis and Indiana. Republicans and Democrats, labor and business, and state and local officials all cooperated to make the Hoosier Dome a reality.

All this happened without any assurance that the city would receive an NFL team. Entrepreneurs take risks, and we were an entrepreneurial city. Actually the risk was not so great as some people imagined, since we were not going to build a freestanding facility out in a cornfield somewhere, a building that would be unsuccessful if the city did not land a football team. We were expanding our Convention Center and our ability to compete for a larger share of the nation's annual $17-billion convention business. We felt that the Hoosier Dome would be successful on its own, regardless of whether we landed a franchise. The general public might think it was empty and call it a white elephant, but such would not be the case. The stadium would pay off because it doubled our exhibit space and provided a large auditorium seating 60,000-plus people, where circuses, tractor pulls, auto and boat shows, conventions, religious gatherings, and rock concerts could be held. Between 1982, when we broke ground for the Hoosier Dome, and 1984, when Irsay announced that the Colts were moving to Indianapolis, we had already booked into the unfinished facility $185 million of new convention business for the latter years of the decade. We also had plans to book high school and college football games there. An NFL team would be icing on the cake. Our projections showed that we could make the project work without it.

The increase in religious convention business hosted by the city since completion of the Hoosier Dome illustrates the point. Indianapolis was the site for 12 percent of the 255 religious conventions held in 1992. The *Indianapolis Star* began a story in early 1993 in which it dubbed Indianapolis the "Crossroads of Religion" with the words: "Welcome to Indianapolis, the mecca of religious conventions." Jack Stone, general secretary of the Church of the Nazarene, remarked: "It's just an ideal place for us and probably most other religious conventions. It's a safe city with great facilities and convenient hotels. And it's a place that has a reputation for being religious, a place where there's a church on many a corner."[19] Our city is fortunate to be the headquarters for the Religious Conference Management Association, which located here when the Hoosier Dome was dedicated in 1984. The organization would probably not have moved to Indianapolis had the city not embarked on the expansion of the Convention Center. An investment in one area pays dividends elsewhere.

Of course, some critics question the wisdom of investing in tourism and convention business. They suggest that the land on which facilities are constructed for such activities could be used more productively for schools, commerce, housing, and parks. They argue that most tourism jobs are "low-paying, offering only subsistence wages," and therefore do not create net economic growth. And they point out that convention trade involves extra costs to the taxpayer for provision of police and fire protection, transportation, sewers, airports, street maintenance, and the like.[20]

These arguments sound hollow to me. Indianapolis has experienced a 385 percent increase in convention business since the opening of the Hoosier Dome, and this in turn has engendered new hotels and restaurants, new jobs for people who might otherwise be unemployed, and new activities for the city such as the Pan Am Games and the Final Four, all of which have had a positive impact on the local economy and enhanced our reputation. Every time a new hotel room opens, two new jobs are created—one inside the facility and one outside. And if an area count is correct, Indianapolis has added 6,296 hotel rooms since 1984.[21]

Hoosier Dome inaugural events were held in the summer of 1984. That year's Mayor's Breakfast (which traditionally kicks off the month of May, when Indianapolis turns itself upside down to celebrate the 500-mile race, undoubtedly the city's most important event each year) was held on the floor of the new domed stadium. It attracted the largest attendance in its history. On July 9 the NBA All-Stars played the U.S. Olympic team coached by Bobby Knight in a game witnessed by more than 67,500 persons, the largest crowd ever to watch a basketball game in the Western Hemisphere. Purdue and Notre Dame played the inaugural football game, followed by Indiana and Illinois. The Colts kicked off their first season in Indianapolis, and the rest, as they say, is history.

The story of the Hoosier Dome illustrates the essential ingredients of the partnership for which Indianapolis became well known during the 1980s: the public sector at the local and state levels coupled with the for-profit and nonprofit parts of the private sector. The mix would change from project to project, but the process was always the same: creative leveraging within the partnership to accomplish a mutually agreed upon goal. In this instance the public sector asked the for-profit part of the private sector for help. These two sectors collaborated to produce a game plan. They approached the philanthropies, and the latter pledged to do their part if the state and local governments did theirs. The state gave the city the opportunity to act. The city responded. And finally the for-profit business community purchased the suites.

Indianapolis is a city where people work together. It is a city that cooperates, a city of partners. And this spirit of cooperation has produced big dividends.

Strengthening the
Infrastructure of
the Spirit

I dreamed of a city that cares as well as cooperates. When
the partnership coalesced, we chose to use it to make
Indianapolis more compassionate and more competitive. We wanted it to nurture what Hal Conklin, a city
council member in Santa Barbara, California, calls the "infrastructure
of the spirit." What this meant to me was building into the attitudes and
policies of our city a meaningful concern for people.

In the early 1970s the City-County Council passed what became
known as the Patterson Amendment, named after its council sponsor.
In essence the amendment stated that the local government need feel
no obligation to pick up the slack if federal monies coming into the city
were scaled back or discontinued. This amendment was aimed primarily at curtailing the funding of social-service programs to alleviate
human need, which is where much of the federal money went. The
amendment characterized the then-prevailing mindset in Indianapolis:
that federal social funds are bad and that they are the work of liberal,
high-taxing, high-spending do-gooders who want to take care of
everyone under the sun.

This attitude occasionally stymied me when I tried to push social-
service programs through the budgeting process. It took almost three
years, for example, to secure a relatively small amount of funding
($150,000) for the Marion County Commission on Youth we were
trying to establish. In another instance, several members of the council
opposed an effort to involve local government in a child day-care study,

saying that child care was the responsibility of parents and we had no business injecting government into the process.

Part of my dream for Indianapolis was that it would become a city where people got along and worked together, but I also hoped that we could be a humane and civilized city where people tried to alleviate others' suffering, heal their hurts, and provide helpful social services. There were many human needs to attend to—housing, neighborhood revitalization, unemployment, substance abuse, gang violence, infant mortality, hunger, illiteracy, and the rest of the long litany of America's urban ills.

As the 1980s evolved, it became apparent that U.S. cities were becoming bifurcated. Most urban mayors could tell a tale of two cities: one prosperous, revitalized, glamorous, and growing; the other neglected, disadvantaged, hurting, and needy. While many Americans basked in the sunshine of broadening opportunity during the 1980s, others lived in the shadows of dwindling resources. The rising tide was not lifting all boats, as demonstrated by the thousands of homeless persons in city after city and the increasing alienation of minorities. Mayors would have to direct attention toward cities' social needs.

Mayors therefore had two tasks: promoting urban growth and alleviating the negative consequences of that growth. As Dennis Judd points out, "Big city mayors, whether minority or white, cannot escape the contradictions between 'trickle down' policies favored by corporations and business elites and demands from neighborhoods and minority populations that want direct, immediate benefits. City mayors will respond to the contradiction differently."[22] As mayor, my response was to try to accomplish both objectives. Human revitalization deserved as high a priority as physical restoration; justice was as important as growth.

One could see signs of the deterioration everywhere, even within the shadows of the Hoosier Dome and the tall downtown buildings that symbolized the emergence of Indianapolis as a growing entrepreneurial city. Rates of drug abuse, gang violence, infant mortality, child and spousal abuse, homelessness, and acquired immune deficiency syndrome were rising. Some neighborhoods looked almost bombed out. Most people believed that the public schools were performing below expectations. Growth was uneven, and the central-city population was declining. The African-American community was seething about police use of deadly force against black citizens. Some citizens were angry because they felt excluded from the benefits of downtown revitalization.

Our community, like the rest of urban America, faced problems more intractable than brick-and-mortar projects. It is easier to build a physical bridge over Fall Creek than to build a bridge of understanding between the minority community and the Police Department. It is easier to put on the Pan Am Games than to reduce the infant-mortality rate. And it is easier to construct a campus for Indiana University–Purdue University at Indianapolis than a network of neighborhood health clinics.

Social problems are more difficult to raise money for and to get people excited about. They do not have the appeal to focus people's energies unlike a glamorous, headline-grabbing downtown development such as the Hoosier Dome. There are few ribbons to cut. Progress comes slowly. Improvements in the delivery of human services bring few immediate apparent results. That makes it more difficult for a leader to bring to the social agenda the kind of synergy that revitalized downtown, as former deputy mayor John Krauss once remarked. Or, to put it in the words of a local religious leader, "Indianapolis is a town that's long on compassion and short on justice." But despite the challenges, we made progress.

Probably the most glaring symbols of the evolution of the social problems that characterized the underside of the eighties were homelessness and AIDS. By the middle of the decade these two issues had pushed themselves to the forefront of our consciousness. In Indianapolis our responses were less than some activists preferred but more than others wanted.

In dealing with homelessness we began by studying the dimensions of the problem through a Mayor's Task Force on Homelessness, which worked closely with our Community Service Council and Commission for Downtown. We made several discoveries. Homelessness was gradually increasing in our city, growing to some 1,500 on any given night in 1985 (and to 2,200 by the beginning of the '90s). The profile of the homeless revealed that they were not a homogeneous group of mentally ill persons or single alcoholic men. They included evicted persons, the unemployed, people recovering from mental illness, abused women and children, and others. Forty-five percent of them were families and women with children. There was no one cause for homelessness; interrelated conditions had put these vulnerable people at risk. Chronic poverty, job instability, domestic violence, mental illness, expensive housing, single-parent households, addictions, rising living costs, and restricted entitlements all contributed, according to Linda

Frick of the Homeless Network. This organization was created as a result of the task force's recommendation that we bring all the service providers under one umbrella, with governmental agencies, civic organizations, and private-sector leadership.

In 1987 the task force recommended that the city develop 100 to 150 new beds for the homeless. Since then, 147 were created, for a total of 670 beds, which seemed adequate. (Some homeless people did prefer to sleep on the streets, and others were marginally housed.) According to Frick, the network's efforts spurred the creation of day programs for homeless adults, uniform data collection by shelters, referral points for families seeking shelter, citywide screening of the homeless population for infectious diseases, collaboration among mobile health and mental health teams, and coordination with the city for long-range planning and disbursement of federal funds.[23] The city provided $50,000 to help establish the Day Center to provide social services to the homeless with assistance from the Salvation Army. The city received more than $2 million of McKinney Act funds for transitional housing needs and more from the Veterans Administration and the Central Indiana Council on Aging.

Essentially the Indianapolis solution was to expand the private sector's capacity to care for the homeless and provide them with appropriate services, rather than make it a governmental function. City governments have not been very successful at running shelters, according to Frick. There remains much to accomplish. The city still does not have a pre-detoxification (sobering-up) facility, which means that we are still using the jail as a drunk tank. Our city is still ineffective at preventing homelessness—it remains relatively easy to evict tenants, because state laws governing landlords are generally permissive and the problem of chronic poverty has yet to be solved. Using men's shelters as exit houses for men coming out of prison or a mental health institution has posed unsolved problems of how best to provide specialized programs for them. And providing transitional housing that spends up to 24 months with good case management preparing homeless people to be mainstreamed remains an unmet challenge.

As for AIDS, we tried to express the ideal of a compassionate city in our response. In 1988 I issued an executive order stating that the city "shall not discriminate against employees or applicants for employment because they are or are suspected of being infected with the HIV virus." We were told that this nondiscrimination policy was one of the first in the country. We made counseling services available to persons with

AIDS in our employ and provided free AIDS testing for all city employees. The city also sought to ensure the safety of city employees who came into contact with blood or bodily fluids on a regular basis.

Education is another area of vital concern. Under the Unigov statute, school systems are run by independently elected school boards separate from local government, with their own taxing powers. Nonetheless, government and business leaders found opportunities to pitch in and help. Twice, for example, the mayor's office helped mediate disputes between the school administration and teachers during contract negotiations. Business leaders rallied to the cause of improving the public schools, as did their counterparts in many other cities.

The Indianapolis Chamber of Commerce involves approximately 350 companies in its varied programs that support education. In the mid-1980s we tried to replicate the Boston Compact at Washington High School. We called it Invest Indianapolis. The aim was to help encourage young persons to stay in school and get their diplomas rather than drop out. Local businesses promised that if high school students would improve their attendance and conduct and finish their courses of study, these businesses would guarantee them first priority for jobs after graduation.

With the help of local business leaders and the cooperation of the local school superintendent, this effort broadened into a more elaborate program known as CLASS—Community Leaders Allied for Superior Schools. Men and women in business not only know that education is too important to leave to the educators; they are also deeply concerned about the quality of the future workforce and want to help promote education reform and improvement. CLASS aims to help restructure the education enterprise, to bring into the workforce graduates better equipped for the changing demands of the new job market and the challenges of responsible citizenship.

One school-related initiative that expressed the ideal of a community where people work together and care about each other was Youth City. Begun in 1990 under the strong leadership of Deputy Mayor Paula Parker Sawyers, Youth City brought together approximately 150 high school students for a week on the campus of the University of Indianapolis. Modeled after Indiana's Boys' State and Girls' State, the explicit purpose of this program was to teach students how local government operates and how local political campaigns are conducted. Youth City also provided these young people with an experience of living together in a harmonious community and looking beyond the differences of black and white, rich and poor, male and female. As they lived in the dorms, ate in the dining hall, walked the grounds, spoke with adult supervisors, elected leaders, wrote and voted on ordinances, and held a mock city council meeting in City Hall, they became friends and comrades. Their differences began to melt away, and the dream of creating unity out of diversity began to come true.

Another constructive example of our city's social spirit was the Campaign for Healthy Babies. In the late 1980s the Children's Defense Fund released statistics showing that Indianapolis led the nation's big cities in infant mortality—deaths before one year of age. Consternation ensued. How could it be that almost 25 babies per thousand in the minority community were not surviving birth? Why had Indianapolis not improved as other cities had since the late 1960s, particularly in the minority population? (By the late 1980s this rate had only dropped 24 percent from that of the 1960s, as compared to 41 percent in Cleveland and 44 percent in Milwaukee.) Moreover, our city was experiencing a widening gap between white and black infant-mortality rates. In 1986 and 1987 black infants were more than 2.5 times more likely to die before their first birthday than white infants. This gap occurs throughout urban America, but it was wider in Indianapolis. And in some areas, we found, infant-mortality rates were far higher than our averages. In these neighborhoods, the populations of which were predominantly low-income people and minorities and where some 2,000 women per year were having babies, there were no clinics. This meant that most expectant mothers would have to take at least two buses to get care and wait in long lines for services at our public hospital, where some 200 persons per day were receiving prenatal care.

To marshal community resources, the Greater Indianapolis Progress Committee held a meeting highlighting the problem. The City-County Council started holding hearings. The city then formed a task force that developed a plan for public- and private-sector involvement. We called it the Campaign for Healthy Babies because a "task force to reduce infant mortality" sounded too negative. Its baseline goal was to reduce the number of newborns with low (less than 5.5 lbs.) and very low (under 3 pounds, 5 ounces) birth weights. A baby born weighing less than 3.5 pounds is 200 times more likely to die than a larger baby. The only way we knew to achieve this goal was to increase the number of women in prenatal care.

The biggest problem to overcome was citizen apathy and the notion that infant mortality is "not my problem, it's someone else's." A council member who lived in the suburbs told me, "I don't know why I should vote for any money for this campaign. It's a problem for the black people downtown, not where I live." This ostrichlike attitude ignored an important point: we are all bound together in our destiny as a city, and what hurts my neighbor hurts me. You cannot have a healthy city if it cannot produce healthy babies. That fact leads to a second important point: it is in the economic self-interest of the suburban constituency to help decrease the incidence of low birth-weight babies who will have great difficulty surviving, because the fight to keep them alive costs many times more than good prenatal care. Riley Children's Hospital does a beautiful job with tiny babies brought in for care, but the sheer economics of the matter suggest that the ounce of prevention is worth the pound of cure. The average hospital cost of care for a very low birth-weight infant (which stays in the hospital an average of 37 days) is approximately $70,000.

Three aspects of the problem needed attention. First was education. We needed to help expectant mothers understand the importance of good prenatal care. Second, we needed to increase access, to ensure that the care would be delivered to persons who needed it. And third, we needed to find the funding to pay for it.

The task force undertook to solve these problems with a good spirit of cooperation. It recommended the establishment of four new health care facilities, comprehensive coordination of prenatal services and primary care, creation of a computerized client record system, more extensive identification and education of at-risk women, and other programs. Ford Motor Company donated $100,000 to help the March of Dimes Foundation purchase a MOM-Mobile (Maternity Outreach Mobile) to travel city neighborhoods distributing information and providing health care. Eli Lilly and Company and the Associated Group lent executive talent. Local foundations provided support. The City-County Council plugged $3 million into the mayor's office budget over two years. Professionals from the Indiana University School of Medicine and Senator Richard Lugar's wife, Charlene, became involved.

The prenatal health care network spread. Four "comprehensive medical teams"—physicians, nurses, other health care professionals, and social workers—began working in six service locations. Five care coordination teams of medical providers in the clinics began working with patients in their homes to assist high-risk women in identifying and accessing a wide range of resources. In 1991 these teams served more than 20 percent of the highest-risk mothers in our city. The health professionals set up a computerized medical record system to coordinate data in eight health care facilities. The campaign mounted an education campaign to send out six messages: women should postpone child-bearing until they are medically and socially in a position to bear healthy children and give them proper care; live healthfully during pregnancy to avoid giving birth to a low-weight malnourished baby; seek out, utilize, and comply with good prenatal care; feed, protect, and nurture new babies; find and use a good pediatrician; and cultivate male responsibility for newborn children.

The effort achieved mixed results. The statistics began decreasing faster than those in other large urban areas, but they have remained too high. By the end of 1991 Indianapolis had dropped from first to 11th in infant-mortality rates among the overall and African-American populations among America's 22 largest cities. The rate for all races declined from 12.2 deaths per 1,000 live births in 1990 to 10.5 in 1991, thanks chiefly to a decline in the white rate from 9.9 to 6.9. Unfortunately, the black rate increased during that period, from 18.9 to 20.7. In late October 1993, however, headlines announced that the black infant-mortality rate in Indianapolis had plummeted, down to 11.2 deaths per 1,000 births as of July. (In the past, it was typical for a long lag time to occur before these statistics could be assembled, so we must view the numbers with caution.) Still, if these numbers are accurate they are good news for Indianapolis, and certainly provide an indication that things are headed in the right direction.

A related task force met with less success. We called it SPIRIT—Strategic Plan For Indianapolis Residents: Investing in Tomorrow. Its purpose was to provide a comprehensive strategy for meeting human service needs in Indianapolis. When I was first elected mayor I had set up a coalition of service providers, involving both the funders and the technicians. Fifteen years later I thought we needed to take a fresh look at the matter. We had received a Community Service Council survey that listed education, support to teenagers, homelessness, infant mortality, drug and alcohol abuse, and support to families as requiring community attention. I thought that a program of strategic planning would help us sharpen our priorities and focus our energies.

When I announced the formation of SPIRIT in my State of the City speech in early 1990, the media belittled it as just another task force. Nonetheless, with a dedicated group led by Deputy Mayor Parker Sawyers and Geoffrey Bannister, president of Butler University, the task force persevered. Its mission was to make recommendations for eliminating overlap in the delivery of social services so that needy persons could be served more efficiently. As a result of its work, the city streamlined the process of evaluating service providers and is integrating the schools and their facilities more effectively within the overall delivery of human services. The city set up a Department of Family and Youth Services and began a visioning effort that incorporated many of the SPIRIT objectives. The task force's proposal to create a city Department of Human Services funded out of existing monies by reorganizing and realigning existing agencies did not materialize, but its request that the city develop a strategic plan for public transportation elicited a new look at Metro, the city's bus company.

Housing brought another opportunity to address unmet social needs in our city. In addition to the homelessness problem, we faced two other issues: how to persuade more people to live downtown and how to encourage the development of more adequate housing for low- and moderate-income people in the neighborhoods.

Urban pioneers were restoring such historic neighborhoods as the Old Northside, Chatham Arch, and Riley Lockerbie. Investments in housing stock in these neighborhoods appreciated throughout the '70s and '80s, and the areas were being revitalized. By the late 1980s the city had enacted many of the recommendations in the original Regional Center Plan. Therefore we set up a second task force of citizens to update the plan and concentrate on making the downtown more user friendly. It established the goal of protecting and reinforcing area neighborhoods as vital elements of the center city, and it addressed the key issue of creating and conserving downtown housing stock.

One of the city's biggest problems is that not enough people live downtown to create the critical mass of vitality that characterizes great cities. A Commission for Downtown study of this problem showed a need for approximately 5,000 new housing units in downtown Indianapolis. The Regional Center Plan, 1990–2010, called on the city to "improve and expand upon existing neighborhoods, including new housing compatible with existing housing, a range of housing types including affordable housing," and it also cautioned the city to "minimize displacement of existing residents by new development, including downtown related projects and thoroughfare projects."

City planners had an idea that one thoroughfare (Tenth Street) should be expanded and pushed straight through a downtown neighborhood to connect the east and west sides of downtown Indianapolis. That "improvement," however, would have dislocated many people in

the Chatham Arch neighborhood, where they were investing in revitalization efforts. Therefore I suggested that the planners abandon their
plans. Emerging and struggling neighborhoods deserve protection, not
destruction, by city policy.

Our goal was always to create safe, decent, affordable housing for
all citizens. Between 1976 and 1991, 7,000 units of affordable housing
were provided. More than $37 million in public investment leveraged
more than $60 million in private investment through Urban Home-
stead, Single Family Rehab, Rental Rehab, Emergency Home Repair,
and Neighborhood Development Fund programs.

In 1985 our administration, with support from the City-County
Council, placed the city's Housing Authority under the authority of the
Department of Metropolitan Development. We believed this step would
make the authority more responsive to the needs of residents and more
accountable to the elected government officials, instead of being an
independent entity answerable only to the U.S. Department of Housing
and Urban Development. At first HUD did not like this plan, but in
view of the fact that our public housing was in dire straits, with a local
TV station doing a series on the shamefulness of the situation ("Shelter
of Shame," it was called), we received permission to make this management change. It proved to be a positive change. In the city's 2,700 units
of public housing, more than 800 were modernized (rehabbed) under
the leadership of the Housing Authority director, Rudy Hightower, and
the vacancy rate was lowered from 17 percent to 5 percent. Forty residents were hired as security personnel, trained at our Police Training
Academy, and made full-time city employees with a total benefit
package. We believed that this would help break the cycle of poverty
and give the tenants a feeling of ownership. The program was the first
of its kind in the country. We achieved another first when we installed a
child development center and kindergarten in two of the communities.
(We tried not to call them projects.) We exceeded the HUD requirements to get off the "troubled" list and compared very favorably to
other big-city programs, but the federal government changed the rules
(for example, by saying that in order to be decontrolled, a housing
authority's vacancy rate could only be 3 percent, and anything above
5 percent placed it on the "troubled" list), so Indianapolis never was
quite able to have its name removed from HUD's list. We were disappointed that our efforts to privatize the management of two public-
housing communities foundered on the rocks of bureaucratic intransi-
gence.

Elsewhere, however, we enjoyed modest successes that combined public- and private-sector resources. For example, with Oscar Robertson and his associates we worked in an old urban renewal area known as Oxford Terrace to develop new single-family housing to be made available through a lease-to-purchase program. Nearby, a $2-million loan was arranged for a couple of entrepreneurs to purchase 50 acres adjacent to the Meadows, a deteriorated shopping center in the 38th Street corridor that literally looked as if a bomb had been dropped on it. This land contained 37 buildings with 647 apartment units. The complex that was built has been named Mozel Sanders Homes, after a leading African-American clergyman. The complex strongly emphasizes self-sufficiency for all residents, and it provides support services toward that end. It has also made a major effort toward resident empowerment; for example, more than 60 percent of the staff members reside on the property.

The city also joined with Eastside Community Investments to complete a financial package to enable it to rehabilitate and construct 29 properties into 51 units of affordable rental housing on the city's east side. We also helped assemble land and develop the sites for Goodwin Plaza, the Citizens Neighborhood Senior Housing Complex, Kenwood Place, and Opportunities Plaza. To the best of my knowledge, the only time the Doxology has ever been sung at a news conference was when we broke ground, with local residents and members of a nearby Episcopalian church participating, for the Goodwin Plaza project in the northwest quadrant of our downtown.

When Judge David Jester of our municipal environmental court (the first one in the nation when we created it in 1978) brought to the public's attention that there were thousands of family dwellings (some estimates ranged as high as 60,000, but a more realistic number was probably 33,000) in our community that were below code, we established a Housing Strategy Task Force. We used volunteer committees and input from all over the city to formulate a plan to guide the city's affordable-housing efforts into the 1990s.

These efforts led to the creation of the Indianapolis Neighborhood Housing Partnership. With some $10 million in commitments from Lilly Endowment and more than that from local banks and thrifts, the organization works primarily with not-for-profit community development corporations throughout the city to provide housing financing and counseling. Its primary mission is to make home ownership mortgages available at below-market rates. "It's affordable housing for people who cannot afford home ownership," said the partnership's president, Tom Creasser. "It's a means to stabilize and renovate a neighborhood."[24] In one project the partnership helped transform 83 vacant, boarded-up properties into rental homes. The project used $1.4 million in financing, which was combined with $1.5 million in city funds to leverage more than $20 million in private assistance to finance low-interest, no-interest, and loan-pool programs. And, as Neal Peirce pointed out, "if all Indianapolis' corporations follow through as full-fledged, not just lip-service partners . . . then their contribution, combined with the extraordinary contribution the Lilly Endowment is making, will create the potential for dramatic breakthroughs" on our community's housing problems during the '90s.[25]

We always considered neighborhood revitalization an important goal that needed to be emphasized because it tends to be overshadowed by more glamorous developments such as the Hoosier Dome. The fashionable criticism at election time was to say that we had ignored the neighborhoods. But the facts indicated otherwise. Utilizing federal, local, and privately leveraged dollars, we initiated a variety of city programs in response to neighborhood housing and economic development needs. City programs were available to answer nearly every neighborhood need, including financial and technical assistance to third-party contractors among our network of community-based organizations for a housing rehab program, offsetting costs for new day-care centers, constructing new housing for the elderly, renovating and upgrading neighborhood parks, and providing low-interest loans to neighborhood businesses to enhance commercial stability and growth.

Our administration spent 25 times as much federal money from the Community Development Block Grant program in the neighborhoods as on commercial space downtown. The billion or so dollars we spent in capital improvements during our 16 years in office included repairs and resurfacing of hundreds of streets and sidewalks, replacement of bridges, park improvements, and new sewers—all in neighborhoods. The overlooked component in a city's economic development strategy is often the infrastructure necessary to support and encourage growth. Between 1980 and 1986 alone, we spent more than $450 million on flood, drainage, and transportation projects in our city.

Also in those years, according to a Department of Metropolitan Development report issued in 1987, the city spent more than $12 million on rehabilitation projects involving more than 4,000 housing units in certain designated neighborhoods and provided more than $2 million in assisting at least 200 neighborhood businesses with facade restoration, interest subsidy loans, and technical assistance. That in turn leveraged a private investment of almost $4 million, which created 289 new jobs while retaining 306. This kind of growth in the small businesses of our city was very significant, especially considering the relatively static employment in many of our larger corporations.

Enterprise zones as a means of revitalizing neighborhoods grew in popularity during the 1980s even though Congress never passed a federal bill authorizing them. Thirty-seven states did pass such bills, including Indiana, so Indianapolis applied for one in a blighted area of our community running north and south along the Fall Creek corridor. Such a zone is defined as an economically distressed area into which business opportunity can be attracted by offering tax incentives, with the hope that increased investment will have positive spin-off effects: neighborhoods will be stabilized, blight reversed, jobs created, and so on. Tax benefits would provide the following: no property tax on business inventory, exemption from gross income tax on the increase in receipts, state income tax credits for individuals purchasing an ownership interest in a zone business and for lender interest income and wages paid to qualified employees, and exemption of qualified employees wages from the state income tax.

We created an Urban Enterprise Association, and things began to move. Cub Foods announced plans to open a 68,000-square-foot store in the Meadows, and construction of a $1.5-million strip mall anchored by Blockbuster Video and a major Indiana chain's drug store began in 1993. The end result? Neighborhood revitalization that would not otherwise have occurred.

An area of city life where progress on the social services–human revitalization agenda is much more difficult to achieve is police-community relations. Community means "coming into unity." This ideal is commendable and highly worth pursuing. A mayor spends much of his time seeking to overcome polarization and hold people together. A few untoward incidents can destroy years of hard work.

In our city, throughout my time as mayor, we tried to make public safety our highest priority. A city needs to support its police and firefighters at the local level just as strongly as the federal government supports the Defense Department. They received the highest annual budgets. That money comprises a local government's defense budget.

We always tried to negotiate new contracts with the firefighters and police unions without ending up in a stalemate or work stoppage. Our ideal was a city that worked, and that meant continuous provision of the services people need, especially those affecting public safety. I feel, to borrow from Calvin Coolidge, that there is no right anywhere, any time, to strike against the public safety.

Once we came close to a strike involving the Fire Department. We had made a very tough decision, in 1977, to terminate the take-home car program in the Police Department. In the ensuing contract negotiations, we offered the police a cash increase to compensate for the loss of the cars. Then the firefighters, who always held out for parity with the police, demanded the same. Negotiations came close to breaking down. But one of my cardinal rules was "Always stay at the table. Keep on talking. Make it work, somehow." I met with the firefighters at 7:30 one cold December morning. Unbeknownst to me, they had called a strike for 8:00, but the breakfast meeting forestalled it, and ultimately the matter was resolved.

We sought to professionalize and modernize the Police Department in several ways. A merit-based personnel system eliminated political clearances from the hiring and promotion process. A new training academy introduced special programs in the use of deadly force and sensitivity to minority concerns. We instituted the use of chemical repellent to cut down on the number of times officers had to use deadly force. We set up a gang task force in cooperation with the prosecutor's office. I addressed every recruit class, at their swearing in, during their instructional time, and at graduation ceremonies. I told class members that I believed in strongly supporting the Police Department in the stressful job it had to do. I promised them a fair shake in disciplinary matters (mistakes of the head would be dealt with appropriately or forgiven if an officer's heart remained in the right place). I reminded them that loyalty was a two-way street, from the top down, but also from the bottom up. We talked about the problems management had in funding the department and discussed the need for police officers to regard themselves not just as law enforcement officers but also as community servants who had to be sociologists, lawyers, chaplains, and ambassadors of good will sending out a message of respect and dignity in all their professional activities. We also utilized the services of a representative of the minority community at the Police Training Academy to conduct classes on multiculturalism, ethnicity, and racism.

We had a strong commitment to affirmative action and equal opportunity. These much-criticized programs had—and have—worthy goals, such as eliminating discrimination in the marketplace and helping minorities enter the mainstream of economic opportunity. They evolved into programs that caused distrust and animosity, but that's not the way they were intended. Ideally, affirmative-action programs would bring more qualified people into the workplace and give them an equal shot at success. The Police and Fire departments rarely constituted a recruit class that did not comprise at least 25 percent minorities and women. Over the years, the percentages of these groups in the two departments gradually increased. The 25 percent figure was a target, not a quota. I put it in place during my first month in office (January 1976) to stimulate a personnel process that would otherwise remain unresponsive to the minority population. We also used the discretion permitted by state law to ensure that the promotion process did not overlook minorities and women if they were further down the list of candidates for consideration. (Only 80 percent of the people at the top of a list had to be promoted.) As of March 1993, 18.3 percent of the Police Department's 968 officers were African-Americans and 14.9 percent were women, up from 9.8 percent and 6.8 percent respectively at the end of 1975.

Also, as part of our efforts to build better relations between the police and the community, trainees took part in "shoot/don't shoot" exercises intended to teach maximum restraint in the use of deadly force without jeopardizing an officer's safety. Instructors used films to train recruits and older officers (in continuing education programs) in the art of deciding when to shoot and when to refrain in making split-second decisions on the street with lives hanging in the balance. Not enough citizens fully appreciate the difficulty with which these decisions are made.

We began moving toward community- (or neighborhood-) based policing, folding it into our regular department operations and being careful not to move too fast. The department was gradually decentralized, abandoning a central roll-call site for the police officers in favor of four neighborhood quadrant headquarters. We instituted team policing, horse and bike patrols, and a foot patrol downtown. Our Crime Watch program regularly put officers in touch with citizen groups, and we had CPOs (crime prevention officers) and Officer Friendly out in the schools and neighborhoods on a continual basis. We participated with businesses and a local TV station in a Crime Stoppers program, encouraging the public to come forward with information that might be helpful in solving crimes.

We installed the greatest possible civilian review of police conduct.

We made it standard operating procedure, for example, that whenever a police-action shooting ended in a fatality, the incident was reviewed not only internally by the Board of Captains and Firearms Review Board but also by civilians on the outside. Only the prosecutor could decide whether to take such an incident to the grand jury, but we made sure that the referral was made not only to that official but also to the coroner, the FBI, and the Justice Department. We also involved civilians in the hiring, promoting, and disciplining of police officers through the Merit Board and the Board of Public Safety.

We also made many efforts to sustain a dialogue with the African-American community. I accepted invitations to speak in many black churches. The chief of police met regularly with minority community leaders. Each month I was in office I participated in a radio call-in show called "Morning with the Mayor" to field questions and respond to concerns from the public. I believed that it was important to keep talking and interacting so that minorities would not feel shut out or kept away from decision makers.

Not everyone in the community was happy with what we were doing or believed that we had gone far enough. Police-action shootings in which there appeared to be reasonable doubt about whether the shooting was justified invariably aroused protests. The most notorious such incident occurred in September 1987 when a young man, Michael Taylor, ended up dead while handcuffed in the back seat of a police car transporting him to the juvenile detention center. According to the authorities, he had killed himself with a gun hidden in his high-top sneakers that had been missed during the pat-down search. Subsequent reviews of the case, both inside and outside the department, established that the young man had either deliberately or accidentally shot himself; he had not been executed by the police. But some critics remained unsatisfied with the conclusion, and resentment lingers.

In controversial cases such as these, certain African-Americans and the local branch of the American Civil Liberties Union accused the Police Department of discrimination against blacks and unjustified use of deadly force. One clergyman went so far as to assert that the department had a philosophy of indiscriminate shooting of black men. Some demanded that we install a black police chief. (We had a black fire chief and director of public safety.) Others wanted the city to establish a civilian review board that would publicly try police officers accused of misconduct. Based on my reading of their materials and discussions with Justice Department officials, I did not believe that such a board would help solve the problem. It would probably engender kangaroo court situations in which antipolice activists would grandstand before the media and police officers would refuse to cooperate unless required to by state law. Therefore I held fast against instituting such a system, believing that the review mechanisms already in place—the grand jury, prosecutor, coroner, FBI, Justice Department, civilian police merit board, and the regular court system—would suffice.

After an incident in 1990 when a young black male suspected of armed robbery, Leonard Burnett, ended up in a car crash after a long chase and was shot to death as he lurched from his car by a police officer who mistakenly believed he was armed, African-American clergy led rallies on the steps of the police wing of the City-County Building and demanded the resignations of the police chief and the mayor. I did not resign, nor did I ask the chief to.

After protests over police-action shootings, police-community relations continued to deteriorate. These relations are always in flux, always needing attention and repair. Tension between minorities and Police Departments are endemic to urban America, as the Rodney King incident in Los Angeles made only too clear, and all urban leaders must look for constructive solutions to this grave and profound problem. My successor took helpful steps in this direction by appointing the first African-American police chief in the history of our city and placing intense emphasis on community-based policing.

A partial answer to the question of how to build public confidence in a Police Department undoubtedly involves giving citizens more input in and control over the department. But we will never find an ultimate answer, in my opinion, because as long as there are men and women in blue out there enforcing the law and criminals breaking it, the two sides will engage in confrontations and feel constant tension.

None of these factors, however, invalidates efforts to pull the police out of the bureaucracy and into the neighborhoods through the Crime Watch program, decentralization, team policing, horse and bike patrols, and so forth. A modest beginning is better than nothing. People want to feel involved and to have a stake in housing, schools, better health care, and police work. To discover new and better ways of governing cities, we will have to unleash people power. As George Latimer, mayor of St. Paul during the 1980s, said, "to really work, programs have to be owned by the people they're serving."[26] Therein lies the best path to the future.

Any discussion of police-community relations brings up the wider issue of race relations. In our city of some 800,000 persons, about 21.4 percent (171,300) are African-American. Our demographics show that Indianapolis has the 16th-largest black community in the United States—larger than the black communities of Birmingham, Oakland, Newark, and Jacksonville, for example. Our city also has a higher percentage of married black families and a lower percentage of female-headed families than other major cities in the Midwest. The city's black community is a working-class community, and our city has the seventh-lowest black unemployment rate among the nation's largest cities, which means that it has the seventh-highest rate of black employment.

During the 1980s, as Indianapolis's job picture brightened, so did employment opportunities for the city's African-American community, and black unemployment declined by 13 percent. A rapidly growing black middle class is advancing beyond the nearly $35,000 per year average income of black households in the more affluent parts of the city. Indianapolis has the 10th-highest black per capita income among the country's top 25 cities, with more than 2,500 black-owned businesses generating a total of $121.7 million in sales.[27] These statistics suggest the presence of a stable African-American community in the city, neither radicalized nor rebellious and certainly not monolithic.

For decades in Indianapolis, as in many other cities, the races have coexisted separately. Indianapolis did not blow up during the riots of the late '60s, but the city was on the edge. Only much hard work by Mayor Lugar and the minority leadership prevented the trauma other cities faced. Today, beyond the world of work, black and white people still live in distinct worlds. The leading African-American pastor in Indianapolis, the Reverend T. Garrott Benjamin, Jr., once asserted that "there are no race relations. We are two different communities in two different worlds that have hardly anything to do with each other."[28]

Through the years and across generations, African-Americans have felt isolated, discriminated against, and "locked out" in Indianapolis. Many of them still do, I'm sorry to say. A beautiful but bitter expression of these feelings was penned by Mari Evans, an African-American who wrote an essay, "Ethos and Creativity," in *Where We Live: Essays about Indiana,* published by the Indiana Humanities Council in 1989. She says that as a child growing up in Indianapolis she learned what it meant to be "locked out" because of color:

> Whether it is a public facility such as a museum, or whether it is a
> public organization, an event, or a school to which a child has been

bussed, the subtleties and strategies of "locked out" are easily read and the impact of them are as psychologically harmful as they are physically limiting. . . . "Locked out" crushes the spirit and rechannels what could be positive creativity into negative creative acts. "Locked out" is something that can be changed, something that must be changed, because for me, even at that early age, it produced an enormous rage, a rage that should not be dismissed as merely youthful and isolated.

She concludes, somewhat hopelessly, "What we find is that racism, in this up-South city at the end of the twentieth century, is like a steel strand encased in nylon then covered in some luxurious fabric. The intent is to avoid, if possible, blatant offenses, to soothe, mollify, if necessary dissemble—while racism, the steel strand, still effectively does the job."[29]

Efforts to counteract racism and melt that steel strand are too important to leave to government alone. The business and professional communities must share the responsibility for establishing a climate of improved relations between the races and implementing strategies that can move our city toward that goal. Schools, homes, service clubs, religious institutions, and social agencies can help change attitudes. I gave mayoral support to the recognition of Black History Month and Martin Luther King's birthday as a holiday. With my encouragement, the Reverend Charles Williams, a mayor's office associate, left to become president of Indiana Black Expo, which has grown into a large event with national and international dimensions. Held every summer, the expo provides an occasion for celebration of the African-American heritage and a forum for discussion of current issues. The city developed job-training programs for minority youth, helping thousands of high school students find summer employment. During the meetings of the Task Force on Human Relations, Reverend Benjamin, of the Light of the World Christian Church, suggested that we start a program called Operation Respect. The timing was not right then, but now—with the cooperation of two leading congregations, one Presbyterian and one Jewish—it is getting off the ground. The goal is to increase the level of respect among people of different races and ethnicities.

What we need is a proactive policy with strong support from the public and private sectors. Our plans and programs tend to be reactive: what can we do to keep our city together? How can we prevent a riot or blowup that will fracture us? What's the best way to keep the peace? A proactive policy would ask other types of questions: What should we do to structure justice into the marketplace? How can our community help find jobs and job training for economically disadvantaged youngsters? How can we remove the blighting influence of drug abuse and gang violence? What more should we be doing to provide good housing, good education, and good transportation for the minority community? If we can build a Hoosier Dome, can we build safe, decent, affordable housing for all our citizens? A community's leadership, along with the media, should wrestle with such questions and find positive strategies for achieving realistic goals in these areas.

Two of our city's leading African-American businessmen have offered helpful insights on this subject. In the *Indianapolis Business Journal,* William Mays, president of Mays Chemical, pointed out that the agenda has shifted from redressing the wrongs of legal and social injustice, which had dominated the '60s and '70s, to achieving economic success in the marketplace. He sees the change of emphasis from civil and political rights to economic rights as necessitating a change in leadership, from lawyers and preachers to business owners and workers. He suggests that the new African-American leadership should offer more programs and fewer criticisms.[30] Gene McFadden, president of Freight Masters Systems, put it this way in a conversation with me: "African-Americans have to make sure that we participate in economic development opportunities. We've got to build black enterprises which are substantial enough to create jobs. We don't have the capital for the most part, which means we are left to the mercy of the community. We're beggars. We want the chance to participate. We need the opportunity to aggregate capital. We can then create the jobs for our community."

Economic action is the kind the African-American community now needs. Leaders must set businesslike goals for achievements such as raising high school graduation rates, lowering infant-mortality and dropout rates, measurably increasing growth in African-American business opportunities, and so on. Such business-oriented leadership will be essential to the achievement of economic equality.

While focusing on specific, attainable goals and programs that can be implemented to achieve them, leaders must nurture a spirit of sensitivity and cooperation in their community. This spirit can be strangled by inattention. It is a spirit of caring about neighbors, and it requires steadfastness of purpose in the face of frustrating obstacles. I always said to my staff in government, "Show that you care. Hang in there. Don't walk away from the table." The attitude or tone of a community is quite important. If it comes across as "that's not my problem" or "I can't be bothered with that," race relations will surely deteriorate. But a strong commitment to justice and compassion can make a tremendous positive difference.

That explains why I felt so strongly about keeping in place an affirmative-action program. "Diversity" cannot be commanded, but a commitment to it can be institutionalized from the top down. The CEO must be on board if it is to work. It cannot be ordered like office supplies; it involves attitudinal change within an organization's culture. I saw our city's commitment to affirmative action in this light. It would serve as a much-needed proactive policy to remedy generations of "lockout." Wider opportunities for women and minorities in the marketplace will not happen automatically. If left to its own devices, the system—which is essentially a "good ol' boy network"—will tend to bring in and promote white males and give business to firms owned and operated by them. The system will discriminate against minorities and women.

This seemed especially true in public safety. Over the years, many relatives of persons on the force and persons who had outside political connections were given preference in hiring and promotions. White males were getting most of the jobs. When I became mayor there were no female firefighters, and minorities made up less than 10 percent of the Fire and Police departments. Without strong executive action, it might have stayed that way. But after we installed our guidelines, the numbers gradually improved. Ten years later the Fire Department's percentages had increased to 13.3 percent minorities and 1.4 percent females, out of a sworn force of approximately 850; the 950-member Police Department was 14 percent minority and 11.1 percent female.

Therefore I was dumbfounded when the Reagan Justice Department filed a motion against our city on April 29, 1985, in the U.S. District Court to require Indianapolis to modify the consent decree we had signed with the Carter Justice Department in response to a lawsuit pending from 1974 that had accused our Police Department of discrimination. We had made progress and had put in place a system that was working quite well, without many complaints or accusations of reverse discrimination. When the Justice Department tried to force us to dismantle our affirmative-action program (and did the same to other cities), I felt it was wrong and decided not to comply.

The motion was wrong legally, based as it was on a very narrow interpretation of one specific case that dealt with layoffs and the seniority system. It was wrong morally, because the founding documents of our country, it seemed to me, affirmed equal rights and opportunity for all. (As a former Presbyterian minister, I also felt that the scriptures of Judeo-Christian heritage affirmed the dignity of each individual before God.) And it was wrong politically, sending out as it did a subtle message that the Republican party was backing away from the fight for civil rights, thereby narrowing the base of the party instead of broadening it.

I stated that we would oppose the motion in the courts and carry the fight all the way to the U.S. Supreme Court, and even if we lost there, as long as I was mayor, Indianapolis would have a voluntary program of acting affirmatively in behalf of women and minorities who for too long had been excluded from the mainstream of opportunity in our country. Without installing a rigid quota system, we would use gender- and race-conscious guidelines within a pool of equally qualified candidates to bring more minorities and women into the Police and Fire departments and promote them through the ranks. How else would they be able to advance in a country where the average woman earns approximately 59 percent of what a man earns for comparable work and the average black family's income is about half of the average white one? The system will not correct itself. It requires a strong commitment and positive leadership from the top down.

Local government officials, like those at other (I won't say "higher") levels, must walk a tightrope between economic growth and social cohesion. Their job is to achieve both. Dennis Judd asserts rather dogmatically that in the 1980s, city officials "neglected the governing task in favor of the economic imperative," by which he means that they were more interested in using the instruments of government to promote economic development than to broker among contending groups and resolve social tensions.[31] That is partially but not entirely true. Many mayors recognize their dual role in the bifurcated cities they are leading, and they work hard to discharge their responsibilities on both fronts. They try to promote growth and distribute the benefits of growth to needy areas and people.

A look at a group in Indianapolis called Dialogue Today will be instructive. Dialogue Today encapsulates the spirit of helping and respecting others. It comprises an equal number of African-American and Jewish women, 100 in all. "We are dedicated to our commonalities rather than our differences," they say. Their purpose is to foster better understanding through dialogue between their two constituencies. The group came into existence after Louis Farrakhan, the Muslim leader, visited Indianapolis and made what these women considered to be racist and anti-Semitic comments; they wanted to smooth things over and promote positive relationships based on mutual respect and appreciation.

The United States espouses the democratic social ideals of human rights, political democracy, and individual freedom, but our country and our cities are hurting because we are becoming increasingly polarized, antagonized, and Balkanized. Whatever happened to e pluribus unum? There's no *unum* left, just *e pluribus;* no one, just the many. The old cohesion has eroded. Every group wants its rights, forgetting that our system of law turns on individual, not group, rights. As Arthur Schlesinger, Jr., observes in *The Disuniting of America,* "the divisions of society into fixed ethnicities nourishes a culture of victimization and a contagion of inflammable sensitivities."[32] That is not the attitude with which a community is built. Dialogue Today has the key: talking things through, exploring differences, being self-critical, maybe even being irreverent and heterodox, and asserting one's point of view and one's self while ultimately letting an evolving discussion bind people together, not drive us apart. These women understand how right Martin Luther King, Jr., was when he said: "We are caught in an inescapable network of mutuality. Whatever affects one directly affects us all indirectly." Our community will disintegrate if we lose our commitment to commonality. The attitude is what matters most, and the opportunity good leaders seize is the one to foster and develop such a spirit.

After the not-guilty verdict came down in the trial of the policemen who had beaten him in Los Angeles, setting off riots (some called them a rebellion) in May 1992, Rodney King plaintively asked, "Can we all get along?" In answering his own question, King pointed us in the right direction: "We've just got to. We're all stuck here for awhile. Let's try to work it out."[33] We must try to build cities that are cooperative and compassionate, shoring up the "infrastructure of the spirit." We will not always succeed. But we must keep on trying to work it out, believing that one day "we shall overcome."

Waking Up Naptown

Indianapolis emerged from its slumber starting about 1965, and today it enjoys a reputation as a major American city. The *Wall Street Journal* labeled Indiana's capital city "the star of the snowbelt," and a Detroit newspaper stated that "Indianapolis is awake year round now." How did we become competitive? And how do we remain so? What philosophy and mechanisms of government can we devise that will enable us to compete for jobs and a better quality of life for our city?

The answer lies in forming the partnership I have already described and in finding a "hook" for economic development and a new approach to governing. We knew, right from the start, that we had to manage better. Perhaps every incoming administration believes that. We wanted to jettison traditional bureaucratic attitudes and try a more innovative, entrepreneurial approach. This philosophy was rather vaguely defined at first but became more crystallized by the mid-1980s. In collaboration with Partners for Livable Places, the U.S. Department of Housing and Urban Development published a little booklet in 1986 entitled *The Entrepreneurial American City,* which characterized the trend pretty accurately:

> This profound change in the way cities operate may best be termed "urban entrepreneurship." Cities are acting as risk-takers and are becoming active competitors in the urban economic game, and the key to each city's success is its ability to invest wisely and to market shrewdly. Urban entrepreneurship entails a new breed of municipal official, transcending the traditional local government roles of delivering services and enforcing regulations. The city's entrepreneurial role includes characteristics traditionally viewed as distinctive to the private sector, such as risk taking, inventiveness, self-reliance, profit motivation and promotion. The bottom line for the public balance

sheet is the enhanced competitiveness of the city, which is critical to urban rebuilding and economic revitalization.[34]

In Indianapolis we did not completely transform our system of governance, but we made several beginnings. We applied this entrepreneurial philosophy both inside and outside City Hall. We sought to manage better, and we took risks to assemble projects that would create jobs and a better future for our city. To become competitive, we first trained our sights inward and concentrated on internal management of local government, knowing that our first job was to run the store well. (The legendary mayor of Chicago, Richard J. Daley, put it this way to New York's John Lindsay, whom he regarded as hopelessly naïve about urban politics, "John, you forget why you were elected—to collect the garbage.")[35] Second, we took the proactive, entrepreneurial philosophy of government beyond service delivery to the task of revitalizating our Rust Belt city.

Every so often, mayors conclude that there must be a better way to manage local governments, and they co-opt private-sector leaders to review city practices and advise them on how to improve things. We did this shortly after taking office in 1976, with a Management Review Task Force. We did it again in the late '80s. We knew that there is always room for improvement, so we constantly sought ways to increase productivity and efficiency. That was a continuous thread throughout our 16 years.

We called the second task force the PEPPER Committee, for Public Entrepreneurship, Productivity, Privatization, Efficiency, and Restructuring. It consisted of 60 persons drawn from a cross section of the city's business, professional, political, union, and neighborhood leadership. Working through 1989 to "undertake a very serious and intensive overview of the management of City Hall, to the end of effecting greater efficiency and innovation," the task force, ably chaired by local businessman P. E. MacAllister, met 23 times and made 110 recommendations about ways in which local government could improve its management practices. We specified responsibility for implementation, established time frames for accomplishing each goal, and gave follow-up orders.

The recommendations included some real blockbusters, in addition to more routine ones such as creating a floating personal holiday to replace Good Friday and a special general liability fund to replace individual agency budgets for lawsuits and handle legal claims against the city. Larger suggestions included transferring the emergency ambulance service to the Fire Department; leasing public golf courses to private operators; seeking state legislation to divert locally generated inheritance tax monies to the county of origin; transferring Bush Stadium from the Parks Department to the Capital Improvements Board, which manages the Hoosier Dome and Market Square Arena; and creating long-range infrastructure maintenance and environmental management plans.

We put some of the shorter-term recommendations into effect, but most of the tougher ones were not accomplished before our administration left office. The mayor-elect asked us not to proceed with the privatization of golf courses, for example, because he wanted to study the problem and make his own moves. Ultimately we ran out of time, and the administration that assumed office on January 1, 1992, began anew with its own effort. Called SELTIC (Services, Efficiency and Lower Taxes for Indianapolis Commission), this task force has gone much further down the road toward privatization and the introduction of competitive bidding into City Hall procedures.

In *Innovation and Entrepreneurship* (1985), business guru Peter Drucker maintained that "to build entrepreneurial management into the existing public-service institution may . . . be the foremost political task of this generation."[36] I was so impressed by Drucker's ideas that I gave copies of the book to all the members of the City Council and my top staff. This, I felt, was the wave of the future. The new megatrend in local government on the horizon in the late '80s was better management. It represented a way to resolve the traditional antinomy between raising taxes and cutting services. There was a third option: do it better. Improve the delivery system. Become more efficient. Streamline and downsize. Do more with less. Privatize. Bring in competition. Break up the traditional government monopoly. Understand the difference between rowing and steering: government policymakers do the steering and have the responsibility for ensuring that essential services are delivered, but neither they nor city workers necessarily have to be the rowers who actually deliver the services. As David Osborne and Ted Gaebler state, "Services can be contracted out or turned over to the private sector, but governance cannot."[37]

When Bob Clark, plant manager of Allison Transmission, introduced us to the management guru W. Edwards Deming, I readily accepted his invitation to attend a four-day Deming seminar with members of the mayor's cabinet and a couple of city councillors. We read Deming's book and tried to put some of his principles to work. We raised tough questions about the wisdom of using job-performance evaluations. We formed quality circles and embarked on a total quality service program. We sent people to Florida to study similar efforts by the Florida Power and Light Company. We conducted training courses and handed out diplomas. To show that this effort was important to the top management in City Hall, I placed our senior deputy mayor in charge of the program. I made clear my belief that excellent customer service starts at the top, and I insisted on signing certificates for employees who completed our total quality service training and handing them personally to each at the graduation ceremonies.

Even before this effort began, we had started to privatize city services. After the blizzard of '78, the Department of Transportation formed contractual relationships with private owners of four-wheelers and other snow-removal machinery to help us clear the streets when the snow reached a certain depth. The department also privatized our street-resurfacing program and much of the street-sweeping work. To be sure, union personnel felt somewhat threatened by these moves, but no one was laid off because of them—and that was the acid test.

Regarding another city department, Public Works, we decided to develop an alternative to public landfilling as a solution for our trash-disposal problems. Although waste minimization and recycling should comprise significant components of an overall strategy, they are expensive and difficult to achieve on a large-scale basis. Continuing to pick up people's trash and dispose of it therefore was our immediate challenge. Landfill space is more abundant in the Midwest than in the East, but we were running out of capacity in city landfills. No one in our county wanted a new landfill in the backyard, and if we went outside the county, tipping fees and transportation costs were bound to increase. We came up with another option: harness new technology. Although the technology was controversial, we decided that incinerating trash and converting it into steam was the wisest course.

The city pursued a joint venture with Ogden Martin Corporation: the construction of a new resource-recovery plant at a cost of $83 million. In the long process of preparing for this project, we worked with local environmental engineers and representatives of the Sierra Club, the Audubon Society, and the Holcomb Research Institute at Butler University. Our main concern was to involve all the right players in the decision-making process so that the public would know that the new facility was environmentally safe and economically sound. We turned over operation of the finished plant to the private corporation, with whom the city had a contract to dump the 2,200 tons of trash it collected each day. The burning trash would create steam, which could be sold to the local electrical power company. The leftover ash (maybe 10 percent of the original volume) was sterile and inert and would be dumped in landfills within our county's borders and outside.

The plant has had a few problems and was fined once for failure to comply with state clean-air regulations. The city avoided a big zoning fight by building the plant on its wastewater treatment plant property, after holding neighborhood hearings and allowing a consensus to develop. The environmental risk was deemed minute: I was told by the president of the local Sierra Club chapter that if a person stood next to the stack for 70 years, he or she would increase his or her risk of getting cancer by one chance in 12 million. We did everything possible to ensure high-quality, clean air and created a watchdog committee to continue citizen monitoring of the plant.

Privatization is not a panacea for every fiscal woe in City Hall. Sometimes a city cannot find a buyer. Sometimes a firm comes in with a low bid to get the business, then raises the price later; that can cost the taxpayer more in the long run. Sometimes the process just does not work. For example, Indianapolis tried to turn over some of its public-housing units to private management, but after six months the private-sector managers were pleading with the city to take the units back.

In 1986 the city spearheaded an initiative that blossomed into a meaningful expression of the partnership for which our city was becoming well known. By harnessing modern technology to a new application, it improved our management capability. We called it IMAGIS—Indianapolis Mapping and Geographic Infrastructure System. The project was a response to legal mandates from the U.S. Environmental Protection Agency to identify and locate all stormwater outfalls, a task that would have been almost impossible using our current records. We also sensed that we could find a way to deliver better service at lower cost to the public and the customers of our local utilities.

The main goal of the project was to improve our management of the county's infrastructure. We wanted to create a computerized map of the entire county on which we would identify all parts of the infrastructure: property parcels, sewer lines, streets, underground cables and pipes for utilities, fire hydrants, storm drains, rights of way, and buildings and other structures. We would do this through a consortium of city departments (Transportation, Public Works, and Metropolitan Development) and the four private utilities in town—gas, water, phone, and power. In other communities, politics had scuttled projects such as this. Therefore, when it became obvious that political quarreling and turfmanship might ruin ours, we enlisted the resources of Indiana University–Purdue University at Indianapolis as an impartial adjudicator of the disputes that arose (such as that between the city's director of public works and the township assessors) and as an efficient operator of the system. The project director and her staff have always worked out of offices on the university campus, where the mainframe computer is housed.

By 1989 the participants had completed and copyrighted the base map, and our city now has a system with some 30 layers of information on it, with additional input still to come from the utilities and townships. The designer of the system allowed for future system growth because we understood that this resource would be changing and dynamic, not static. The valuable information on the maps can be purchased by engineering firms, realtors, surveyors, title companies, cable TV firms, airlines, and other potential users. A food chain even bought some of the information to help it in routing its delivery trucks. Utilities can use the maps to generate more revenues by identifying potential customers who live near their lines but are not hooked up.

The end result of the project has been improved services without staff increases. The Public Works Department can use it to track maintenance of storm sewers, and the complaints tracked by the system can identify problem areas: where it needs to create better drainage, where drains are clogged, and so forth. The department can target work orders more efficiently; all work done in a neighborhood or councilmanic district can be quickly summarized, and capital projects can be mapped more easily. Duplication of effort is eliminated, because now there is only one base map as a reference point; each service deliverer does not have to develop its own. And the consortium approach keeps every partner alert: everyone has input and everyone is expected to contribute, so the information on the map remains reliable, consistent, and up-to-date and everyone has a sense of ownership and responsibility about the project.

There is no other mapping system this extensive in the country, to my knowledge. The public-private partnership in Indianapolis pulled off something unique, which we hope will be of great benefit to our community for years to come. Because the move to privatization is now sweeping local government across the country, it is conceivable that the city government in Indianapolis someday will consider selling IMAGIS to a private company. In the judgment of many, this move would be unwise, because it would break up the partnership and the various participants might have lower levels of involvement; and that might lead to the inclusion of unreliable information. It will be most effective if all partners have a stake in it.

In 1976 the Indianapolis chapter of internal auditors invited me to address the group. In preparing for this speech I was surprised to discover that the city had no internal audit program. I discussed this matter with the group, and concluded that we should try to establish one, because it seemed like a sound business practice and a handy management tool. County officials did not want to participate ("I don't want any city bureaucrat telling me how many paper clips I can buy" was a not untypical response), so we had to be content with an internal audit division for the city alone. It was authorized by the City-County Council, and over the years it issued some 12 to 15 reports annually on different city departments and agencies. These reports were so dry that the media routinely ignored them, even though they were on public file in the council office. But the reports provided extraordinary help in managing cash flows, tracking personnel, catching innocent errors or conscious wrongdoing, and handling accounts. The mayor and city controller respected the independence of the division. We never told them what to do or what implications a report should have. The work of this division saved us much grief and helped us avoid considerable trouble every year. In retrospect the establishment of this program strikes me as one of the best things we ever did.

We also instituted other financial practices, and these prevailed throughout the time I held office. We converted our accounting from a cash flow to an accrual system. Our able and respected city controller, Fred Armstrong, and I believed that the city should begin issuing annual financial statements so that the public, and more particularly the rating agencies in New York, would know where we stood financially.

We hired external auditors and started producing the annual city financial reports in 1977, in conformity with commonly accepted rules of governmental finance reporting. Fred and I made periodic trips to New York to meet with the national bond rating agencies. We met with Moody's, Standard & Poor, and Fitch to discuss our city's numbers and its overall investment climate and economic health. Our goal was to achieve and maintain (if possible) a triple-A financial rating, because we knew how much money that would save the taxpayers whenever we issued debt. The rating agencies were impressed by the resilience of our strong and diversified economy, by our prompt payment of our bills, by our timely financial reports, and by our openness in discussing any problems we encountered. They rewarded us with the triple-A rating throughout most of the 16 years we were in office. That translated into savings for our taxpayers, because the higher the rating when debt was issued, the lower the interest rate that had to be paid.

It is a mistake to float bond issues to cover normal operations. Sometimes, however, external forces require it. The city never did this, but in the division of labor within Unigov between the City of Indianapolis and Marion County, the county is responsible for welfare. Township trustees handle poor relief, and several times during the years I was mayor we found that the Center Township trustee, who was coping with the heaviest welfare load, in downtown Indianapolis, was overspending his budget. State law did not require him to match expenses to income, and the poor people on his doorstep had to be cared for. Consequently the courts ordered the City-County Council to authorize bonds to cover these shortfalls. Because it was such a bad practice, I considered refusing to sign the ordinances. City legal advisers, however, told me that to do so would only make the matter worse, so I reluctantly acquiesced. The state will have to initiate reforms before long or the financing of poor relief and welfare will become fiscally intolerable.

Of the top 50 cities in the country, only 15 of them ended 1991 with a budget surplus, and Indianapolis was one of them. At year's end our city reported an unreserved balance of $301 million. It was our practice to project incoming revenues conservatively and monitor expenses closely, department by department on a daily and weekly basis, so that we could control expenditures. Thanks to these practices, we usually ended a fiscal year with a surplus of about 5 percent in our operating balance. We were sometimes criticized for living off our surpluses, when we were simply rolling surpluses, if any, over from one year to the next to keep the property-tax rate down. This simply struck us as good management. We did not encourage departments to spend all the money budgeted for them.

In late 1991, *City & State* magazine ranked the top 50 cities in fiscal strength. It put Indianapolis fourth on the list. We ranked 49th out of 50 in the number of city employees per 1,000 population (that is, second fewest) and 38th in long-term debt per capita. Our city was weakest in the percentage of our pension funds that was funded (12.28), but evidently this low rating was counterbalanced by high marks elsewhere in the complex formula that analyzed creditworthiness, financial management, long-range planning, and budget numbers.

In issuing debt for the city, we followed three rules of thumb. First, we would not allow debt service to make up more than approximately 10 percent of our total budget. Second, we would try to keep our bonded indebtedness in all our different bonding districts from exceeding 50 percent of the total capacity permitted by state law. And third, unlike the county, which had a different problem, we would not float long-term debt to solve near-term shortfalls in the operating budget. These conservative management principles seemed to pay off for us: our reputation as a well-managed city is well documented. In its edition of October 29, 1990, *U.S. News and World Report* featured "boom" and "gloom" cities; it put Indianapolis in the former category, comprising cities that were coping well with the undertow of the national recession. The magazine stated that we "ran a tight fiscal ship" and had "a conservatively managed budget."

In the mid-'80s, public opinion began to turn against general-obligation bond issues backed by the full faith and credit of the city because of their perceived adverse impact on property-tax rates. This sentiment reflected the trend that started in California with the Proposition 13 tax-relief vote.

In 1985, shortly after being awarded the Pan Am Games for 1987, the city proposed a $47-million bond issue for 14 neighborhood revitalization projects. We knew that we would have to prepare for the games quickly, and we tried to couple this need with the needs of our neighborhoods. Consequently the proposed bond issue included a project that would have built housing for 6,000 Pan Am Games athletes scheduled to come to our city in the summer of 1987. The facilities for the athletes' village were going to be located in downtown Indianapolis, and after the games we would turn these units into permanent housing stock for the city. The proposal passed overwhelmingly in the City-County Council, and I strongly supported it as a positive long-range contribution to the revitalization of our neighborhoods.

The proposal would raise taxes, however, and here we immediately ran into difficulty. We learned how easy it is to set up a table in a shopping center with a sign on it saying, "If you don't want your taxes raised, sign here." That is essentially what happened when the Indianapolis Taxpayers Association galvanized its forces. The bond issue became known as the "Pan Am bond issue," and a lot of citizens did not want any of their tax money going to help the games, which they considered a frill. As one newspaper columnist put it, he could not see what the renovation of a building at Belmont and Washington streets had to do with the Pan Am Games (the answer was easy: nothing) and therefore could not support the bond issue.

This experience certainly taught us the importance of marketing a program. Opponents misrepresented our cause, and we never effectively countered them. In the end, more people signed petitions against the Pan Am bond issue than for it, and it was defeated. (Later that year, the school board was defeated on a proposed bond issue for capital improvements for the same reason: it would raise taxes.) The Pan Am athletes were housed at Fort Benjamin Harrison on the northeast side of our county, thanks to the tremendous cooperation we received from the U.S. Army. The real losers were the neighborhood residents who signed the petitions opposing this proposal.

Sometimes officials must raise taxes if they are to govern responsibly. Unfortunately, it is easy for a political opponent to castigate someone who has raised taxes, user fees, and the like while holding office. I learned this lesson thoroughly in 1990 when I ran for Indiana secretary of state. All an opponent has to do is add up the revenue increases, put $2 million of TV advertising on the airwaves, and win the election. The people of Indiana were told a shocking statistic: Hudnut had raised taxes 27 times as mayor, and we certainly did not want a person like that holding statewide office. Our campaign did not defend against the charges well. We should have shot right back: yes, we raised taxes, and we did it to build a great capital city for Indiana, a city that works, where in the past 15 years more than 100,000 net new jobs have been created, more than 5,000 new businesses have opened their doors, $11 billion in new construction permits have been issued, and the property tax rate today, whether you believe it or not, is lower than it was when I took over as mayor in 1976.[38] But we did not do that, and we lost the election.

Nonetheless, it is entirely reasonable to raise taxes to fund education, public safety, and the delivery of other basic services when the only alternative is to reduce these services. It also makes sense to raise taxes to initiate projects such as the Hoosier Dome that lead to an infusion of vitality into a community. In endorsing my candidacy for secretary of state, one newspaper editorial stated,"There's a difference between wild spending and wise spending."

Oliver Wendell Holmes, Jr., once remarked that "taxes are what we pay for civilized society." If the alternative is a crumbling mental health system, an understaffed Police Department, or an underfunded public school, perhaps a city should raise taxes. The number of taxes is not nearly as important as the reason for the taxes and the size of the total tax burden. At the end of 1990, according to *City & State,* Indianapolis ranked 41st out of the top 50 cities in the country in general fund revenues per capita, a pretty good indication that our city had a relatively low tax burden.

We undoubtedly made errors of judgment about taxes over the years. By and large, however, we were managing a city that worked, without having to endure huge layoffs or confrontations with the unions or deferred infrastructure maintenance. A city that does not work well discourages investment. Economic health requires that the city's infrastructure be maintained and city machinery run smoothly. Consequently I believe that the tax increases we instituted were justifiable. Without the local option income tax, the police and fire pension funds would be empty. Without the surcharge on our phone bills, our community would not enjoy enhanced 911. Without occasional increases in the property tax, folks who work for local government would not receive wage or benefit increases, and we would be unable to make capital improvements. To those who criticize, we might well ask: which workers would you lay off? Which fire station would you close? Would you pick up the trash only once every two weeks? Which streets would you leave till next year to resurface? Which emergency runs would you not make? You cannot have it both ways forever—continuing levels of services and flat levels of funding them. At the end of the '80s and into the '90s, we went three years straight without raising income taxes and four years with a flat property-tax rate. Even so, raising taxes or fees is sometimes a necessary evil and cannot be avoided unless the public prefers a drastic curtailment of services.

The tax revolt and pressure not to raise taxes had a salutary effect. They compelled us to become more creative in our financing mechanisms. The tax revolt is here to stay, we realized, and we had better come up with new ways of raising money and operating local government, because the taxpayers were saying loud and clear that they did not want their taxes raised. By this time we had already arranged the financing for the Hoosier Dome without using property-tax money; it was done with revenue bonds, a method we would use again in building our resource-recovery plant. We also began to use tax increment financing (TIF). In a TIF district, taxes on the improvements on a property would be plowed back into the project to help service the debt contracted at the front end when the money was borrowed to do the project. The disadvantage of this finance mechanism was that it could be seen as keeping monies from being distributed to other governmental entities, such as school boards. On the other hand, if the project did not materialize, there would be no money to distribute. Our opponents used the same arguments against tax abatements, which we also granted under certain circumstances, on both real and personal property, to attract development. The unanswerable question was always whether the project would not have been undertaken or would have moved somewhere else if we had not granted the abatement or TIF. That is an issue, like so many others of government policy, on which reasonable people can differ. We established TIF districts to help fund projects such as the downtown mall, which was also financed with moral obligation bonds, and the United Airlines maintenance facility at the airport.[39]

In 1985, with the help of the state legislature, we established the first municipal bond bank in the country, the Indianapolis Local Public Improvement Bond Bank. This bank is a financial tool the city can use to consolidate and more effectively manage its debt. The bank manages debt at lower costs and under more favorable borrowing conditions than the city's 14 qualified entities—such as the airport, thoroughfare system, bus system, public libraries, and public works—could do independently. The bank can pool the municipality's efforts, which allows rating agencies to evaluate the municipal bonds as a single offering rather than individual issues from the qualified entities. It also simplifies debt management, because the bank can easily borrow money on a short-term basis until a window opens in the market for a more favorable long-term note. Since its founding, the bond bank has issued approximately $680 million in bonds.

Our high bond ratings would indicate that our financial-management practices were successful. Government performance is extraordinarily difficult to evaluate. In business, performance seems more straightforward, because at the end of the year one can look at the bottom line. Government, however, really has no bottom line, unless ending the fiscal year in the black rather than the red qualifies. Indianapolis did that regularly.

The nation recognized Indianapolis as a well-run city. One magazine called us "an urban center to watch." A survey rated us the tenth-best city in the United States in which to do business. The controller and mayor received national awards. In rating us Aaa, the New York rating agency, Fitch, gave us high praise: "Indianapolis has displayed a high level of economic stability and resilience . . . population declines have been reversed . . . debt levels are modest . . . conservative budgeting has provided good balances."

In 1976, the year I assumed office, the tax rate was $4.08 and the city had 5,304 city employees, according to the city controller. When I left office at the end of 1991, the tax rate was $3.91 after two reassessments and the city employed 5,096 people. Both sets of figures show a decrease of approximately 4 percent, which compares rather favorably with the 149 percent increase in the Consumer Price Index during that time. The city's assessed value increased by 208 percent, and its budget rose by 176 percent. According to the annual financial report for 1991, the city's savings account had a $330-million balance.

Marketing the Store, Not Just Minding It

T rying to run a tight ship by managing City Hall's affairs as well as possible was only half the story. The other half involved looking outward, exporting into economic development the proactive entrepreneurial philosophy of government that was driving our internal management. A city cannot attract new business opportunities if it is not a creditworthy organization whose sewers and bridges are not collapsing. Responsible city officials, however, are more than caretakers. They need to market the store as well as mind it. Our city policy had two goals for making the city more competitive: to invest in its human and physical resources and aggressively attempt to capitalize on economic opportunities with every tool at our disposal.

In making investments, job training comes before jobs, and education is too important to leave to the educators. Everyone should help—government, business, labor service organizations, and teachers and parents—if we as a country are going to achieve the laudable goals set forth in the America 2000 program initiated by President Bush and the nation's governors. They set their sights high. By the year 2000, the dream is that all children in our country will start school ready to learn, that the schools will be free of drugs and violence, that every adult American will be literate, that the high school graduation rate will increase to at least 90 percent, that all students will demonstrate competency in the core subjects of English, math, science, history, and geography, and that the United States will be first in the world in science and math achievement.

But nontraditional forms of education also require support. Manufacturing represents a shrinking fraction of the nation's output and employment, but its methodologies are changing as the economy moves from the smokestack to the computer. Therefore job training and retraining have become crucially important. The shift to services is inevitable. My colleagues at the Hudson Institute believe that "the key to domestic economic growth" is increased productivity and worker output in the service sector. The number of persons engaged in manufacturing, farming, and mining will decline; job prospects for professional, technical, managerial, sales, and service jobs will far outstrip the opportunities in other fields.[40] Meeting these needs will require job training and retraining programs, so that workers in service industries such as health care, education, trade, finance, insurance, real estate, and government will have the necessary communications and word-processing skills.

What does it say about our educational system that McDonald's spends $450 per person to train new employees in how to do their jobs behind the counter? People often remark that we do not want to become a nation of hamburger flippers. If we don't, we must invest in education and training, which the Hudson Institute's William B. Johnston calls "the primary systems by which the human capital of a nation is preserved and increased." He concludes:

> As the economies of developed nations move further into the post-industrial era, human capital plays an ever more important role in their progress. As the society becomes more complex, the amount of education and knowledge needed to make a productive contribution to the economy becomes greater. . . . Between now and the year 2000, for the first time in history, a majority of all new jobs will require postsecondary education. Many professions will require nearly a decade of study following high school, and even the least skilled jobs will require a command of reading, computing, and thinking that was once necessary only for the professions.[41]

In addition to the programs previously described that were designed to further the community's partnership in the education enterprise, a few others deserve mention. We started a Mayor's Tutoring Program for employees inside City Hall who needed help with their reading and writing skills. Surprising as it may seem, we discovered that we had employees who were very limited in these areas, so we established the program in which other city employees tutored them on city time. Most of the students enrolled in the program benefited from the experience. Students progressed according to their own comprehension levels. The average length of time to complete the program was six months to one year. Supervisors noticed immediate improvement in productivity and employee self-esteem. Because of the confidentiality of the program, it was difficult to market it to employees who needed the service. Some supervisors felt that participation in the program was a way of getting out of performing regular duties. Student and tutor matches were critical to the program. Most were successful. Occasionally students had to be rematched when the tutors left the employment of the city or changed jobs and could no longer participate in the program. These instances made student progress a little tentative, and some students lost interest altogether. But overall the program was a success.

We also placed strong emphasis on continuing education. We hired outside professionals to help our workforce upgrade its skills in areas such as answering the telephone and typing.

During the 1980s we placed more than 15,000 economically disadvantaged youths in summer jobs through our Partners 2000 program. In 1989 the organization shifted its focus from a job-placement-only strategy to a year-round effort aimed at summer public-sector employment for 14- to 16-year-old at-risk youth attending public schools.

The city-supported OIC (Opportunities Industrialization Centers) was led by the Reverend Mozel Sanders and after his death by Joe Matthews. Two OIC programs initiated in Indianapolis with city support received national attention. One was a program with a local firm, Navistar, to involve business and industry in job-training program design and curriculum development. We invited OIC to help Navistar recruit minority applicants who would receive basic vocational-directed skills training inside the plant. This program became a model for the development of the PICs (Private Industry Councils) that were put in place throughout the country in the '80s after the passage of the Kennedy-Quayle Jobs Training Partnership Act. The city and state often used funds provided by this act in putting together packages to encourage private investment. The other OIC program involved cooperation with the city in establishing an early childhood development center at one of our public housing sites. We found that working with these children aged three to six years made it possible to meet their families and develop a more holistic approach to their needs. We discovered mothers, for example, who could not work because they had to obtain child care. When they became involved with OIC, they found their way into the job market.

The Indianapolis Network for Employment and Training is making a remarkable contribution to the city. It was founded in the early '80s to combine public-employment, job-training, and workforce development services under one umbrella. Working with disadvantaged persons, laid-off workers, school youths, food stamp and welfare recipients, and general jobseekers, the network served 8,564 persons in fiscal year 1991–92, with a budget of $8.8 million. Its programs include job-readiness workshops, workplace literacy, transitional services for the homeless, retraining services for workers affected by downsizing, road readiness (to help adults with low reading levels pass tests for a commercial driver's license), and in-school remediation for at-risk youngsters aged 14 and up.

In my State of the City speech in January 1985 I addressed the problem of environmental protection, suggesting that the connection between clean air, clean water, and people's health is only half the story. The other half is jobs. Our city's economic development potential depends on how well we safeguard the environment. I said, "Dirty air and loss of jobs are directly related. A cleaner environment means more business opportunities."

When a group of Indianapolis leaders visited with Ford's vice-president for North American operations to discuss the possibility of bringing a new production line into the empty Western Electric building, his first question was "What's your environmental scan?" AT&T had announced the plant closing in 1983. The city was searching for new uses for it. One possibility was a Ford Motor Company production line. This use, however, would have entailed painting, which would have added to our air-pollution problems. Therefore nothing came of the conversations, because the city could not guarantee sufficient steps elsewhere to offset the additional degradation of air quality that this new manufacturing process would create.

Indianapolis is classified as a "marginal nonattainment" county by the U.S. Environmental Protection Agency, and the city's effort to get off EPA's list has been ongoing. Of the four categories involved—ozone, particulates, sulfur dioxide, and carbon monoxide—compliance with the ozone requirement is the most difficult to attain. In my 1985 speech I advocated a complete ban on open burning (we were the largest city in the country without one), which was subsequently adopted. We also took steps to pave dirt alleys and parking lots to reduce the number of fugitive dust particles. But the state was not interested in helping us by mandating vehicle emissions testing, and without state backing there was little the city could do to combat the ozone problem created by tailpipes, because some 100,000 cars per day commute into Indianapolis from outside its jurisdiction. The city has achieved compliance in the other areas, but ozone remains elusive. With a voluntary vehicle emissions inspection program, painting operation regulations, an antitampering program on used cars, and stage-one vapor-recovery systems now in place in Marion County, the city is close to attainment of the ozone standards. It continues to work on its plan, although I do not see how the problem will ever be solved until the state gets into the act.

By 1985 our city's water pollution problems had diminished considerably. During the late '70s, Indianapolis undertook what was at the time the largest public works construction project in the United States, the building of a tertiary treatment plant to clean our treated wastewater before discharging it into White River. The plant cost more than $200 million. Its construction was mandated by the EPA, and it was built with 75 percent federal funding and 10 percent state assistance. We believe that our treated wastewater is more than 98 percent clean. Since this facility was built, our biggest problem has been accidental spills.

We followed up during the '80s with considerable effort in the treatment of our sludge. The city generates more than 600 tons a day. The mass is dried, then incinerated, and the residual ash is buried in old lagoons on the plant property. The city, with help from the EPA and the state, undertook a $105-million renovation of the sludge-incineration plant, making it the most modern in the country, according to former Public Works director William Shassere. During the dedication ceremonies, each participant received a button that bragged, "We're Number 1 in the Number 2 business!"

The new resource-recovery facility reduced our need for new landfill capacity, although it should not be construed as a complete substitute for source reduction and recycling. More needs to be done in these areas. In 1985, because of the heated emotionalism with which this subject was being debated in our community, I observed that we needed to find "a rational solution that is the healthiest and best for Indianapolis" and reaffirmed my intention to proceed. Some have criticized us for building the plant, but the obvious question is this: what would you have us do with the 2,200 tons of trash our community accumulates each day, which it is the city government's responsibility to pick up and put down somewhere? Reducing the amount generated is certainly part of the answer, as is recycling. But in a city as large as Indianapolis, a multifaceted approach probably makes the most sense.

There is not a city in the United States that does not have infrastructure problems—either the preservation of deteriorating streets, bridges, sewers, parks, stormwater systems and buildings or the construction of new ones. Some estimates of the nationwide total expenditures needed run as high as $800 billion. As its 100th-birthday present to the city in 1990, the Indianapolis Chamber of Commerce generously donated time and talent to study our infrastructure needs. In his PEPPER Committee report, P. E. MacAllister had warned that "there is a definite need for the development of a Public Awareness Program which will emancipate people from their normal lethargy about how good things are and enlighten them on the dangerous degree of disrepair into which our infrastructure has fallen, the amount of dollars we are accumulating in belated reparations to the systems and the impending calamity that awaits the taxpayer if we continue to stall action till it becomes even more expensive."

Probably the most prudent steps a city can take to improve its competitive position is to invest in job training, education, and infrastructure. Subsidies and incentives to attract business play a part in the economic development of a community. But they are not a substitute for the expenditure of funds on these other matters. As writers in the *Journal of Urban Affairs* noted, "the keystone for urban economic development is investment in the education and training of the labor force" and "improving an area's infrastructure is a productivity enhancing policy that serves to improve the area's competitiveness."[42] My successor, Stephen Goldsmith, gave this matter serious attention and devised a plan to devote $519 million over three years to fund 477 capital improvement projects. Said Mayor Goldsmith, "The competitive survival of our city and the needs of our children demand that we consume less of our budget operating for today and more preparing for tomorrow."[43]

The Chamber of Commerce report issued 52 recommendations in 1991 after some two years of work by more than 200 persons. This group too had an acronym: GIFT—Get Indianapolis Fit for Tomorrow. The report called for the city to invest $1.1 billion in its infrastructure during a ten-year period. This money was to supplement the approximately $1 billion that our administration had already spent in the previous 16 years. The key question, of course, was where the city would get the money to pay the bill. The Chamber of Commerce recommended new taxes; but at a time when taxpayers were saying loud and clear that they did not want new taxes or increases in existing taxes, the challenge would be to devise other ways of accomplishing the objective.

Consider one example. The city had lost some $4 million per year during the '80s because of cutbacks in Federal Aid to Urban Highways funds. That equaled the cost of resurfacing some 60 miles of streets each year. Therefore I decided to recommend to the City Council that the city exercise an option, provided by the state, to enact a surcharge on license plates—commonly called a "wheel tax"—to make up for the loss of federal revenue. In these situations our choice seemed to be reduced to increasing taxes or decreasing services. One thing neither the Reagan Administration nor the Congress ever made clear to the American people during the '80s was that cuts coming out of Washington would force these difficult choices on local governments. The people never understood the connection. By the end of the decade, people had become sure that any tax increase was bad. But we chose the politically riskier course of "enhancing revenues." We opted to implement the wheel tax, the funds from which—$4 million in round figures—would be dedicated to street resurfacing. That would enable us to avoid falling further behind in street maintenance.

Our successors in the Goldsmith Administration and the City-County Council have decided to pledge half of these wheel tax funds to a bond issue floated in 1993 and to be paid for over the next 15 years. The bond issue will raise money up front to resurface a massive amount of street and sidewalk mileage. The city will not need to increase property taxes, and our streets will receive a tremendous infusion of investment. That is fine, and it certainly will make the incumbents look good. But—and this is the downside—the plan will tie the hands of future administrations, which will not be able to use the money for resurfacing because it has already been pledged toward debt service on the current bond issue. My administration chose not to take this route when we had the chance, after putting in the wheel tax. We did not think it would be fair to future generations of leaders, who would have to pay off the debt and yet be unable to use that annual infusion of money for their own resurfacing plans. Sometimes a short-term gain causes long-term pain.

In addition to projects that required funding, GIFT, through its chairman, Ray Humke, laid out constructive management and policy suggestions for handling infrastructure problems more effectively: implement a city capital budgeting process, establish an office of capital development, and initiate a departmentwide strategic-planning process complete with centralized performance measures and a system to help prioritize projects when allocating funds. These were good management ideas, but our administration had no time to implement them before leaving office. Perhaps I had erred over the years in the decisions I made in this matter. I had always felt that capital budgets were nothing but dream lists that provided city officials an opportunity to list everything they could imagine. I considered capital budgets to be meaningless documents because they contained no means of finance. Therefore I asked the department heads to come up with annual capital plans that we could realistically hope to accomplish. I let them do their own prioritizing. Whether a more centralized system would work better is uncertain.

In the early '80s, the city promulgated a plan, with the assistance of Central Research Systems, David Birch of the Massachusetts Institute of Technology, and local business and professional leaders, for the city's economic development. The plan became the roadmap for the Indianapolis Economic Development Corporation.[44] We viewed two things as bedrock truths. First, even though the country was making a transition from the Industrial Age to the Information Age, with the sun setting on smokestack industries and rising on computers, word processors, and telecommunications, it would be a mistake to ignore manufacturing. Manufacturing would always be the backbone of the economy, even though by 1980 our city had twice as many jobs in the service sector as in manufacturing, a complete reversal of the situation just after World War II. Therefore we had to retain as much of our manufacturing base as possible. And second, most of the job growth would come from small businesses, not large ones. We knew that Indianapolis was demonstrating a remarkable rate of growth in company start-ups, along with small-firm (twenty or fewer employees) growth superior to the rest of the nation. Entrepreneurial risk takers appeared to be abundant, and we wanted to keep it that way.

The plan recommended that certain industries be targeted for priority retention/expansion and attraction efforts: industrial automation, telecommunications, instrumentation and test equipment, health care technology and services, software, and consumer electronics. All these industries developed during the '80s, but so did others: agribusiness, biotechnology, electronics, transportation, and "back-office" businesses. The plan recommended certain strategic mechanisms to support the effort to capitalize on our city's resources and assets, among which it mentioned "numerous business start-ups, a growing pool of young, well-educated people, and a promising foundation in 'leading edge' industries. The mechanisms included an industrial development corporation, enhanced support for education, innovative development finance, a technology-oriented complex, a three-way partnership between business, government, and education, and high-profile leadership support."[45] Looking back from the vantage point of the '90s, one can safely say that most of these mechanisms were established in Indianapolis during the '80s, with very positive results for job growth in the city. The city took a balanced approach to economic development: we worked with small and large businesses, downtown and in the suburbs, with Democratic and Republican developers. The point was to create jobs.

We worked with Allison Transmission's management and labor leadership to promote the kind of cooperation that would make it possible to capture an engine contract. Boeringer-Mannheim, manufacturers of medical diagnostic equipment, on the northeast side of town, was a sleeping giant that awoke in the '80s, with zoning and infrastructure assistance from the city. Mike-Sell's, the potato chip manufacturer, opened a new 45,000-square-foot snack-food production plant in Park Fletcher after the city, using its property file, helped identify a suitable building. The city helped Allstate Group Insurance Company arrange a tax abatement for its new regional claims operation. Target put up a new building in our west side because it needed a larger distribution center to service 100 stores. Ford Motor Company embarked on a major retooling program, securing 3,000 jobs with a $230-million investment after the city obtained personal-property tax abatement and employee training assistance. We also kept the General Motors Truck and Bus operation going (it used to be a Chevrolet plant) in what the managers told me was the largest steel-stamping program in the country. Indeed, during the '80s Indianapolis enjoyed great success in the retention/expansion business. It turned out to be a grand-slam home run for us.

When International Harvester (now Navistar) began to decline in the early '80s and many of the company's jobs seemed to be headed for Mexico, the city and state geared up to help keep them here. The plant

landed a $500-million, five-year, renewable contract with Ford to pro-
vide a 6.9-liter engine for its heavy-duty pickup trucks and vans after the
city provided assistance with tax abatement and the city and state provided job-training funds. (The millionth engine rolled off the assembly
line in late 1992.) The United Auto Workers proved to be flexible and
forward-looking in its thinking, as was the state. The General Assembly
passed the "Harvester bill," which authorized tax abatement on personal property as well as real property, that is, on manufacturing equipment as well as improvements to the capital plant. This legislation
provided tremendous positive development potential for us, as did the
"dinosaur building" bill passed a few years later, which provided incentives for the redevelopment of old buildings.

To enhance our position in the global market the city had established a foreign trade zone at the airport, "a legally secured area outside of U.S. Customs territory" where foreign and domestic goods
might enter to be stored, distributed, exhibited, assembled, or combined with other products without paying duty or with the payment
delayed, thus significantly improving a company's cash flow. We told
Navistar that the zone would consider its application for subzone status.
If approved, this status would allow the company to realize savings on
duty and inventory taxes on imported goods. The idea never materialized, but it does illustrate one way a city can try to become competitive.
In 1988 for example, merchandise valued at $51 million moved
through the foreign trade zone from Japan, Germany, Spain, Italy, and
Pakistan. Medical equipment, automobile production parts, audio components, electronic parts, textiles, and machinery comprised the list of
products.

The city and state package leveraged some $36 million of scarce
capital investment from Harvester, saved more than 300 jobs, and
began the plant on an upward swing. Looking back, Tim Cooney of
Navistar remarked, "We would have been extinct without your help."
Entrepreneurial management, new product lines, sophisticated manufacturing equipment, enlightened labor leadership, and public-sector
assistance all combined to avert the shutdown of a plant and foundry
that employed some 1,500 persons, to say nothing of the 1,500 jobs
dependent on doing business with Harvester that were retained elsewhere in the economy. This would not have happened if the governmental entities involved had been disinterested.

Indianapolis competed with other areas for the location of a new
business opportunity that represented a combination of the resources

of Eli Lilly and Dow Chemical. The company would be known as Dow-Elanco. After the project was completed, it would employ approximately 1,100 men and women, and the company estimated that it would generate about $1.5 billion in annual sales, enough to put it in the middle of the Fortune 500. The city and state worked with the leaders of these two companies to arrange a package of transportation improvements and other incentives at a location on the far northwest side of the city.

The private sector brings a challenge in the form of an opportunity, and the public sector must try to help put the pieces together and make the deal work, in a true partnership. The bulk of the city's efforts, though not the bulk of the media's attention, has always been directed toward medium-sized and small business opportunities. Nabisco Foods was being wooed by other metropolitan areas, for example, but when the city offered personal-property tax abatement and training funds to use in an overhauled Indianapolis industrial site, the company decided to stay here. It announced a $40-million investment in a new margarine plant, retaining 170 jobs and creating 60 new ones. That story has been duplicated many times during the past two decades in Indianapolis.

We were not always successful in these efforts. We lost some big ones, such as a Chrysler minivan plant, an Inland Steel cold roll mill, H. J. Heinz Pet Foods, the national headquarters of the Presbyterian Church, and a large Conrail customer-service facility. If you bat .300, you're in the major leagues, and we were hitting at least that well throughout the '80s. Without a doubt, willingness to tolerate failure is a sign of entrepreneurial leadership. It accompanies a willingness to take risks, and every time a deal is put together, there is a risk that it will fail.

A local government's quiver contains a large number of arrows with which to hit the bull's-eye of job creation and enhanced business opportunity. Tax abatement, zoning, job-training funds, enterprise zones, economic development (industrial revenue) bonds, federal funds such as Community Development Block Grant dollars, infrastructure improvements, tax increment financing, grants and loans, guarantees, land acquisition powers, tax credits, foreign trade zones, economic revitalization areas (we made economic development and the removal of blight and economic obsolescence a criterion for the creation of such areas), dinosaur bills, and more comprise the arsenal of incentives that must be "customized" for each project. No single tool does the job.

It must be recognized that these incentives can be abused or used ineffectively. Tax abatement decreases revenues. Enterprise zones create discrepancies between wages and taxes of those inside the zone and those who live and work outside. (This factor explains why we ran into strong opposition from labor and neighborhood associations when we started working on the zones.) Some claim that these policies derive from false premises: according to Dennis R. Judd, "the overwhelming scholarly consensus is that tax incentives offered by local governments do not materially influence investment decisions."[46] It can also be argued that spending money (or should I say, losing money?) on tax concessions erodes a local government's fiscal capacity to strengthen education and infrastructure and other services essential to an area's economic future. And some argue that the incentives do not always lead to the jobs promised.

The Urban Policy Research Institute in Dayton recommends "abandoning strategies that rely on pumping millions of dollars into publicly leveraged downtown revitalization projects" in favor of streamlining the regulatory process, exempting self-employment income from a city's income tax, and suspending zoning laws to encourage business development.[47] Harold Wolman and associates argue that public incentives should be eliminated altogether: "State and local governments should seek to strengthen the competitive advantages of their business environments through policies that enhance productivity, such as education, worker training, and infrastructure development. State and local policies designed only to create government induced cost differentials by subsidizing specific businesses should be eliminated. State governments should prohibit local governments from engaging in interjurisdictional competition through tax concessions."[48]

That approach might work in an ideal world. Academics may well pine for a perfectly level playing field. In the real world, however, the competition is extraordinarily keen, and if a city does not create customized incentives, it will probably lose businesses to one that does. Without these incentives for companies to enhance their competitive position, many economic development projects would not happen in the first place, and little money or jobs would ever be generated beyond what was currently available.

In 1990 and '91, for example, Indianapolis granted almost $900 million of tax abatement, mostly in the industrial and personal-property categories, with a tiny amount of residential and commercial. Much of this abatement went to Eli Lilly for the development of its Technology Center and other projects, which received staggered three-, six-, and ten-year approvals. It was projected that 4,226 jobs would result from these abated projects. There is, of course, no guarantee that these numbers will prove accurate. Without the abatements, however, the private-sector firms might not have undertaken these projects, and the city would have been deprived of the investment and the resulting jobs.

Properly devised customized incentives can help make a city competitive. Most cities use them. Certainly Indianapolis did. As David Carley, former director of the city's Department of Metropolitan Development, remarked, "We changed local government's functions in this town because we became an active player in the economic development game and a partner with the business community." We had an aggressive progrowth strategy, unlike the antigrowth mentality of some cities.

Through the Indianapolis Economic Development Corporation, the city began a "Visit Indy" program that coincided with the 500-mile-race weekend each year in late May. The corporation invites guests from companies around the world to spend three days in the city to become exposed to our business potential and quality of life. It also developed a mailing list of some 300 companies around the country and sends them brochures and videos extolling the virtues of doing business in our city. Through the '70s and '80s, our job was to create growth, unlike the Sun Belt cities, whose job was to manage it. By the late '80s, however, our priorities were shifting more to growth management, as we reaped the positive results of our development strategies.

Even though there were many similarities between our city and others in how we sought to stimulate our local economies, Indianapolis had two policies that in combination may well have been unique: a strong commitment to downtown revitalization and the utilization of arts and sports to promote development. Coupled with an effective working partnership between the public and private sectors, these policies produced dramatic results as "India-no-place" became "India-show-place."

We knew that a city's identity, its image, is created by its city center. Call up the names of San Francisco, Chicago, or New York and your mind's eye centers on an image. But that was not necessarily so for Indianapolis, where a relatively nondescript city center combined with flight from blight as residents and businesses abandoned it for the suburbs. I saw our mission as downtown revitalization.

As we looked outward in the mid-1970s, we saw a distressing trend of emigration from the center city. This movement was creating a doughnut effect, with most of the development occurring on the periphery and the central core of the city becoming hollow and inert. A powerful symbol of this process occurred when the federal government removed the area offices of the Department of Housing and Urban Development to a suburban location. They eventually returned to downtown, but the initial move always struck us as a startling revelation of the problem we were facing.

This trend has continued. Today, central cities are facing tough competition from "edge cities" like Carmel on the north side of Indianapolis and Greenwood to the south, which are being developed as middle-class enclaves outside the urban area. This Information Age phenomenon has been well documented by Joel Garreau.[49] Where once there were cow pastures, cornfields, and small villages, offices and malls have sprung up. Jobs have migrated from the central city to these safer, sanitized havens, leaving the poor, the minorities, and the elderly behind and posing for many cities the challenge of coping with the flight of wealth to the periphery of their jurisdiction, where the tax rates are lower and the living is easier. Since World War II, Americans have tended to equate the American dream with how far they live from the center city, but unfortunately, economic development is more like a string than a rubber band: it does not stretch; it moves.

A generation ago, people loved to shop at attractive downtown department stores. But shopping centers began to spring up nearer to where people lived, then malls came to the suburbs, and now we create "edge cities." The wealth and jobs moved, and downtowns declined. Buildings emptied, people who could afford to move away did so, infrastructure grew older and more expensive to maintain, and decay and "urban thanatopsis" set in.

Tax-rate differentials helped stimulate the flight to the suburbs. Several factors influence this trend, but higher taxes in the central city (compared to the suburbs) certainly serve as a disincentive to stay downtown. For example, a $10-million office building with an estimated assessed value of $2.21 million would have to pay $217,306 in taxes downtown but only $100,081 in suburban Greenwood.[50] Mayor Goldsmith has pointed out forcefully how this puts downtown at a terrible disadvantage. Unfortunately, no mayor can control the downtown tax rate because the public schools, poor relief, and independent municipal corporations all have taxing powers over which the city exercises no control.

I perceived our job to be one of reinforcing the core. With our director of Metropolitan Development and the City-County Council, I created a development policy designed to counteract the forces of urban abandonment. We wanted to encourage urban reinvestment without discouraging suburban investment. We liked to say, "You can't be a suburb of nothing." We told people we did not want our city to become a doughnut with all the good development taking place outside the beltway and downtown becoming an empty hole; we wanted it to be like a good cookie, solid throughout.

There are three ingredients for successful downtown revitalization: a certain frame of mind, conscious public-policy decisions, and use of the tools available. An attitude of partnership between the public and private sectors, of cooperation and trust, coupled with a commitment to the vision of a revitalized central core, plus the patience to stay in the program for the long haul and not expect instant results, together make up an essential first step. So do public-policy decisions that recognize the importance of the planning process. Government has to reach agreements and articulate a vision about the kind of development to pursue (residential as well as commercial and industrial) and where it will go. And government has to use all the tools at its fingertips—land-usage powers, tax incentives, financing, grants, infrastructure mainte-nance, crime fighting, off-street parking authority, public transporta-tion, and even eminent domain—to make the dreams come true.

Eminent domain must be used sparingly and carefully. It can easily make government a bulldozer that tramples private businesses and homes and replaces them with asphalt in the name of the public good. It can also cost the taxpayers a lot of money, because a city has to buy—or spend—its way out of eminent domain once a price is established, and that may not be to the common good. In a five-year period, when the city purchased some $60- to $70-million worth of real estate, we used eminent domain only two or three times.

One example of our city's downtown development policy was the tennis complex we wanted to build as a permanent home for what was then, in the 1970s, the U.S. Tennis Association's Clay Courts Champion-ships. Indianapolis had been the home of this tournament for years. Originally the games were played at a private country club. Later they moved to a public suburban racquet club. In 1977 the time seemed right to invite them to settle in Indianapolis permanently. To accomplish this goal, we needed to have a permanent facility for the tournament.

City Hall offered to participate if the new complex were situated in downtown Indianapolis. We believed it would serve a useful public pur-pose. It would be a year-round facility which members of the public could enjoy, located on the edge of the downtown campus of Indiana University–Purdue University at Indianapolis (IUPUI). No bond issue money would be available, however, if the facility were built in the suburbs. That settled it; the complex was built downtown, a $7-million project including a center court with a 10,000-seat stadium and several ancillary courts. It was funded with $4 million from a city redevelopment bond issue and $3 million from the private sector—half from Lilly Endowment and half from the sale of rights to 100 box seats at $15,000 apiece. The partnership we had forged began to reverse the outward migration with a step toward downtown revitalization.

Former Indiana lieutenant governor John Mutz believes that one of the most important developments in the history of Indianapolis was the decision in the early 1960s to locate an Indiana-Purdue joint campus in downtown Indianapolis. He is correct. The campus has evolved slowly, from small beginnings in the early 1970s into a major player in the Indianapolis market. With its 29,000 students, 8,000 employees, $434-million annual payroll, and construction programs over the years that have amounted to much more than $1 billion, IUPUI has become an essential component not only of our downtown revitalization efforts but also of our economy. The city worked with the university in two primary areas: transportation planning and the construction of certain sports facilities on its property. In this case, town and gown have enjoyed a mutually fructifying relationship over the years.

The university collaborated with the city in an important revitalization project along Indiana Avenue near the campus. This historic stretch in the northwest quadrant of the downtown area, where the roots of the African-American community ran very deep, had seen better days by the 1970s. Lockefield Gardens, the second-oldest public-housing project in the country (with walls three feet thick), had fallen into vacancy and disrepair. It was surrounded by a fence, weeds were rampant, glass windows were broken out, and doors swung to and fro on rusty hinges. Businesses along the avenue languished. Crispus Attucks, the black high school where Oscar Robertson and his fabled basketball teams of the mid-'50s soared to national prominence, was undergoing thorough changes as desegregation took hold. The jazz halls where famous musicians such as Wes Montgomery, David Baker, Earl Grandy, J. J. Johnson, Slide Hampton, and Jimmy Coe had played had fallen silent. What could we do to promote revitalization?

The federal judge who had presided over the court-ordered desegregation had informed the city that renovating Lockefield for family public housing would cause racial compounding; therefore we had to find another option. Moreover, historic-preservation considerations prevented us from rebuilding the entire complex. We considered a recommendation that all of Lockefield Gardens be razed, but we rejected it after a set of hearings in Washington where Senator Birch Bayh argued against demolition. We then regrouped and formed a coalition. Leaders from City Hall and the Greater Indianapolis Progress Committee formed a partnership with neighborhood leaders along the corridor, the Health and Hospital Corporation, HUD, and the university.

We eventually devised an action plan. The city would declare a portion of the corridor an urban renewal area and make funds available to MEDIC (the neighborhood leadership group) to retain a consultant to come up with a plan. It also would work with HUD and the private sector to accomplish the restoration of up to 275 units of Lockefield Gardens housing and the construction of more than 250 units of new housing there and another 150 units for the elderly on the other side of the avenue, build a new street through the area, and "undertake other improvements and rehabilitation in the area calculated to assist in its revitalization." The university took some of the land for its medical school campus but agreed not to move any farther into the corridor.

State Representative William Crawford placed these actions in perspective at a groundbreaking ceremony: "As a youngster who grew up in Lockefield Gardens and for eight years walked by this very site daily on my way to St. Bridget's Grade School, I can remember what this area once was. I see it as it is now, and because of the leadership of Mayor Hudnut, I am confident that it will be an area we will all be proud of in the future. Because of his leadership, we can see what can happen when we talk to each other and not at each other. Thanks to him, we have, in the historic 1980 Memorandum of Understanding, a vehicle that can become a model plan for neighborhood development because it emphasizes cooperation and dialogue over competition and divisive debate."[51] The situation has turned around. Bloom has replaced blight, Lockefield Gardens is fully occupied, and the avenue is coming back to life.

It takes time to rebuild urban areas. The chapters keep unfolding. Our progress was slow and steady, but it did happen, as the dramatic changes in our skyline attested. We worked with American United Life for 18 months before it decided to come downtown rather than move to the suburbs from the midtown location it was outgrowing. We cleared out almost 30 pieces of property, vacated a street, and moved a sewer. We offered tax abatement to the insurance officials. In the end, these corporate leaders made a pioneering decision: they would build a new office building downtown.

We partnered with other companies and developers in a similar fashion, offering city services and incentives to persuade them to assist us in reinforcing the core of our city. We spent a great deal of time working with Eli Lilly, our city's largest employer and most important corporate citizen, in the development of its campus on the south side of downtown, where a mammoth research facility and technology center, new administrative offices, parking garages, a new production facility for human insulin, and a home for the new Cray-2 supercomputer are now located. We vacated streets, relocated a sewer line, pledged $44 million toward the reconstruction of a couple of major thorough-fares, and worked on some river levies. Lilly committed approximately $1 billion to new capital projects it could have built anywhere else in the world. This decision to invest more in our city was essential to our ongoing growth, but without the city's help Eli Lilly could not have accomplished it.

Some people criticized us for the displacement of a dozen or so homes and businesses by this development, but we felt that the development's benefits far outweighed the costs, either financial or personal, and we were glad to cooperate. The whole point of economic development is to benefit the majority of the people who live in your community (expansion of the tax base being an important corollary), and you do not help the locals by letting businesses move out.

New buildings began springing up on our downtown skyline during the booming, speculative 1980s. Visitors who had been away from the city for a while remarked on its startling change for the better. I began to wonder if our city was becoming overbuilt, but I did not feel it was the local government's place to tell business leaders not to build. We had to save downtown from deterioration by encouraging investment there.

To help develop an antilitter mentality, we created a Clean City Committee and made a conscious effort to keep the downtown area clean. The city established the first municipal environmental court in the nation. It committed substantial Department of Transportation resources to downtown cleanup, sweeping the streets and sidewalks six nights a week. The Police Department contributed new initiatives, such as horse patrols, bicycle patrols, and foot patrols. Buses were rerouted to keep them off historic Monument Circle in the heart of downtown and to break up traffic congestion. We beautified Monument Circle, at the heart of our city and state: we laid down bricks on all its spokes, created a winter ice-skating program, and roped off the area for festivals during warm weather. We sold people individual bricks with their names on them for $25, to build a sense of ownership in our spruced-up downtown. I recall attending a coffee hour at church one day when a conservative old-timer scolded me about the bricks, saying they were a frill and warning me that if I went ahead with the project, I would lose the next election. He was wrong.

The historic Indiana Theater on Washington Street (the old National Toll Road running through the heart of the city) came close to being demolished by the wrecking ball but was saved at the last minute. It was restructured with the help of federal Urban Development Action Grant money into three new theaters and made the home of the city's Repertory Theater. The Indiana Roof, where hundreds of high school proms had been held in the World War II era, was restored and tied in to a new Embassy Suites hotel constructed on the site of the old Claypool Hotel, which had burned down in the 1960s. On Monument Circle the decrepit Circle Theater was refurbished in a partnership between the city and the Indianapolis Power & Light Company, and, with its good acoustics and beautiful adornments, it became the new home of the Indianapolis Symphony Orchestra, which moved downtown from Clowes Hall on the Butler University campus. Another repertory theater established itself in the historic German watering hole and gymnasium, the Athenaeum. Pan Am Plaza replaced a relatively derelict block of buildings in the heart of downtown, after the city acquired the land and a private developer, Michael Browning, built a 12-story building at cost, complete with underground parking and two ice-skating rinks.

Across from Pan Am Plaza, Union Station was restored. Erected in 1888, it was the first union station in the country, but since the last train pulled out in the early 1970s this ancient building had been empty. A group of investors led by Bud Tucker, a local realtor and early pioneer in the revitalization process, purchased the station with the hope of restoring it. But that proved too costly, so the city stepped in to help. We knew that if we did nothing, Union Station would continue to decay. The roof was already leaking terribly. Therefore we pulled together some $17 million of public monies to save the station. Our goal was to preserve this historic structure and provide it with an adaptive reuse as an intermodal transportation center. We persuaded a private developer and a consortium of local banks to become partners with us, and ultimately the $60-million restoration project that created a festival marketplace full of boutiques, restaurants, and food courts, coupled with a 274-room Holiday Inn and Amtrak station, became a reality. In its first year it employed 1,700 persons and did about $50 million worth of business. It has been open for nearly seven years and is paying approximately $1 million annually in taxes.

The largest downtown revitalization project we undertook, and certainly the most controversial, was the Circle Centre Mall. Our original vision called for several city blocks, chiefly occupied by buildings that were either empty or about to become so, to be redeveloped into a downtown shopping mall, complete with anchor stores, a couple hundred retail outlets, theaters, possibly a hotel, underground parking, second-level walkways, and a "winter garden." We envisioned a project (which was subsequently downsized) that might employ on a temporary basis some 3,400 construction workers, then create 4,300 permanent jobs inside the complex with a possible ten- to 15-year payroll of $112 million. The plan called for the city to acquire the land, raze the buildings, and prepare the site, then for a private developer to build and operate the mall. We initially estimated that the total project might cost as much as $750 million. The city's portion would be financed basically by lease payments from the developer (the city would own the land) and the creation of a tax-increment financing district that would generate property-tax revenues that could be allocated to the debt service on the project.

We took the first steps in the late 1970s and early '80s with the restoration of the Indiana Theater and the old Wasson's department store building, plus the construction of a new office building, One North Capitol, to replace some deteriorated urban structures, and the new Embassy Suites hotel. The dedication of the Merchants Plaza–Hyatt Regency complex, begun in the Lugar years, also helped promote the new life downtown.

During the '80s the city worked on its side of the deal—land acquisition and site preparation—and the developer on his—design, financing, and tenants. The state legislature and City-County Council came into play, and the city borrowed $230 million to fulfill its commitments. The land was acquired, the derelict buildings torn down, and the site prepared for the foundations to be laid. The design went through several phases and changes as time wore on, but the developer's commitment never wavered.

Unfortunately, the Circle Centre project was so large and complex an undertaking that it could not be completed before the economy began to sour in the late '80s. It became almost impossible to arrange financing for commercial projects, and some major retail outlets backed away from their tentative commitments to the developer, Melvin Simon and Associates, and the city.

Critics howled. They argued that the project was too speculative, that it was wrong of the city to be giving so much money to a rich developer, that it would be better to abandon the plan than go forward, that the egos of those involved were preventing a prudent retreat, and that people would not come downtown to shop. The mall became a political football, with my opponents demanding to know exactly how it would be financed, ridiculing it as a foolish undertaking, and alleging that I was putting taxpayers' money in the pockets of some of the country's richest businessmen while ignoring the problems of the little guy.

By the end of 1990, things looked bleak. No major anchor had been signed. Saks Fifth Avenue had pulled out. It became obvious that the May Company wanted to close its big downtown store, L. S. Ayres, which was an Indianapolis landmark. The developer was not even close to arranging financing. Huge holes pockmarked the downtown landscape. And the city was on the hook for $230 million. The city believed that the downtown acreage it owned would remain a good long-term asset even if the mall did not materialize, but that was only an option of last resort. We decided to push ahead.

In November 1990 I asked for time on the agenda of the Corporate Community Council to discuss the problem. The mall was not going well, largely because the private developer was having such difficulty arranging his financing, which amounted to more than $100 million. I said that we were at a critical juncture in the city's history. If the mall failed, our national image would be severely tarnished. People would see us as a city that could not finish what it started. Our high bond rating would be lost. Downtown revitalization would stall. Would the corporate community be interested in forming some kind of consortium to become partners with the developer?

As had happened so often before, the feelings of partnership that had developed over the years came into play. I visited with the CEOs of several major Indianapolis companies. The Corporate Community Council appointed a committee to work on the project. Many meetings were quietly held. Ultimately, with Eli Lilly and Company taking the lead, a dozen companies signed on, finalizing the agreement in September 1991. The consortium pledged a total of more than $50 million to help reduce the nut the Simons had to crack. The companies would be partners with the Simons; they would not be making a grant. The companies would take an equity position in the project and would enjoy a preferred rate of return. It was a prudent investment but also a very generous display of civic spirit.

The derelict buildings were razed in the late '80s, deliberately, for two reasons: to keep the project moving forward and to remove blight from our city's downtown core. The holes in the ground became eyesores for more months than one cared to count, but they were not replacing buildings that were full of people working; they replaced empty buildings that had been for the most part vacated and boarded up.

In October 1991 we held a public ceremony to pour cement to start construction of footings for the mall. Again we felt it was important to show progress. At approximately the same time, the developers signed Nordstrom as a major anchor department store. Parisien signed on in 1992. The completion date might be pushed back to 1995, but the prospects were brighter. The dream would come true in a matter of time.

The jury is still out on urban malls. Most of them have been financial disappointments. The recession of the early 1990s has not helped them, nor has their inevitable association with urban problems such as crime and traffic. The philosophy about downtown shopping malls is changing, to help them compete with their suburban counterparts. Entertainment, focused around food, drink, and music, coupled with an emphasis on families, has assumed a status equal to that of shopping. According to the *Wall Street Journal,* these malls are "trying to recreate the sense of downtown as a community gathering place."[52] Certainly the ever-changing design of Circle Centre embodies such hopes, but it will be years before we know if they will pay off.

Patience is hard to learn in a society that wants immediate gratification and insists on instant results. Unfortunately, development projects have to be produced in a regular oven, not a microwave. They require patient nurturing and a willingness to wait quite a while for a long-range return on a short-range risk. The payout comes up front, and the payback comes much further down the road. In this case, it seemed unacceptable to do nothing and let further erosion set in downtown. Furthermore, from some peoples' perspective, the mall was the best neighborhood project we could undertake, because a healthy downtown will support inner-city neighborhoods.

In downtown revitalization projects such as Circle Centre, a city must dream about what can be, and the private sector has to devise a project responsive to the opportunity outlined in the city's plan. In this case there were three factors: risk, return, and management. The city would fill the financing gap with some form of public incentive or assistance, but it would stay out of the management. The city put some $5.7 million into the land acquisition under Pan Am Plaza, possibly $250,000 into refurbishing the Circle Theater, and $17 million into Union Station. We were always looking for a creative spinoff. In the redevelopment of Lockefield Gardens and those 747 units of obsolete downtown public housing, the city contributed $197,000 to the deal and used repayments on loans elsewhere to enhance the credit that made it possible for the developer to participate.

Leveraging Amenities

W hen the downtown portion of the Indianapolis Water Company Canal was given to the city, Congress made some monies available for the restoration of this "historic transportation way," thanks to Senator Richard Lugar. We combined this money with funds from Lilly Endowment and the city and spurred much development along the canal's borders, from a brand-new fire station to townhouses to a mini industrial park. In projects such as the canal restoration, we understood and practiced what was called "the economics of amenities."

In November 1984 the Urban Land Institute described Indianapolis's economic development strategy as "leveraging amenity infrastructure." In analyzing what differentiates the efforts of cities to attract jobs and business growth, the authors concluded that it was "the particular packaging of the tools and the specific objectives of the strategies." They quoted a report by the U.S. Department of Housing and Urban Development noting that economic development is an art, not a science, and "as such it draws heavily on the intuitive and creative skills of its practitioners." What made Indianapolis unique was the way it packaged and promoted amenity infrastructure—our convention center, sports facilities, museums, and facilities for the performing and visual arts—as tools for job creation and economic expansion. Active support for such facilities stems from a recognition that traditional capital facilities, "although necessary, are hardly a sufficient basis for economic development."[53]

Promoting amenity infrastructure can produce two advantages. First, it can help produce jobs directly for the construction, maintenance, and operation of the facilities. Second, it can enhance a city's competitive position by making it more attractive to potential investors. Cultural and sport facilities achieve goals beyond their immediate missions.

Few people pause to consider the economic impact of the arts. Usually the public and the politicians they elect regard the arts as a frill, a plaything of the very wealthy. While I served as mayor, local government plugged about three-quarters of a million dollars per year into local cultural institutions, usually only after heated council debate, editorial opposition from both newspapers, and complaints from arts leaders that our support was too skimpy. I always considered this money well spent, even though it was hard to come by. A city probably should identify a source other than the property tax for these funds, but channeling them to the agencies through the Arts Council of Indianapolis, which was created for this purpose, does get them out to the grassroots organizations, where they can do some good. The city also provides capital support for the arts through grants and loans that make projects like the renovation of the Circle and Indiana theaters possible.

Statistics assembled by the Indiana University Center for Urban Policy and the Environment for the Arts Council in a 1993 profile of the arts in Indianapolis[54] illuminate the economic impact of the Indianapolis Museum of Art; the Children's Museum; the Repertory, Cabaret, Civic, Circle and Phoenix theaters; the symphony; the Eiteljorg Museum of American Indian and Western Art; the Warren Performing Arts Center; Clowes Hall; the ballet; the opera; the Indianapolis Quadrennial International Violin Competition; the annual MacAllister Opera competition; and all our other cultural institutions, to say nothing of the art galleries, theaters, and performance clubs located in Broad Ripple Village and along Massachusetts Avenue downtown. More than 3.4 million visitors attend arts events in Indianapolis each year. Some 12,500 volunteers support the arts. The arts organizations employ more than 2,300 persons and have a collective budget of approximately $40 million. Government support for the arts in Indianapolis accounts for only 6 percent of local budgets, as do corporate contributions (national averages are higher, about 10 to 11 percent).

Cultural institutions contribute to the enhancement of the quality of life for many citizens, not just wealthy patrons. For example, the Children's Museum has a special program to address the needs of neighborhood children, most of whom are economically disadvantaged. The Neighbors Program offers a variety of special activities and programs for its participants, such as printmaking, performing arts, hiking, computers, simulated missions to Mars, and a historical look at African-American culture. The program administrators hope that as neighborhood children work together on these projects, they will improve their self-confidence, their interpersonal skills, and their knowledge through exposure to new people, experiences, and ideas.

All of this suggests that a commitment to the arts pays off handsomely for a city. Of course, the arts enhance the quality of life. Organizations that express the creativity of the human spirit in its exploration of the aspirations and frustrations in the human heart are intrinsically good for a community. They tap into the eternal amid the ephemeral. The great achievements of composers, dancers, painters, sculptors, actors, writers, and poets, along with those of youngsters and amateurs and lesser-known professionals which adumbrate the greater works, are works of art that tower over the wrecks of time, and they will be with us to make our civilization richer and finer long after the successes and failures of men and women in politics and fields of battle and commerce have vanished. The arts also contribute to the festival quality of urban living, giving people programs and events to enjoy as they celebrate the gift of life in a city environment. Art fairs, food fairs, ethnic festivals, and the like bedeck the city calendar throughout the year, giving people ample opportunity for recreation, enjoyment, and enlightenment.

Also, the indirect benefits generated from the arts community are immense, beyond the immediate impact of the jobs they create, particularly when the economic multiplier of amenity investments is considered. As we shift toward an information- and service-based economy, amenity infrastructure helps a city create a comparative advantage. A continuing commitment to the arts increases our advantage in the competition for business.

The same can be said for sports, which turned out to be the hook on which our city pegged much of its revitalization effort. Watching our progress, the *Boston Globe* observed, "The city was tired of being called India-no-place and Naptown and written off as a neon cornfield. . . . So Indianapolis decided . . . to become the amateur sports capital of America, built $168 million worth of facilities and has since brought in more than 250 national and international events."[55]

For several generations, going back to before World War I, Indianapolis had been known as the home of the Indianapolis 500 automobile race, "the greatest spectacle in racing," if not in all of sport. The city had benefited greatly through the years by the investment of various entrepreneurs, chiefly the Hulman family, in the Indianapolis Motor Speedway. Hundreds of thousands of people come to the city each May to participate in and enjoy the events associated with the race—qualifications, the 500 Festival Parade, the Queen's Ball, the Mayor's Breakfast, the Mini Marathon—as well as the race itself. The economic impact of "the month of May" has been extraordinary (precise figures are hard to come by, but the figure of approximately $60 million is common), and certainly the race has given Indianapolis a worldwide reputation. The addition of the NASCAR Brickyard 400 in 1994 did nothing but enhance the Speedway's impact on the city's economy.

Nevertheless, without denigrating the contributions of the race to the city's image and economic base, Indianapolis had to move beyond its image as a place where "they watch the race one day a year and sleep the other 364." Could we build on the sports theme made obvious by the race and turn it to positive economic development advantage? Could we use sports, which, like the arts, constitute a legitimate end in themselves, to burnish our image and stimulate investment? We felt that this was worth trying and implemented a strategy to market our city through sports.

In 1976 and 1977 we sought an answer to the question of how Indianapolis could become more competitive. What were our assets and how could we build upon them? We held retreats in Boston and Bloomington in late 1976 and early 1977. At these think-tank sessions we discussed this question with the help of a facilitator from the Massachusetts Institute of Technology, Constantine Simonides. Every city has to build on its strengths. We did not have the mountains of Denver, the bay of San Francisco, the beaches of Florida. The challenge was to figure out what our assets were and to capitalize on them. We could work for a hundred years and never be a great shipbuilding town; that was just not in the cards for Indianapolis. But we did have some positive things going for us. We concluded that our strengths included the following:

- a central geographic location, which would help us become a distribution center (our motto was "the crossroads of America");
- a heavy investment in pharmaceuticals, chemicals, and medical instrumentation;
- a substantial commitment to health, represented by the presence of the second-largest medical school in the country at IU, and Purdue's know-how in areas such as agricultural productivity and fitness;
- an expanding capability in the convention and tourism business.

Weaving these thoughts together, we found a theme in the matrix: competition, fitness, sports.

Sports! What a way to build on the inherent advantages our city possessed and the base laid for us by the 500-mile race. With their galvanizing effect on the human spirit, sports offered an attractive way to draw people's attention and enlist their cooperation in a partnership across the lines that so easily and often divide them. We would use sports to promote job growth, attract new business, enhance our image, transform us from a branch town to a destination city, and propel us toward major league status. Sports could motivate people to rally round. They have an energizing effect that other causes—such as building a steel mill or making us the insurance capital of the country or improving city housing—just do not possess. How about becoming the "amateur sports capital of the country"?

Indianapolis needed an emphasis like this one at just this moment in its history. The city was somewhat divided. Unigov was relatively new, and a true sense of community had not yet taken hold. Morale was low in the Police Department because of changes in command, newspaper investigations, and outside political interference. The hotly contested mayor's race of 1975 and the fierce rivalry among the city's banks discouraged cooperation. The city needed a leader who would exercise a reconciling and unifying influence, a coalition builder who would bring people together around new visions, new themes, and new projects.

In early February 1976 my last conversation with Gene Beesley, past chairman and CEO at Eli Lilly and Company and then chairman of Lilly Endowment, centered on this subject. We had been at a "visioning" meeting at Stouffer's Inn, and as we stood in the parking lot afterward, chatting (little did I imagine that this magnificent leader in our city would die of a stroke just two days later), we discussed the importance of overcoming the rivalries between the banks by building a spirit of partnership. Another key player at this juncture, the board chairman of our city's largest bank, the late Frank McKinney, Jr. (who had been an Olympic gold medal winner at IU), was quick to point out that we had to get people working together for Indianapolis beyond their private interests. We needed to create a unifying theme that would overcome people's commitments to private gain with a commitment to the public good.

During this period, late 1976 to early 1977, the city cemented those ties that bind, in the commitment McKinney spoke of. The process of consensus building concerned a style of leadership. It involved inclusiveness, base touching, sensitivity, patience, and working with people rather than telling them how things were going to be. Because of this, people gathered round something transcendent. Sports provided the rallying point for the partnership that became the hallmark of the Indianapolis story.

To move in this direction, however, we would have to build facilities to host the competitions that would come to town. There was great excitement at the turn of the decade, when the newly formed Indiana Sports Corporation landed the National Sports Festival for 1982. This accomplishment required a gigantic leap of faith, however, because we did not have facilities in which to host the event. Winning the competition gave us a deadline. Soon a natatorium and track-and-field facility replaced declining buildings and weedy properties on some downtown land owned by Indiana University. The tennis facility and Market Square Arena were already completed. We built a world-class velodrome and started work on the Hoosier Dome. By 1987, when the Pan Am Games came to Indianapolis, the city had added new soccer fields and the only internationally recognized rowing course in the United States (at Eagle Creek Park). All told, the city constructed some $170 million worth of facilities, with a mix of public and private money.

Supplying the glue that held it all together was Lilly Endowment. Across the country, as I tell the Indianapolis story, people ask whether we could have accomplished what we did without Lilly Endowment. I always say no. Indianapolis would not be what it is today without the tremendous support for these initiatives—and many others—from the endowment. Its generosity during the past 20 years has been a huge blessing.

We had hoped that our citizenry would also use the facilities we built. We have to do more work in this area, but we have made a start. The city has 143 parks, and we must increase our community's awareness and appreciation of the recreational opportunities they provide. As Leon Younger, the city's director of the Parks Department, has said, "Parks create the opportunity for wealth to exist. . . . Good parks represent a resource that can change the way people think about their city." These special facilities are public, and they certainly add value to our city. On any given day, one could probably find people playing tennis at the tennis center, rowing on Eagle Creek, swimming in the Natatorium, working out at the Fitness Center, and attending meetings or events in the Hoosier Dome. Access to these facilities for low- and moderate-income folks was an important part of the overall strategy in building them, but we must nurture their use.

While constructing the facilities, we worked on persuading national governing bodies for various sporting activities to locate here. The American Athletic Union moved here in 1978. The American Academy of Sports Medicine came a few years later. Governing bodies for more than a half-dozen national amateur athletic organizations—rowing, synchronized swimming, gymnastics, track and field, water polo, canoeing and kayaking, and diving—came to town. We wanted to develop an institute of sports medicine and secure accreditation as an official Olympic training center, but these ideas never really worked out, although a fitness and training center was built. (It is called the National Institute of Fitness and Sport, NIFS.)

A group of younger leaders in our city, headed by attorney Ted Boehm and Lilly Endowment president Jim Morris, realized that a volunteer organization was not going to be able to market the facilities we were building and orchestrate the athletic events that our city had begun to attract. So they incorporated the Indianapolis Sports Corporation in 1980 and hired a staff headed by Sandy Knapp, a genius in the field of attracting sporting events and putting them on in first-class fashion. The first big one was the National Sports Festival in 1982. Seeing some 4,000 to 5,000 athletes from all across America dressed in their green, white, blue, and red colors standing in the American Legion Mall in downtown Indianapolis for the opening ceremonies covered by ABC sports, alongside members of the Olympic Committee chaired by Bill Simon, was a moment of glory for our city. Then came the Pan Am Games in 1987 and the NCAA Final Four in 1991, with many other events along the way. From its inception to now, the Sports Corporation has hosted more than 250 single- and multi-sport competitions in Indianapolis, ranging from the White River State Park Games for Hoosier boys and girls to world championships in gymnastics and track and field. These events have provided a substantial economic return for the investment made and have enhanced our quality of life and our reputation as a can-do city.

In a sense, we succeeded too well. The corporation has become a model everyone wants to follow. It has put us on the cutting edge of a real growth industry. At its inception there was only one other such organization in existence (in San Diego); now there are about 100. Every time Indianapolis has done something in this area—the Final

Four, the Pan Am Games—we have taken it to a level that others want to copy. The corporation deserves much of the credit for that. People want to hold events here because they know they will be well attended, well organized, and well financed.

The Pan Am Games in the summer of 1987—coming on the heels of two national conventions, the National Association of Counties, and the National Council of State Legislatures—stretched us to the limits. But the event was certainly a high-water mark in the history of our city. The games involved some 6,000 athletes from North, South, and Central America. Approximately 40,000 persons volunteered to help the local organizing committee, dubbed PAXI (Pan Am Ten, Indianapolis), host the events during a three-week period. Worldwide media attention focused on our city. Visitors and tourists came by the thousands to watch the competitions. The opening ceremonies, colorful and dramatic, were orchestrated by the Walt Disney folks at the Speedway. The vice-president of the United States came to town to open the games.

Assessing the economic impact of these events is far from a precise science. The Final Four in 1991 had an estimated $39-million impact. The Pan Am Games brought in approximately $175 million. That was their direct contribution to our economy, measured in terms of dollars spent and rolled over. (The number came first from the Indiana University School of Business as a preliminary estimate. Later, looking at the figures from preevent traffic through our city for planning meetings, ticket sales, hotel-room nights, construction activity, purchases in business locations during that period of time, vendor and concession sales, and so on, it seemed as though the ballpark figure was correct.) We experienced some surprises: restaurants did not do nearly as much business as we had anticipated or hoped, but local appliance stores, where visitors walked in with handfuls of cash to buy portable radios, did much better than expected. Intangible benefits from the games were even more difficult to quantify. What kind of price tag can we put on the positive exposure our city received throughout the Western Hemisphere from the games? The publicity for these events was mostly favorable, and it did a great deal to enhance our image and enlarge the city's national and international reputation. People read the sports pages, and sports put us on the map.

In mid-1993 the Indianapolis Chamber of Commerce released a study it had commissioned on the economic impact of amateur sports in our city for the years 1977–91. Conducted by William A. Schaffer and Associates, the report concluded that the payoff for the city of this "high-risk, unknown endeavor" had been quite substantial. An investment of $164 million (in 1991 dollars) by government (27 percent), philanthropy (55 percent), and the business community (17 percent) attracted $1.05 billion to the Indianapolis economy from outside sources. And as this money circulated, gross revenues to businesses rose by $1.89 billion, much ending up as wages paid to city residents, some returning to the state and city as tax revenues. City residents received $683 million in personal income from the amateur sports strategy, thus producing a return on investment of 64 percent per year, a rate "well above that of most business investments." By 1991 the research could identify 526 jobs created directly in amateur sports organizations and facilities, not counting new jobs created indirectly by the infusion of new money into the economy, as manifested in significant improvements in shopping, restaurants, and cultural amenities. The study further noted that the experience Indianapolis had with amateur sports not only made available to our citizens an extensive array of health-enhancing recreational facilities "unparalleled in other cities" but was also instrumental in attracting unrelated economic development ventures such as the United Airlines maintenance facility.

Past success, however, does not guarantee future achievements. The increase in competition from other cities, the aging of the world-class facilities built in the '80s that necessitates additional expenditures, the volunteers' fatigue that inevitably sets in, the end of the novelty effect, and other such factors mean that a city has to sustain its amateur sports strategy through continuing efforts on the part of city leadership. While Indianapolis is not large enough to host the Olympics, there are many other valuable events to pursue, and the Indiana Sports Corporation will have that ongoing responsibility, which it will fulfill as long as it receives community support.

The sports strategy included more than amateur events, of course. Our professional baseball franchise, the Indianapolis Indians, had been a staple on the local scene for three-quarters of a century. Our city had also emerged on the hockey map, with the Racers, the Checkers, and then the Ice taking us through several chapters of minor league professional hockey. We were elated when the Indiana Pacers were accepted into the National Basketball Association, and we worked hard to keep them here through several generations of ownership. At one point we even held a telethon to help them out of a precarious financial situation. We traveled to Florida in search of new owners but finally ended up negotiating a deal with the Simon brothers right in our own backyard. Mel and Herb Simon bought the Pacers franchise, took over its assets and liabilities, and secured the rights to revenues generated at Market Square Arena, which they would operate. If they ever sold the Pacers, the city would receive half the proceeds. The city would cover the maintenance and utility bills of Market Square Arena through its Capital Improvement Board, which owned the structure. The agreement, negotiated in 1983, entitled the board to 50 percent of the positive cash flow.

Some have criticized the deal as being too lucrative for the Simons. Perhaps it was. The agreement may have to be renegotiated. Nonetheless, the team has stayed here. Would our city be better off without the Pacers? I think not. If we had lost our professional basketball franchise to Sacramento, which was a real possibility, our reputation as a major league city, so hard to establish, so important for our competitive position, would have been severely tarnished.

This major league reputation was immeasurably enhanced by the arrival of the Colts in 1984 from Baltimore. The Hoosier Dome awaited, a giant step forward in establishing Indianapolis as a competitive city. We had built it as an expansion of our Convention Center, but we had made it big enough for professional football. We had the benefit of a study by Stanford Research Institute that rated Indianapolis high as a potential NFL city, and we were hoping to acquire an expansion franchise. The big decision was whether to construct the dome for baseball use also. Actually we thought that the dome could be reconfigured for baseball if we acquired a major league franchise. We had decided to save about $7 million by not installing retractable seats, figuring that if we needed them for baseball, they could be added later. We visited major league baseball commissioner Bowie Kuhn, and when he and his people told us the dome could be configured for baseball, judging by the blueprints we showed him, we thought we were all set.

Later those predictions proved incorrect; the Hoosier Dome was not well situated for baseball, being sandwiched between a set of railroad tracks and the wall of the convention center. We ended up with an oblong stadium with no retractable seats; we dropped the idea of playing baseball there after an old-timers' game proved that the overhang from the second deck would obstruct long fly balls. We also realized that baseball in the dome would produce major scheduling conflicts with our convention business. Further studies concluded that Bush Stadium, where the Indians play, could not be adapted to major league specifications. Therefore we left the matter at that point. If a major league baseball team decided to come to Indianapolis, assuming our city could handle it, we would build a new open-air 40–45,000-seat facility in the downtown area.

It has been said that luck usually strikes those who are prepared. As one of the great golfers remarked, "the more I practice, the luckier I get." Indianapolis was lucky to land the Colts, but we were also prepared. We did not steal the Colts; Baltimore lost them. The Colts' owner, Bob Irsay, had been shopping his NFL franchise around. Even though the NFL owners decided in 1983 not to expand, which was a great blow to our hopes, NFL owners still had the power to relocate their franchises. Al Davis had moved the Raiders from Oakland to Los Angeles. After the Colts moved, Bill Bidwell took the Cardinals to Phoenix, and the Jets moved out of Shea Stadium into the Meadowlands. Irsay felt as though Baltimore had abandoned him. Attendance had dwindled, the stadium had deteriorated, and Irsay was being maligned in the local media. He had looked at Phoenix, Birmingham, Jacksonville, Memphis, even New York. After the 1984 Super Bowl, Tom Shine, an Indianapolis businessman who headed Logo 7 and was well connected in the NFL, called the Colts and suggested to Mike Chernoff, Irsay's right-hand man, that they consider Indianapolis, which was building a stadium. Chernoff came in for a visit. Shine showed him the new facility. The Colts were interested. And so were we.

Thus began a six-week negotiating odyssey that ended in early April. Dave Frick, now in private practice, did our negotiating pro bono. He was backed up by a group I assembled that became known as the 706 Club because we met in Room 706 of the Columbia Club in downtown Indianapolis to discuss the deal as it progressed. Our objectives were a favorable long-term lease with the option of local ownership if the franchise changed hands. The Colts also wanted a favorable lease and financing terms, coupled with assistance in relocation costs and a pledge of local support. The negotiators ended up with a 200-page document that was definitely not a giveaway. The city would build the Colts a practice facility, the Colts would share in streams of revenue generated by their arrival, we would guarantee them a certain level of support ($7 million of local radio, TV, and ticket sales for 12 years, which has never been called on because attendance has remained sufficient), and we would agree to subsidize the difference between the prime rate and 8 percent on a $12.5-million loan, if necessary.

In return the Colts would pay us to play in the Hoosier Dome ($250,000 per year, 5 percent of ticket revenues, and day-of-game expenses to approximately $100,000 per year) and the city would benefit from about $2 million of revenues from parking, concessions, suite rentals, and advertising. In addition, we calculated that the economic benefit to the city would be about $35 million per year and that the intangible benefits of national recognition would be substantial. It seemed like a good deal.

For Baltimore, it certainly was not, and the midnight departure of the Colts generated ill feelings that still remain. On the tenth anniversary of the Colts' departure, a reporter from Baltimore called me up for an interview and asked if I had any regrets over the pain I had caused his city, and whether or not I thought what we had done was "immoral." I repeated my same view to him again that I had held for ten years: Baltimore lost the Colts, Indianapolis did not steal them. Actually the Colts were forced to move from Baltimore immediately, under the cloak of darkness, because the Maryland legislature had passed a bill in late March 1984 giving government the right of eminent domain over the Colts property, and the governor was preparing to sign it. If we had given advance warning, temporary restraining orders would have flown, lawsuits would have been filed, and the Colts would have been tied up in court for months or years. But no matter. The competition had been won, and the Colts were coming to Indianapolis.

During the negotiations, one night in February 1984, Indianapolis played host, as the city does annually, to the Sullivan Awards dinner honoring America's outstanding amateur athletes. The media pounced on me at the dinner, asking about the Colts negotiations, in effect inquiring why we were trying to steal the Colts from Baltimore. I said, "What am I supposed to do? Sit on the sidelines and watch the river of history flow by and eat bonbons? Of course I'm going to compete. Any mayor worth his or her salt is going to be a fighter for their city, and do what they can to attract jobs and economic development."

Nonetheless, legitimate questions can always be raised about the extent to which a city or state should provide incentives for a business to relocate in its area. There is a real battle being waged constantly for jobs and economic growth in our country: city versus city, downtown versus suburbia, region versus region, state versus state—with no end in sight. As these battles were fought during the '80s, people began to ask whether governments were giving away the farm. Were they being bribed by private-sector companies, held up for ransom, squeezed, played off against one another? Nobody liked it, but everyone played the game because no alternative seemed to exist, except to sit on the sidelines and watch the business go elsewhere.

Illinois governor Jim Edgar thinks it is time for domestic disarmament: job-hungry states should shelve some of the heavy artillery known as incentives. Edgar says governments should cool these bidding wars: "A lot of governors want to disarm, but they don't want to disarm unilaterally."[56] But we cannot expect these bidding wars to cease soon. As *City & State* magazine concludes, "Government officials may badmouth incentives from time to time, but it is obvious that incentives are the tools politicians hate to love." Political leaders are elected to be ambassadors and advocates for their constituents, and most of them want to be aggressive about it and are therefore unwilling to say, "We pass," when an opportunity such as an NFL franchise or a United Airlines facility materializes on the horizon.

The Indianapolis strategy—using amenity infrastructure to leverage economic development activity—paid off in many ways. Investing in sports created business opportunities and jobs. Take, for example, the case of Western Electric. Its Princess telephones were manufactured in a 1.8-million-square-foot plant on the east side of Indianapolis, which employed approximately 8,700 people at its peak in the late 1970s. In September 1983 AT&T corporate leaders in New York announced that the plant would be closed, citing the building's obsolescence, judicial rulings regarding divestiture, and competition from overseas. Therefore, even though the governor and mayor traveled to the Big Apple to talk with the CEO, AT&T phased out the operations and closed the building.

I appointed a task force to look into new uses for it, but nothing much happened for a few years until two businessmen from Rochester, New York—Neil Norry and his son Lewis—came along. The Norry Company had some experience with Indianapolis, having owned the Printing Arts Center located in the Real Silk Hosiery Mills. It specialized in giving new life to old buildings such as the Packard building in Detroit and the Stromberg Carlson plant in Rochester. After much negotiating, the Norrys bought the Western Electric plant and turned it into a warehousing and distribution center. Capitalizing on its location at a major interstate interchange, they built a Hampton Inn beside the plant. With the help of the city a road was constructed around the property and Schneider Trucking Company located a regional headquarters on the other side of the plant, creating approximately 500 new jobs for our community.

Although Neil and Lewis were already familiar with the city, what caught their eye was the impetus that sports had given Indianapolis during the 1980s. They read about the city on the sports pages. They understood that the city was using sports as a major economic development tool and that sports were part of a total strategy of community revitalization. They considered Indianapolis an up-and-coming city— energetic, progressive, and dynamic; in short, a city worth investing in. Therefore they bought the plant. Without the reputation the city had developed as a result of its commitment to sports, the Norrys might not have decided to do the deal.

Also at this time, entrepreneurs began opening new restaurants in Indianapolis, building new downtown skyscrapers, and adding new hotel and motel rooms. The Hoosier Dome expanded our Convention Center, and convention business skyrocketed. Unquestionably the coming of the Colts aided these efforts, but they were also part of the city's general economic surge in the '80s. Some of the activity was spurred by the nationwide economic expansion of the '80s, but part of it was clearly a payoff of the sports strategy as well, which made us a much more competitive city.

A city cannot rely on just one game plan, however, in its economic development. To stay competitive with other cities, we will have to develop new strategies, such as a heavier emphasis on the arts or air cargo or automobiles. The challenge in the '90s is to sustain the momentum of the '80s and ride the winds of change creatively. We have reached a high plateau, and we must stay there while continuing to do well in the sports area.

Consider the Circle City Classic, a joint venture between Indiana Black Expo and the Indiana Sports Corporation. Played here each October, it features two predominantly black college or university football teams and has an estimated $10-million impact on the city. This event always fills the Hoosier Dome, and approximately 45 percent of the 62,000 attendees are visitors to our city who fill up all the hotels within a 45-mile radius. This event ranks just behind the 500-mile race as the second largest hotel-night event of the year in our city. The event has been growing steadily, and the challenge facing the city is to nurture it, not start a new one.

Harvesting Plums

By the end of the 1980s, as the economy decelerated, the competitive base laid by the initiatives of the previous decade put Indianapolis in a strong position to contend for one of the juiciest economic development plums to come along in many a year—a new maintenance center for United Airlines.

On November 21, 1991, the *Arizona Republic* carried an article on Indianapolis. It observed that the United Airlines maintenance facility, along with the U.S. Postal Service mail-sorting hub, were two of the "highest profile economic development plums in the nation this year." They exemplified "the Indiana capital's ability to overcome enormous odds and hook the kind of businesses other cities drool for." It credited the success to the public-private sector partnership that had developed during the previous two decades. "Having won both projects over dozens of competing bidders within a span of two weeks last month," the article continued, "Indianapolis has gained a national profile for what residents call an unusually close cooperative relationship between government and business that's especially important during these tough economic times. It is this public-private blend of civic spirit that built the Hoosier Dome, lured the National Football League's Colts from Baltimore and established Indianapolis' reputation as an amateur sports center a decade ago."

And what was the project we landed? A second (the first was in San Francisco) United Airlines Maintenance Operations Facility, MOC II. It would occupy a 2.9-million-square-foot building plus other buildings for office, administration, and supply space, to be constructed at a cost of more than $800 million on 300 acres of Indianapolis airport land to provide comprehensive airframe and power-plant maintenance service on United's entire fleet of Boeing 737s, which numbered some 200 planes, with the expectation of doubling that number in the next ten years. The 50 Airbus A320s United expected to add in 1993 would be serviced there also. The facility would be so large that 17 737s would be able to fit under its roof at the same time. MOC II would be a seven-day, 24-hour-a-day operation with state-of-the-art technology, expected to cut the average maintenance time from 28 days to as little as 18 days per plane. Some 6,300 jobs would come on line, with an annual payroll of some $250 million. And it was estimated that the project would create another 18–20,000 jobs indirectly in central Indiana. United suppliers and vendors would probably do approximately $100 million of business annually in our economy.

Worth pursuing? You bet!

Landing MOC II was a "consummation devoutly to be wished." It would bring to fruition two decades of partnership and aggressive economic development strategies, with sports in the background, which had become the theme of the Indianapolis story. Everything led to this. It tied the themes together. "The amateur sports strategy became a glue that held together a growth coalition of public and private interests," said Mark Rosentraub, associate dean at Indiana University's School of Public and Environmental Affairs. Observing that the city was "reaping the rewards from the decisions and investments it made during the economic contractions of the 1970s and early '80s," Rosentraub commented: "There hasn't been an explosive growth. There has been a good, steady base of expansion."[57] In short, this huge economic development plum fulfilled the efforts of Indianapolis over a quarter of a century to become competitive in the face of the insidious decline of the Midwest's traditional economic engine and consequent loss of high-paying manufacturing jobs that threatened so many Rust Belt cities.

In late 1989 UAL sent letters to states east of the Rockies and south of the Mason-Dixon Line requesting proposals on possible sites for a new maintenance complex. Ironically, Indiana was not on the original list. United wanted a warm-weather location, where it could work year round outdoors as well as inside, and our state did not fit that requirement. How Indianapolis made the initial cut therefore is a story in itself.

The City of Terre Haute found out about the United request for proposals and persuaded the State of Indiana to support it in submitting an independent package. Indianapolis heard about the Terre Haute proposal, and we alerted our Airport Authority officials, who had also heard of the proposed facility in a roundabout way. If Terre Haute could apply, why couldn't we? Our airport officials called United to ask whether the Indianapolis airport could apply for consideration. They were told that they had missed the cut-off—mid-February 1990—and that United would not accept any unsolicited proposals after that. But we were not to be deterred. Our deputy mayor, John Krauss, and our director of Metropolitan Development, Mike Higbee, sensed the economic potential of the deal, and Dan Orcutt, director of the Airport Authority, felt that Indianapolis had something unique to offer in the form of land ready for construction.

They discussed the matter with me, and our conversations inspired a decision that seemed modest at the time but in retrospect appears momentous: Indianapolis would throw its hat in the ring. "Let's go for it" was the response, just as it was six years previously when it appeared that the Colts might be looking for a new home. Orcutt sent United a letter reiterating our desire to join the competition. United called him on March 13 and said, "OK, you have two days to get a proposal in to us." Elaine Roberts, deputy executive director of the Airport Authority, spent the next 48 hours preparing our initial proposal, which went, with letters from state and city officials, to the Chicago headquarters of United Airlines on March 15. Our foot was in the door.

We could have decided not to pursue the matter. Too risky, too big, too uncertain, too little chance of success, too costly if we got it. We could have played it safe, but we decided to give it a try. Our entrepreneurial spirit prevailed once more over the forces of caution and skepticism. We felt that this project represented such a large economic development opportunity that it would be almost irresponsible not to seize any chance to get in the running. And we knew we could always opt out of the process later if it turned sour.

In March we filed the unsolicited proposal with UAL from the Airport Authority, and we followed it a month later with a more complete one. Unbeknownst to us, more than 90 sites originally applied for consideration, but by the end of 1990 the list had been pared way down, and only nine remained. Before long, in 1991, the list was further reduced to four finalists: Louisville, Denver, Oklahoma City, and Indianapolis.

At each step of the process we conscientiously tried to keep political and business leaders in the decision-making loop so that they would not be caught by surprise later. We also tried to understand how each step we were taking would affect our economy. At each bump up in the bidding war, we and the state took time out to analyze the figure closely and perform a cost-benefit analysis to see if the return continued to justify the outlay. We analyzed the impact of the new level of commitment on elements such as tax base, tax revenues, job creation, and new investment that would be created, to see how broad a net we were casting and ask the fundamental question: is it still worth it?

We went out of our way to understand our competition. We kept an eye on the other cities so that we would know what to put on the table and not get too far ahead of them. We subscribed to a newspaper clipping service to keep abreast of our competitors' negotiations with United along with related factors, such as their utility rates, labor costs, weather, airport land availability, and public controversies surrounding the proposals.

As the bidding escalated, Indianapolis managed always to hang in with the others. There were several reasons for this outcome. For one thing, we had an excellent site. The airport had been doing much prudent landbanking during the previous 20 years; we could offer 300 acres of land free and clear of any encumbrances (except for a minor environmental hazard—the possibility that the Indiana bat had a sanctuary nearby). In contrast, one of our competitors, Louisville, was at a severe disadvantage because its airport did not have this kind of land ready. It would have had to endure a protracted condemnation process and relocate many displaced homeowners. "Indianapolis was ready," as one local business leader, Richard Notebaert, president and CEO of Indiana Bell, pointed out in a retrospective for the *Indianapolis Business Journal.* "We were prepared. The groundwork was laid and the infrastructure was in place. We didn't go to United with plans we would implement if they would choose us: we went to them with a description of what we [had] to offer right now."[58]

Second, by mid-1991 the state and the city were working closely together. We were presenting a united front to the teams of private-sector officials on the other side of the table. (United had an A team, composed of financial people and others in top-level positions who did the negotiating, and a B team of technical engineering staff.) We gave them the secure feeling that we would deliver on our promises and not become bogged down in political bickering. Probably my announcement that I was not going to run again for reelection and would be looking for work in the private sector after my fourth four-year term (ending December 1991) helped inspire the new spirit of cooperation. But no matter. United saw clear bipartisan cooperation between two levels of government. The governor, the mayor, and their negotiators had become a team and were working closely with good faith and in earnest. I worried about Republicans resenting my alliance with the Democratic governor on the project—success would give the governor something to brag about in the future—but I was much relieved when the chairman of the Indiana Republican party said to me, "Bill, you did the right thing."

Such cooperation paid off handsomely, and it was a rewarding experience. If the city and state had jockeyed to claim the credit or if the negotiations had been used to gain partisan political advantage, the deal might never have materialized. After it was finished, people often commented about how refreshing it was to see a Democrat and Republican working so well together for the good of their constituents. It doesn't happen very often. (We might note in passing that Kentucky hurt itself by not manifesting this kind of partnership. The governor did not include the mayor of Louisville in the negotiations, and the city's airport authorities were left pretty much outside the loop, all of which hurt the final bid.)

As already implied, the Indianapolis Airport Authority proved to be an indispensable partner with the state and city. Its officials deserve much credit for making the deal happen. Not only did they carry most of the up-front costs of preparing our proposals and do most of the early legwork in one 90-hour week after another, but at every step along the way they signed the agreements being negotiated, along with the state and the city. The internal documents constantly referred to the three entities as "The Partnership."

The partners also included private-sector leaders—again, something that did not have to be manufactured, thanks to our city's long tradition of public- and private-sector partnership. United undoubtedly noticed how well we all worked together. In a speech to Indiana economic development officials on September 29, 1992, Rick Street, United's vice-president for airport affairs, identified "the great cooperation between the public and private sectors that obviously has been nourished here over the last twenty years" as a key factor in United's decision. He said: "in many major cities, that is not the case. Politicians and business leaders often become adversarial, and the economy of the community suffers as a result. But that has not been true here."

We should note two examples of this partnership. Organized labor tried hard to help. Street spoke of our city's "excellent track record for harmonious labor-management relations, especially in the construction industry," as another factor in our successful bid. "When you're building an $800 million facility with tight deadlines, you don't want it stifled by strikes and picketing and frivolous work rules that impair efficiency at the job site." When we were advised by UAL that our construction cost figures were higher than those of the other cities, we approached the local unions to see how we could shave costs. They agreed to use more lower-paid apprentices, and they also pledged not to strike or hold any other work stoppages, so that United could be confident of meeting its construction deadlines. (The first building was completed within budget and on time in early 1994.)

In another example of the kind of cooperation that truly made a difference, technical people assembled behind the scenes to pull together background information and do the nitty-gritty legwork, while Mike Higbee and Mark Moore, representing the mayor and governor respectively, did the higher-profile negotiating. The Airport Authority brought together personnel from city and state departments and the utilities in an all-day session to answer a hundred technical questions United's B team had posed. The Indianapolis Economic Development Corporation collated important information from the phone and power companies. According to Indiana Bell's Notebaert, when telephone company representatives met with United in August, "We told them about fiber optic capabilities and route diversity. We described central office switching equipment and emergency back-up power suppliers, carrier access rates, network service capability, and a number of other subjects. . . . The other city utilities did the same. Each in turn gave overwhelming evidence that they have planned for the future, that they have made good choices and wise investments in their physical facilities."[59] In short, teamwork paid off for Indianapolis.

So did a professional negotiating manner that kept most of the conversations and correspondence quiet, confidential, and off the front pages of the newspapers. This is a third reason why Indianapolis was able to stay competitive. There is no question about the importance of this point. Denver, the odds-on favorite to win the competition, hurt itself badly by allowing political wrangling and details of the deal to spill out in public. Premature disclosure of a city's offer only tipped off the others, enabling them to sweeten their proposals. Of course, the participants planned to bring a wider circle of public officials and the media into the loop. But going public too early and submitting our proposals to intense scrutiny and second-guessing, with all the political posturing and criticizing it would have entailed, would have served no useful purpose. Indeed, it would probably have scuttled our chances. You cannot negotiate deals like this (or the Colts) in public.

The fourth reason why we stayed competitive is that we managed to include just enough financial incentives to stay in the running at each step. We never led the chase, but we never lagged so far behind that we failed to make the next cut. By the end of 1990, when the list had been pared down to nine cities, the city and state had almost $150 million on the table in grants, loans, and tax abatement. Six months later the figure had escalated to $170 million. It climbed by $20 million more by the end of the summer, and on October 16, 1991, we received a call saying that only four cities were left in the running, that they were all invited to come to Chicago the next day to make their presentations, and that Indianapolis would certainly be welcome, but we were "about $135 million short."

Actually we were lucky to have our foot still in the door. After the dust settled we found out that the name of Indianapolis did not initially appear on that October 16 calling list. The negotiating team had dropped us off. Somebody higher up had pulled rank, however, and given the order to reinstate our name. Why?

Certainly for some of the reasons listed earlier, and certainly the financial package we had put together had kept us in the ballpark. But nonmonetary considerations also contributed, as we discovered in subsequent public and private remarks by United officials. We did not offer the most cash and incentives. Rick Street later stated, in his 1992 speech, that "the financial side of the package" was not "the deciding issue." We put together what he called "an attractive proposal" even though we came late to the bidding, and in the end our incentives package "was very competitive with other cities." On October 23 United chairman Steve Wolf told us, "You did not have one dime too much on the table." He did not discuss the merits of the four final proposals—which would have invited the other cities to make invidious comparisons. But it can safely be said that there were many reasons why Indianapolis was awarded the contract, and money was only one of them.

We had a beautiful site all ready to go—300 acres free of condemnation proceedings, demolition work, and zoning battles. The Indianapolis Airport Authority had an excellent reputation in the industry. This track record helped, as did our proximity to Chicago, home of United's headquarters. The airport's foreign trade zone helped, as did the news that the U.S. Postal Service would construct a new distribution center on our property. As Street remarked, "everything we learned about the Indianapolis airport suggested they were ready to play in the big leagues of American aviation."

The fact that our airport was seldom closed for bad weather did not hurt, even though United had initially confined its search to warm-weather cities. Specialized training for United's mechanics and engineers, to be made available through Purdue and Vincennes universities, enhanced our package. United was impressed by the "abundant supply of skilled labor" in our area and the promises of the universities to beef up their programs to fill the forthcoming manpower needs. Other factors publicly mentioned by United officials included the quality of life in central Indiana, the moderate cost of living, "all the amenities of a major urban center," our willingness to make a long-term commitment coupled with the capacity to deliver on what we promised, the diversity of our economy, and the financial viability of the state and city. The state's constitution prohibits it from deficit spending that piles up debt, and the city's triple-A bond rating and "great track record for paying its bills" impressed United's management team. Finally, Wolf mentioned an intangible factor, the "spirit" of the agreement. In the long run, many small pluses added up to a victory for Indiana and Indianapolis.

On October 22 we received word that Wolf wanted to see the mayor and the governor as soon as possible. We agreed to meet in the governor's residence the next morning, not knowing whether we had won. We knew when we came home from Chicago that we were still short, by perhaps as much as $85 million, so we worked feverishly over the weekend to move the numbers in our favor and close the gap, arguing with United's negotiating team about the way they discounted some figures to present-day value, how they valued our commitments on things such as the cost of labor and power, and so on. The governor and I had talked late one night about how much further we could extend ourselves, and we agreed that in the last escalation of our offer, instead of splitting the sums equally—as we had been doing but which I did not think the city could afford any longer—we would go one-third city and two-thirds state.

I went to the meeting on October 23 primed with responses to the questions I thought the UAL chairman would ask, the most important being how do I know that you can deliver on your commitment if you will be going out of office at the end of the year and we don't know who the new mayor is going to be? By this time, both mayoral candidates and the leadership of the City-County Council had been briefed on the negotiations, and I thought I could handle the question.

But it never came. Steve Wolf walked into the room, shook hands with the governor and me, and said, "I'm glad we're coming to Indianapolis. Please give me a few hours to notify the other cities and their senators, and then you can release the news."

We exchanged a few thoughts about the deal. During the course of our conversation, I asked him whether we could have confidence that United would be around ten years from now: its balance sheet showed more liabilities than assets, and in 1991 it was losing more money than it was taking in. He responded that United was a survivor and that despite the difficult times in the airlines industry, the company would make it, along with American, Delta, and possibly a couple of others. We shook hands and went our separate ways.

For me this was an extraordinarily emotional moment. I was about to leave office, and we had just landed the largest economic development deal in the country. We had competed against 92 other cities and won. All that business, all those jobs, would be coming to Indianapolis in the next ten years. As I realized this, a lump developed in my throat, just as when I walked into the Hoosier Dome with Bob Irsay in early April 1984 to introduce him to the Indianapolis community after he had announced he was moving his NFL team to our city, and some 20,000 people stood up to cheer.

We had a month to finalize the agreement—30 days to negotiate final terms with United and persuade the community's political leadership and the public that this deal could be financed and was worth ratifying. And between November 21 and year's end we would have to put the funding package together, enact the necessary ordinances, and complete the rest of the paperwork.

That was a tall order, but not impossible. It required herculean amounts of work, hundreds of hours of discussion, untold numbers of meetings, public hearings, private sessions with lawyers, delicate but deep conversations with the mayor-elect and his representatives, briefings and planning sessions with members of the city council, touching base with other elected officials, neighborhood associations, and union officials, background sessions, news conferences, and much else. I canceled a speaking engagement in Italy in order to stay close to the scene. The governor worked on his end of the deal. When Steve Wolf returned to town on November 21, we had everything ready and held a gala public signing ceremony in the governor's office. By December 31 the rest of the job was pretty well completed.

When the dust settled, what had we agreed to, and did it make sense? United committed to locating, constructing, and equipping the MOC II facility at the Indianapolis airport with an investment of at least $800 million by December 31, 2001, and to have at least 6,300 full-time employees with an aggregate payroll of more than $250 million working there by the end of 2004. The airline also promised to use reasonable efforts to engage the services of and procure goods and supplies from minority- and female-owned business enterprises. And it agreed to help the state and city induce other private entities to locate significant new economic development projects in Indiana.

A unique feature of the agreement entailed a penalty provision if United failed to meet these investment and employment goals. United would reimburse the city and state based on a proportional repayment of the incentives provided, one-third for the investment and two-thirds for the level of employment goals. The *Indianapolis Star* called this stipulation "savvy work."[60] In an article quoting economic development experts with a national perspective, the *Star* said "it appears to be a blockbuster deal that will change the way communities compete and the way they ask companies to guarantee their promises." Holding companies accountable in writing to repay the taxpayers' incentives if the promises of jobs and investment are not fulfilled was "truly unique," according to a professor at the University of Southern California in Los Angeles. "Someone had a real light bulb idea," said Jon P. Goodman. "This is clearly a good deal for United and a good deal for Indiana."

Not everyone thought it was a good deal, however, primarily because the price tag was high—too high for some people, but a price that others thought was worth paying to garner the benefits it offered. The Airport Authority promised to deliver 300 acres in "construction-ready condition" to United by the end of 1992 and make improvements, such as access roads, taxiway connectors to a runway, sewer lines, and utility access. The airport would lease the site to United. The airport would issue up to $850-million worth of tax-exempt special-facility revenue bonds, which would be offset by the amount of tax increment financing bonds and other instruments United might utilize. The airport would pay back the special-facility bonds out of United's lease rentals and would pay off the tax increment financing bonds from personal property taxes on United's equipment collected in an Airport Development Zone to be established by the Metropolitan Development Commission.

The state agreed to a grant of $15.2 million to United to pay costs of the project and to issuance of tax-exempt revenue bonds to provide $159 million for the MOC II facility. Hendricks County, which stood to gain much development from the deal because of its location just west of the airport, provided an $8-million incentive. Indianapolis promised to issue its tax-exempt revenue bonds within 90 days of the signing of the agreement, to provide $111.5 million for the facility. United would pay no real property taxes (no businesses do at the airport) or state corporate-income taxes. Each government also agreed that none of the costs or expenses of the project would "in any manner be paid, directly or indirectly, from airport rates, charges, or landing fees."

Arranging the city's side of the financing was extraordinarily difficult. In our briefings of the City-County Council leadership, we had continually discussed the possibility of using an economic development income tax to cover our costs. That would have amounted to a 0.1 percent increase in people's income taxes, and if we reduced the county option income tax by an equivalent amount, it would be a wash for the taxpayers. Other possibilities on our complete list of financing options included general obligation bonds, sale of city assets, tax increment financing, reducing homestead credits, a regional economic development income tax, airport revenues, and so on. The council leadership supported us every step of the way, asking tough questions and doing due diligence with us, but also understanding the tremendous opportunity ahead.

The mayor-elect had been skeptical in his campaign comments about the United deal, and he had made a no-tax-increase pledge. Therefore after the election we had to work closely with him and his people to ensure that the plan we submitted to the council would enjoy his support. We believed our plan of creating a new economic development income tax coupled with reduction in the county option tax was the option of choice, but the new administration did not consider that acceptable, so it would have had a rough time in the council elected in November 1991. (It had to be enacted, according to state law, in the first quarter of the new year, and without a special act of the state legislature—which the governor and the chairman of the House Ways and Means Committee did not support—the old council could not pass it in November or December of 1991). Therefore we had to come up with a different idea.

In our deliberations on this issue, we outlined certain parameters acceptable to everyone involved in the decision—the old and new mayors and City-County Council members, to say nothing of the public. They were as follows: no new taxes, no service cutbacks, no reduction in homestead credits, capturing of new airport growth revenues, and encouragement of creative funding approaches. The basic idea was to derive as much revenue as possible from the growth to be experienced at the airport in the next ten years. We had an $11 million to $15 million annual nut to crack, and to get there we proposed estimated revenues ranging from $12 to $17 million, to be derived from property and income taxes from the benefited district, energy savings, service charges, debt-service savings, and savings from refinancing of longer-term debt. This was more complicated than our original plan, but the new mayor and his people wanted it, and I felt obligated to support it and advocate its acceptance.

To float the city bonds, county option income tax funds were pledged, but it was clearly understood by the council, the administration, and the public that they would not be drawn down and that the revenues mentioned earlier would actually be utilized for the debt service. The City-County Council spelled this out carefully in the ordinance it passed toward the end of 1991 to fulfill the city's part of the agreement. It did this to reassure the Fraternal Order of Police leaders, who felt threatened by the county option proposal because so much funding for the Police Department came from that source.

Was the deal too sweet? Some thought so. Was it fair? Some thought not. Conservative writer Fred McCarthy, a former president of the Indiana Manufacturers' Association, called it "a $110 million bribe to a private corporation to locate in the city." He went on to say that "there are citizens of Indianapolis who need public assistance but who will never benefit from the 'economic development' schemes so widely touted as 'progress' for the city." He concluded that "for some years, the city of Indianapolis has been run with a sadly misguided set of priorities."[61]

A respected local businessman, Tom Binford, writing in his regular column in the *Indianapolis Business Journal,* expressed sympathetic understanding for the difficulty public officials have when operating in a marketplace where these kinds of auctions occur. He wrote that we seemed "to have done an excellent job within those parameters," but he said he was disturbed by the process of "buying jobs" and felt that we should give more thought to the ramifications of this process.[62]

The editors of the *Indiana Policy Review* expressed harsher criticisms. According to their calculations—based on the conclusion they wanted to arrive at—we had put up $630 million for a "promised" 6,000 jobs, which amounted to more than $100,000 per job. Of course they thought that was much too high a price.[63] (One could figure it another way, however, dividing the dollars by the total number of jobs attributable to the project, which would imply a much lower cost per job.)

In *City & State* magazine, an unidentified economist pointed out the downside of the commitments of city money to economic development. Hudnut "is fond of saying, 'I got the Colts, the Pan Am Games and built the downtown,' but we have yet to see what the rate of return on those particular investments has been. What we do know is this city is going to be paying off the debt into the next century."[64]

These are legitimate public-policy questions. Did we pay too much? That's hard to calculate, but to the mayor, the governor, and those in the legislatures who supported their decisions, the benefits seemed to justify the commitments. Did this deal put too big a load on small governmental units? Decatur Township officials who lived near the airport complained that the burden on their infrastructure would become too heavy and there would be no funds to finance it, because the tax increment financing would plow the revenues back into the project and not distribute them to the townships. This may have been true, but there was no way of ascertaining how many of the new employees at United would live in Decatur Township. Moreover, without the tax increment financing, there would have been no deal. Often those who complain about public commitments of tax-abated dollars and the like forget that these incentives are essential to a project and the revenue increases it brings, that nothing would happen without them.

Was the deal fair? Should we have given the money to small businesses in small amounts? That is what the Republican candidates for governor and lieutenant governor of Indiana in 1992 argued. And Sam Staley, an urban economist at Wright State University in Dayton and president of the Urban Policy Research Institute, maintained that "traditional approaches to revitalizing urban areas appear to be nothing more than financial black-holes. . . . Cities need to shift their focus away from large, publicly leveraged downtown revitalization projects . . . and concentrate on cultivating small businesses and entrepreneurship."[65]

Certainly it is true that most of our business growth comes in smaller increments than 6,300 jobs. Looking at the growth of jobs in Indianapolis and the record of our administration in assisting smaller businesses, however, it would be unfair to suggest that we were interested only in big deals. We wanted to hit singles as well as home runs. But the home runs received most of the attention. We might also note that some of these larger dollar amounts simply could not have been assembled for smaller deals, because they were either earmarked for specific projects, such as the Hoosier Dome, or largely derived from the project itself, as with the United deal.

Some people criticize government tax incentives as inherently unequal—they are given to some, not to others. Public-private partnerships are not universally admired. Former IU professor Robin Paul Malloy, who is now at Syracuse University School of Law, criticizes them as acting in restraint of trade. He asserts that they prevent Adam Smith's "invisible hand" from doing its work and that they foster rule by an elite hierarchy.[66] Reviewing this book, Washington and Lee University law professor Denis J. Brion asserts that "classic liberalism seeks to maximize freedom, individual liberty and human dignity through capitalism and the free market as counterbalanced by a limited state," whereas "partnerships, by contrast, . . . are part of 'ever increasing trends toward central planning, communitarianism and statism.' "[67] In another review, Paul Brietzke of Valparaiso University calls urban politicians "pyramid-building pharaohs . . . appear[ing] to suffer from Edifice Complex[es]." He maintains that such politicians spend "scarce resources on prestigious buildings . . . [to] enhance the 'lifestyle' of the upper middle class through a gentrification that attracts this group's political support."[68]

To such criticisms the mayor (and probably the governor, although he can speak for himself) can only respond as follows: were we to pass up the opportunity to bring 6,300 jobs into a new $800-million facility that would generate an annual payroll of a quarter-billion dollars and indirectly account for 18–20,000 more jobs in this area, 12,000 new homes being built, and $100-million worth of new business being done annually, and let that development go elsewhere, we would not be doing our best for the people who elected us. The folks in 92 other cities would love to have made the cut. They didn't, and we did. They would give their eyeteeth to be in the position we are in. They all consider this a coup. The market is unerring in its accuracy. MOC II is unquestionably the most significant economic development deal in the country. It has value. Ninety-three cities could not all be wrong. Probably only time will tell whether this was a good deal for everyone. But we believed that our leap of faith was prudent and would be justified by subsequent events, and so we forged ahead. I really think that this kind of risk taking is what leadership is all about.

Marion County and Indianapolis made a greater sacrifice than the state did, for more of the benefit will go to the state than to the city. The state might see it otherwise, because it put up more dollars than the city. But the state will collect the sales tax and income tax, and unless the new workers live in Marion County, local government will not receive that revenue directly. Nonetheless, we concluded that we would all benefit indirectly by the growth that will occur. What helps one helps all.

When the happy event was celebrated in the governor's office on November 21, the broad consensus seemed to be that we had won a significant victory that had positive long-range implications for the city and state economies. We were taking a risk, in true entrepreneurial style, but we believed that it was a prudent one. The bread we were casting on the waters would return to us severalfold. Top business, labor, and political leaders of our city and state attended the ceremony, and when it came my turn to speak—after UAL's Wolf and Governor Evan Bayh—I remarked that "today is one of the greatest and most exciting days in our city's history." Thanking United for its commitment to our city and state and expressing my gratitude to all who had worked so hard to make this dream come true, I referred to the "month-long process of intense, tough negotiations" carried on day and night for the past 30 days "to address thorny issues and resolve horrendously complex problems."

I did not sugar-coat the challenges that lay ahead: financing the deal, preparing the site, gearing up to attract the spinoff businesses that would serve United and drive other parts of our economy well into the 21st century, organizing our postsecondary institutions to train our citizenry so it could take advantage of these high-skilled jobs, and developing joint planning on economic development with our neighboring counties. But I pledged that we would be faithful, hardworking partners with United in this gigantic undertaking. "We stand united for United," I concluded. "Indianapolis will meet these challenges. We are a can-do city. We are a city that says 'yes' to opportunity."

No Conclusion,
Just a New
Beginning

C ities are the laboratory in which the experiment of American democracy is being conducted. There is no guarantee that the experiment will succeed. The cities might explode. The experiment might fizzle out. Or the experiment can work. Usually the end result represents a mixture of the possibilities—success here, failure there. Not all the dreams come true, but progress can occur and positive results can be achieved.

In the minds of many, Indianapolis came off the sidelines in the past three decades, emerging as a major player among the nation's cities. The *Hartford Courant* observed that "in Indianapolis, they've learned to think regionally, to aggressively encourage economic growth, to establish a common vision and pursue it with a vengeance and to spread the cost among all (or at least most) of the people who benefit. It's a formula that's lifted America's twelfth largest city out of a tailspin and made it one of the most livable places in America."[69] One can only hope that the quality of life for our citizens has changed as much and as well as our skyline, where 34 new buildings sprang up during the 1980s.

In saying this, I recognize that it would be a serious error to claim too much success. Indeed, Indianapolis has enjoyed positive change and growth since 1965, particularly in the 1980s, as seeds planted earlier flowered and the rising tide of the national economy lifted many boats. But we did not entirely reverse the urban decline that affected Indianapolis as well as most other big cities. The physical infrastructure of this old industrial community continues to deteriorate. Crime remains too high. Too many people are still too poor. Poverty and unemployment still cast their shadows across the lives of too many citizens. In the hearts of many, hopelessness and alienation have taken firm hold. Race relations can always be improved. Indianapolis may have achieved desegregation, but true integration is still a distant dream, as is the removal of the invisible "glass ceiling" that prevents many women and minorities from rising above a certain level in the corporate pyramids in our town.

The agenda remains unfinished. We completed many projects, but many remain. The neighborhoods always need more attention, as our community continues the fight against blight and flight. One wonders whether the old concept of "minigov" will be born anew. We continue to strive to provide safe, decent, affordable housing for low- and moderate-income people, and public housing that is well managed and an asset for the city instead of a liability. Downtown will prosper only when more people start living there. The flow of business ownership out of state is threatening to make our city a branch town, with only Eli Lilly and Indianapolis Power & Light remaining in the ranks of large home-owned employers. The job of retaining and nurturing existing businesses will never end, and it needs the maximum possible support from government.

The Campaign for Healthy Babies will bring infant-mortality rates down if it receives an institutional home in the city. As the city grows, a more regional approach to issues that transcend obsolete governmental jurisdictional lines—such as trash disposal, transportation planning, and zoning—would make sense. We must reform education to utilize innovative ideas about how to educate our children better. And we can only hope that the scourge of drug abuse and gang violence will abate when everyone takes up arms against this sea of troubles and refuses to leave it all to government.

The drawer of unfulfilled dreams is pretty full. In the sports realm we do not have major league baseball or hockey. If major league baseball comes, and with it a new stadium, could we make Bush Stadium available to the American Legion as the permanent home of its annual World Series? We have discussed building an Olympic training facility, as well as a Wall of Fame at the Hoosier Dome to memorialize outstanding Hoosier athletes, but we do not have them yet. In transportation, could we build a bike bath along the old Monon tracks and down the canal, or develop that corridor as a light rail or bus system? Might a rapid surface-transit system some day connect Union Station and the Indianapolis airport with Bloomington and West Lafayette, or a high-speed railway link our city to downtown Chicago? Should we try to build a second-level walkway and automated guideway system tying the major downtown buildings to one another along with White River Park and the Indiana-Purdue campus, or a series of connector tunnels doing the same thing?

Indianapolis is waking up to its international dimension, which we can enhance through new sister-city relationships with several cities around the world in addition to those already in place with Cologne, Scarborough, Taipei, and Puerto Allegre. The city can become more global by developing the airport's capability to move cargo as well as passengers globally and linking Indianapolis to Europe with direct airline service.

Several plans and hopes are still on the table. The city must complete White River State Park and beautify and better use White River. During my last year in office, I suggested to the chairman of the incoming Corporate Community Council that an umbrella agency be created to yoke the different entities now in place promoting Indianapolis into one comprehensive coordinated body called "Indianapolis Tomorrow." The arts need a permanent source of funding (a penny on the hotel-motel tax is the one most frequently suggested) and the city has to develop a strategy for using the arts to promote city development and tourism, now that the sports strategy has leveled off. Could Indiana Avenue become a northern Bourbon Street, alive once again with jazz and entertainment? We have also discussed the formation of a medical and biotechnology research park adjacent to the Indiana-Purdue campus, stretching north along the canal toward Methodist Hospital. President Daniel Felicetti of Marian College has suggested that we can do a better job of utilizing our institutions of higher education as a community resource, which could stimulate our effort to become competitive in this postindustrial era. Perhaps we could develop an institute of sports medicine in cooperation with the academic institutions in our city.

Dreams, dreams, and more dreams. Some are unrealistic, but others may yet come true. Chapters in the life of a city begin and end, but the book never closes. A city's life is forever unfinished. Conclusions are really new beginnings, and positive possibilities keep appearing. We are surrounded by opportunities brilliantly disguised as insoluble problems. Those who love the city and its people must never abandon hope.

I trust that most people will see the evolution of Indianapolis during the past two decades and more as a positive one. This narrative has highlighted the city's progress toward the goal of becoming more cooperative, compassionate, and competitive. Now there is new leadership, a new agenda, and new hope. As I see it, the near future for the cities of America will involve at least five items:

1. The emphasis on economic development and job creation will continue. Building Circle Centre Mall and the MOC II facility are huge undertakings. But most new jobs come from expansion in a city's small-business sector. Here the partnership between government and business can continue to be productive. A city cannot ignore decaying infrastructure, and people will see quality-of-life issues as affecting a city's ability to compete. Also, cities will understand better the importance of working cooperatively and transcending parochialism. In the emerging global marketplace, regional metropolitan areas, sometimes called "citistates"—not cities, not states, nor even nation-states—are the key competitors, and collaborative partnerships between different governmental jurisdictions and between the public and private sectors will help a city compete successfully in the dynamic world economy.

2. Reforming education also will be important. No community, state, or country can compete without an educated workforce. Studies show that the United States has the largest percentage of functional illiterates of any industrialized nation; business spends $30 billion each year just to get employees up to a functioning level; six in ten major companies say they have trouble finding employees with basic skills; 82 percent of America's prisoners are high school dropouts; one million high school students drop out each year; on international math and biology tests, U.S. students ranked last; and on and on. Traditional education methodologies may be obsolete today. New initiatives will be launched. Schools will be restructured. Educators will realize that if modern business requires different mental skills from those needed earlier, the curriculum may have to deemphasize older disciplines such as algebra, trigonometry, and calculus in favor of newer ones such as logic, statistics, and probability. Education is becoming the most important part of our infrastructure, because it makes a community more competitive.

3. As stewards of the earth and its resources, we cannot ignore the environment. As cities cope with mountains of trash and degradation of

air and water, they will have to pay more attention to recycling, resource recovery, tree planting (one tree produces enough oxygen for one person to live for one year), antipollution efforts, and the general philosophy of thinking globally and acting locally.

4. People who have been left out of the mainstream will be coming in—minorities, women, gays and lesbians, children born at risk, economically disadvantaged persons, persons with AIDS, and so on. Cities will have to affirm diversity so that those who have been weak can become stronger. Empowerment will thus comprise a major strategy for enlarging a sense of ownership in the process and product of government. On issues such as child care, health care, elder care, tenant ownership, neighborhood-based policing, and community-based decision making, it is time for cities to distribute the power and benefits of economic development more widely.

5. Governments at all levels will have to learn to manage better. The public's grave concerns about tax increases and the diminishing resources and reduced expectations about government's role will require creative new approaches to increase government's effectiveness. These new approaches will have to transcend the simplistic alternatives of increasing revenues or decreasing services. City governments will utilize techniques such as downsizing, rightsizing, privatizing, and breaking up top-heavy, centralized bureaucracies and their monopolies by injecting more competition into the service-delivery process. The public will elect to office increasing numbers of candidates who show promise of implementing these methodologies. The taxpayers want government to be run in a more business-like manner, even though government is not a business. People will call these options by various names—enterprise management, retrenchment management, reinventing government—but their ultimate concern will be efficiency and effectiveness, not turf-building and politics as usual.

Looking down the road, one wonders whether the cities will survive. Significant forces are pulling them apart. The telecommunications revolution is reducing the need for people to be physically together to confer with one another. Fax machines, telecommuting modems, personal computers, e-mail, and two-way videos are making information transmission easy, cheap, and fast. Throughout this century we moved people to where the information and office work were. But as we head into the 21st century we are discovering that moving information—and office work—to where the people are makes more sense.

Commuting in a car downtown to work in an office is on its way to becoming obsolete. Suburbanization and the development of "edge cities" is sapping vitality from the central core. Fears about crime, poor services, high taxes, and poor education are prompting people to move to the suburbs if they can afford to, leaving behind neighborhoods where residents live in deepening poverty. The rise of regional approaches to governance that cross old jurisdictional boundaries— such as solid-waste districts and transportation coordinating authorities—is making city governments less important in the decision-making process. The proliferation of choices is contributing to the demassification of society and decentralization of government.

Consequently the urban landscape is flattening out. Series of smaller centers of commerce and governance are ringing the cities, setting up centrifugal forces that will not be reversed over time. The challenge facing the cities will be to remain intact. They will, if they address the coming agenda, yoke onto regional partnerships, raise the density and tighten up their fabric through deliberate public policies that concentrate the core, maintain pedestrian-friendly streets, keep their taxes down, and manage change creatively.

I find the words of urban-planning consultant William H. Whyte encouraging in this matter. In *City: Rediscovering the Center* he concludes that

> it is the big cities that face the toughest challenge. Will their centers hold? Or will they splatter into a host of semicities? At the moment, the decentralization trend seems dominant. . . . But one can hope. I think the center is going to hold. I think it is going to hold because of the way people demonstrate by their actions how vital is centrality. . . . The problems, of course, are immense. To be an optimist about the city, one must believe that it will lurch from crisis to crisis but somehow survive. . . . What has been taking place is a brutal simplification. The city has been losing those functions for which it is no longer competitive. Manufacturing has moved toward the periphery; the back offices are on the way. The computers are already there. But as the city has been losing functions it has been reasserting its most ancient one: a place where people come together, face-to-face.[70]

Of course the cities will survive. That is what this book is all about. We *can* meet the challenges and overcome them. We *can* make our cities livable. We *can* help create jobs, retain a tax base, and improve the quality of life. The Indianapolis story is one of qualified success. It is an ongoing saga, the final chapter of which will never be written. The city will change mightily in the future, as it has in the past, but at the heart of the state of Indiana, there will always be . . . Indianapolis.

NOTES

1. *Newsweek*, September 9, 1985, 26.

2. Quoted in *Indianapolis Business Journal* (advertisement for CLASS), June 15–21, 1992.

3. Edward A. Leary, *Indianapolis* (Indianapolis: Bobbs-Merrill, 1971), 167.

4. Leary, 168.

5. Leary, 215.

6. Leary, 216.

7. John Gunther, *Inside USA* (New York: Harper, 1947), 387, 910.

8. Leary, 220.

9. Dennis R. Judd, *The Politics of American Cities,* 3d ed. (HarperCollins, 1988), chap. 6.

10. Leary, 224.

11. C. James Owen, "Indianapolis Unigov: A Focus of Restructured Executive," paper prepared for the Wichita Assembly, March 13–14, 1992, Wichita State University, Wichita, Kansas.

12. Quoted in Owen, 4.

13. *Indianapolis News,* July 14, 1987.

14. Quoted in Owen, 10.

15. David Osborne and Ted Gaebler, *Reinventing Government* (Reading, Mass.: Addison-Wesley, 1992), 52.

16. Dan Carpenter, *Indianapolis Star,* May 9, 1991.

17. Leary, 232.

18. Inter-Community Visit Report, Greenville, N.C., Chamber of Commerce, 1991, 2.

19. *Indianapolis Star,* January 10, 1993.

20. Judd, 393–94.

21. My source is the Indianapolis Project.

22. Judd, 418.

23. *Indiana University School of Public and Environmental Affairs Review,* vol. 12, no. 1.

24. Quoted in *Indianapolis Business Journal,* April 13–19, 1992.

25. Neal Peirce, speech to Corporate Community Council, 1991.

26. Quoted in Osborne and Gaebler, 39.

27. WTLC, Profile of the Indianapolis Black Community, 1992.

28. Quoted in *Indianapolis Star,* February 21, 1993.

29. Mari Evans, in *Where We Live: Essays about Indiana* (Indiana Humanities Council, 1989), 30, 41.

30. *Indianapolis Business Journal*, November 23–29, 1992.

31. Judd, 406.

32. Arthur Schlesinger, Jr., *The Disuniting of America* (Whittle Direct Books, 1991), 64.

33. Quoted in *Los Angeles Times*, May 2, 1992.

34. Robert P. Duckworth, John M. Simmons, and Robert H. McNulty, *The Entrepreneurial American City* (Washington, D.C.: Partners for Livable Places, 1986), 5.

35. Quoted by Gary Rivlin, *Fire on the Prairie* (New York: Holt, 1992), 11.

36. Peter Drucker, *Innovation and Entrepreneurship* (New York: Harper, 1985), 186–87.

37. Osborne and Gaebler, 45.

38. Annual Financial Reports, City of Indianapolis; James Steele, Controller, City of Indianapolis; County Business Patterns compiled by the U.S. Census; the Bureau of Economic Analysis of the U.S. Department of Commerce; the Indiana Department of Employment and Training Services; Indianapolis Chamber of Commerce; City of Indianapolis, Department of Metropolitan Development, Monthly Statistical Report; William Hudnut, State of the City address, January 11, 1991.

39. With moral obligation bonds, the full faith and credit of a city do not back them. They are not a guarantee. Morally, a city has to notify its legislative body that a deficiency exists and the bonds could fall into default. The council then takes whatever action is necessary to remedy the problem, or the default would occur.

40. William B. Johnston, *Workforce 2000* (Hudson Institute, 1987).

41. Johnston, 116.

42. Harold Wolman et al., "National Urban Economic Development Policy," *Journal of Urban Affairs*, vol. 14, nos. 3–4 (1992) 226, 229.

43. Quoted in *Indianapolis Business Journal*, September 14, 1992.

44. "A Strategic Plan for the Industrial Development of Indianapolis: Economic Analysis and Strategies," Central Research Systems, Inc., May 1982.

45. Ibid., v–vi.

46. Judd, 407.

47. Newsletter of the Urban Policy Research Institute, vol. 1, no. 3 (1992).

48. Wolman et al., 230.

49. Joel Garreau, *Edge City: Life on the New Frontier* (New York: Doubleday, 1992).

50. *Indianapolis Business Journal*, October 12–18, 1992.

51. Quoted in William H. Hudnut III, *Minister/Mayor* (Philadelphia: Westminster Press, 1987), 169.

52. *Wall Street Journal*, November 16, 1992.

53. Rita J. Bamberger and David W. Parham, "Leveraging Amenity Infrastructure: Indianapolis Economic Development Strategy," *Urban Land*, November 1984, 12, 13.

54. Laura Littlepage and Mark S. Rosentraub, *The Economic Importance of the Arts in the Indianapolis Area* (Center for Urban Policy and the Environment, 1993).

55. *Boston Globe*, May 31, 1992.

56. This and the following quotation appear in *City & State*, October 19, 1992.

57. Quoted in *News & Observer,* Raleigh, North Carolina, November 24, 1991, 3F.

58. *Indiana Business Journal,* November 18–24, 1992, 7A.

59. Ibid.

60. *Indianapolis Star,* December 1, 1991.

61. *Indiana Policy Review,* March-April 1992.

62. *Indiana Business Journal,* December 23, 1991.

63. *Indiana Policy Review,* vol. 3, no. 1 (February 1992).

64. *City & State,* August 24, 1992.

65. News release, Urban Policy Institute, Dayton, August 28, 1992.

66. See Robin Paul Malloy, *Planning for Serfdom: Legal Economic Discourse and Downtown Development* (Philadelphia: University of Pennsylvania Press, 1991).

67. *Indiana Law Review,* vol. 25, no. 3, 685ff.

68. Quoted in ibid., 741ff.

69. *Hartford Courant,* May 24, 1992.

70. William H. Whyte, *City: Rediscovering the Center* (New York: Doubleday, 1988) 7, 341. See also Holly Hughes, "Metropolitan Structure and the Suburban Hierarchy," *American Sociological Review,* vol. 58 (June 1993) ("Results demonstrate the continued dominance of the center city, even in these multi-nodal metropolitan areas. Despite deconcentration of population and employment, the metropolis remains oriented toward the center city more than toward any suburban city. However, some suburban cities are occupying increasingly dominant positions in the metropolitan system") and Jon C. Teaford, *The Twentieth Century American City* (Baltimore: Johns Hopkins University Press, 1986), 153 ("America, by the 70's and 80's has created a cluster of cities . . . the central city no longer being central to most metropolitan areas . . . but became one of many metropolitan clusters. Thus the central city was not dead; it had simply become one more suburb, yet another fragment of metropolitan America serving the special needs of certain classes of urban dwellers. Central cities of the 80's housed the poor and elderly, but they also attracted young middle-class single persons and childless couples. . . . Meanwhile, the central city downtown remained the hub of finance, government, and business services").

The Reverend William H. Hudnut III, congressional candidate, opens Blacks for Hudnut headquarters in September 1972, flanked by Mayor Richard G. Lugar of Indianapolis, left, and Julius F. Shaw and John W. Mosley. *Star* photo by Bud Berry.

Sworn in by outgoing mayor Richard Lugar, William Hudnut becomes the thirty-ninth mayor of Indianapolis, January 1, 1976. *News* photo by Horace Ketring.

Mayor Hudnut demonstrates his
trashball hook shot to plug Indianapolis's
postblizzard grime-removal campaign, April
1978. *Star* photo by Jerry Clark.

When one-year-old Nisha Marie Ahamad, born during Indianapolis's blizzard of '78, meets Mayor Hudnut at a "Remember the Blizzard" party in January 1979, even his hockey hat fails to impress. *Star* photo by Jerry Clark.

The Indianapolis Department of Transportation's Jack McKenzie and other workers move their operations to Harlan Street and find a willing helper in Mayor Hudnut, April 1979. *News* photo by Bob Doeppers.

A mayor's work is never done, and sometimes it means
helping schoolchildren cross the street, as Mayor Hudnut
discovers during the Hoosier Motor Club's traffic safety
program in September 1981. *News* photo by Tim Halcomb.

In his second term as mayor, William Hudnut and his
city receive a signal honor when Indianapolis is named
one of ten All-American cities, April 1982. *Star* photo by
D. Todd Moore.

It's back to the streets for Mayor Hudnut as he helps
George W. Dawson, Lee Clark, and Tim B. Bush plant a
tree, April 1983. *Star* photo by Jerry Clark.

Annetta Tanner, who won a home for one dollar in the city's Urban Homestead Program when Mayor Hudnut drew her name from a fishbowl, gets a hug from the mayor, October 1983. *News* photo by Patty Espich.

William Hudnut, mayor of a city that built a dome and then found an NFL team to come fill it, chats with Indianapolis Colts owner Bob Irsay in the Hoosier Dome, April 1984. *Star* staff photo.

The mayor keeps as cool as the kids in a game of ring-around-a-fire-hose, kicking off the Indianapolis Fire Department's Operation Cool Down in mid-July 1985. *Star* photo by Frank H. Fisse.

Possible sale of the closed Western Electric
Company plant is the topic of Mayor Hudnut's
talk with the media, May 1987. *Star* photo by
Bud Berry.

Mayor Hudnut goes to the scene after an Air Force jet fighter crashed into the Ramada Inn near Indianapolis International Airport in October 1987, causing multiple fatalities. *News* photo by Jim Young.

A reflective Bill Hudnut addresses his supporters following his victorious campaign for a fourth term as mayor, November 4, 1987. *News* photo by Jim Young.

After pulling the lever that activated the wrecking ball that finally began demolition for the billion-dollar downtown Circle Centre Mall, Mayor Hudnut is all smiles in March 1989. *News* photo by Joe Young.

Looking more like Uncle Sam than an
honorary leprechaun, Mayor Hudnut steps
out smartly in the St. Patrick's Day parade,
1989. *Star* photo by Bud Berry.

Basketball great Oscar Robertson joins Mayor Hudnut at a groundbreaking for more than a hundred single-family homes to be built by Oscar Robertson & Associates, March 1989. *News* photo by Mike Fender.

Having built the big Hoosier Dome, Mayor Hudnut kept finding ways to fill it—this time with the 1997 NCAA Final Four basketball tournament, announced in July 1989. *Star* photo by Ron Ira Steele.

After delivering a truckful of snow to the home of "Wishing for a Winter Wonderland" essay contest winner Jimmy Brigham, Mayor Hudnut joins the sixth grader for a sled ride just before Christmas, 1990. *News* photo by Jim Young.

Although Circle Centre Mall seemed a long time coming, Mayor Hudnut is delighted to show off its hole, August 1991. *Star* photo by Jeff Atteberry.

William H. Hudnut III in the autumn of his
mayoralty, September 1991. *Star* staff photo.

Mayor Hudnut and Indiana Governor Evan Bayh announced United's choice of Indianapolis International Airport for its new operations center, only a few days before Hudnut completes his sixteenth and final year as mayor. *Star* staff photo.

PART TWO

ACADEMIC CRITICS

Fiscal Health

LAURA LITTLEPAGE, MARK S. ROSENTRAUB,
AND MICHAEL PRZYBYLSKI

Was Indianapolis a fiscally healthy city at the end of William Hudnut's term as mayor? If one considers the city's Aaa bond rating, Indianapolis was certainly considered fiscally sound. But are bond ratings a valid measure of the fiscal health of a city and its various communities?

Measuring any community's fiscal health is a complex challenge. Cities have many parts, and one community can be fiscally healthy at the same time others are not. This is even more possible in a city such as Indianapolis where important services are provided and financed at the township level. For example, within the City of Indianapolis there are nine public school systems, each independently financed, and several different police and fire departments that are also independently financed.

With arrangements such at these, measuring the fiscal health of a city is difficult. At one extreme, fiscal default (revenues received are insufficient to satisfy budgeted allocations) is obviously a definition of poor fiscal health. However, a balanced budget, or even a budget surplus, is not necessarily a measure of good fiscal health if the level of services provided is inadequate to meet the needs of citizens or to enhance the city's economy. Bradbury illustrated the difficulties in defining fiscal health by creating two separate standards: (1) budgetary fiscal distress, or the inability to balance the budget, and (2) structural fiscal distress, or the "inability of residents to receive a reasonable level of services for a reasonable level of sacrifice" (1982: 34). There are also many other different and more elaborate measures of fiscal health and stress (Ladd and Yinger, 1989).

Others have suggested that managers and students of public finance should look beyond a singular declaration of fiscal health and focus their attention on numerous indicators of fiscal status and stress. Ladd and Yinger's efforts (1989) are representative of the important work done to identify many factors that are designed to alert mayors and their managers to fiscally desirable or undesirable situations. The responses to these sorts of warning lights remain left to a city's leadership. In arguing for multiple measures of fiscal health, Ladd and Yinger note that the complexity of a city's health requires information on numerous indicators and trends.

However, confusion can be produced by a process that uses multiple measures when some indicators of fiscal health are positive while others are negative. When this occurs, normative judgments must be made to reach a final determination of whether a city is fiscally healthy. For example, low expenditures by the public sector for any particular service might not necessarily mean low levels of service. Low wage levels and material costs could mean production costs are lower for similar levels of outputs, yet in many instances it is difficult to measure outputs (Ladd and Yinger, 1989; Howell and Stamm, 1979; Bahl, 1984). Furthermore, even if inputs from the public sector (wages, materials, etc.) could be controlled, there is still the possibility that outputs are the result of extensive expenditures by the nonprofit or private sectors or of contributions of time by volunteers (Rosentraub, Harlow, and Harris, 1992). And low expenditures could ultimately mean low taxes, which would be viewed as a sign of fiscal health by some, while others might be concerned whether low taxes meant low levels of outputs. The difficulty in measuring outputs frequently means proponents of low taxes find that their preferences are more commonly accepted as a guidepost of fiscal health.

Faced with the complex problem of defining and measuring fiscal health, it is not surprising that the popular media and many elected officials and professional groups look to a city's bond rating as a simple measure of fiscal health. Each year—and more often during elections— civic, business, and popular publications report on the fiscal health and strength of cities. For example, in December 1991, three of the top five most "fiscally strong" cities chosen by *City & State* magazine (San Diego, Indianapolis, and Dallas) had Aaa bond ratings. But shortly after this report, the Indianapolis Public Schools faced a severe budget crisis, the City of Indianapolis had to forgo raises for its employees, and the city made two very large investments for economic development. Was Indianapolis's Aaa bond rating hiding some deep-seated financial problems? To answer this question we first tried to determine whether a city's bond rating measured fiscal health, then looked behind the factors that produced Indianapolis's Aaa bond rating.

Do Bond Ratings Measure Fiscal Health?

To determine whether bond ratings measure fiscal health, we developed a model that included numerous indicators of fiscal health in an effort to both predict bond ratings and explain the differences in bond ratings between cities. We then tried to predict these bond ratings using measures of each city's fiscal and economic environment.

The model was quite robust in illustrating that the bond rating a city receives can be considered a reliable summary measure of fiscal health. In addition, we also found that nonprofit activity was significantly related to a community's bond rating.

The third, or nonprofit, sector, as demonstrated by United Way contributions, was positively related to bond ratings. A city with a very active nonprofit sector, it would seem, experiences less pressure to provide certain services and thus has lower costs. The model showed that the percent of a city's budget spent for interest on debt, the unemployment rate, racial minority population, and home ownership were all good indicators of a low bond rating. These factors seem to reflect the potential for poor fiscal health owing to their demands on the tax base. Furthermore, the ability within a city to shift the tax burden for residential services to commercial and industrial property would also imply a greater tax burden for a community with less business property (Mullins and Rosentraub, 1992). But property tax payments as a percent of total taxes was positively associated with bond ratings, as would be expected, because a major portion of property taxes can usually be exported outside the community.

Bond ratings, then, can be used as a measure of a city's overall fiscal health. Our model, however, did not include at least one factor that can possibly influence fiscal health: the quality of municipal management. Part of the problem in assessing effective management and stability is the insufficient amount of data that exist to measure these concepts.

Indeed, accurate measurement probably requires detailed case studies. Stability can be measured in terms of length of time since there was a change in political party, but many cities have nonpartisan elections and in other cities the differences within the same political party can cause instability even when two mayors are from the same party. In addition, stability can be a negative factor if a city is poorly managed.

To provide limited insight into the possible effects of management on bond ratings we used our model to predict the bond ratings of all cities with Aaa evaluations. We assumed that some portion of any positive deviation between the predicted value and the actual rating was actually a measure of the bond rating company's assessment of management and stability. As the table illustrates, Indianapolis, Minneapolis, Omaha, and Portland had the largest positive residuals of the cities listed. They also were among the cities that had the largest residuals for all 86 cities. Quality management, then, does make a difference and can compensate for weaknesses in a city's economic position in producing a Aaa bond rating.

1990 Actual and Predicted Bond Ratings

	1990 Actual	Predicted	Difference (Residual)
Los Angeles	7 (Aaa)	6.1	0.9
San Diego	7 (Aaa)	7.0	0.0
Indianapolis	7 (Aaa)	5.6	1.4
Des Moines	7 (Aaa)	7.0	0.0
Minneapolis	7 (Aaa)	5.6	1.4
Omaha	7 (Aaa)	5.1	1.9
Charlotte	7 (Aaa)	6.9	0.1
Raleigh	7 (Aaa)	6.4	0.6
Portland	7 (Aaa)	5.4	1.6
Dallas	7 (Aaa)	6.4	0.6
Madison	7 (Aaa)	6.6	0.4

Bill Hudnut's tenure in Indianapolis illustrates the importance of management in securing a high bond rating. If economic factors alone were considered, Indianapolis's bond rating should not have been Aaa. However, Indianapolis's history of management and stability provides some insight into factors that might be considered valuable by bond rating agencies. Indianapolis was managed by just two individuals from 1968 to 1992, Richard Lugar (eight years) and William Hudnut (16 years). Both were also from the same political party and the transition from one mayor to the other was done with minimal staff changes. These individuals brought stability and nationally recognized good management (*City & State's* all-star management team) to the administration of the city.

This stability might have changed if Indianapolis had not undergone consolidation with Marion County (Unigov). Even though many functions (schools, police, fire) were not consolidated, the entire county elects the mayor. In 1960, before adoption of Unigov, 20.6 percent of Indianapolis's population was African-American. After Unigov, the black percentage fell to 18 percent even though the number of African-Americans increased by 37 percent in absolute terms. In 1990, 40.9 percent of the population in the old boundaries of Indianapolis was African-American, almost twice the average for the Unigov boundaries. Today, while 22 percent of the city's population lives within the old boundaries of Indianapolis, 45 percent of all households in Indianapolis earning less than $10,000 live in this area. A concentration of disadvantaged residents affects the demand for services (Ladd and Yinger, 1989). If Indianapolis had not been consolidated, demands for more services and higher spending could have produced more changes in administrations.

Behind Indianapolis's Aaa Bond Rating

Bond ratings do measure a city's fiscal health, but our model suggests that if economic factors alone were considered, Hudnut's Indianapolis would not have received a Aaa bond rating. The Aaa bond rating was a result of effective management and leadership as well as stability in local politics.

What economic factors did this effective management and leadership overcome? By the end of Hudnut's tenure, Center Township in the city's core had become home for much of the city's low-income population. By 1990 more than two-fifths of all of the township's households were classified as low-income (150 percent or less of the official poverty

level), and more than 45 percent of the entire city's low-income population lived in Center Township. This low-income population had to pay
the taxes to support several local services, including schools and police
and fire protection, without the assistance of higher-income households
in other townships (see figure 1). Furthermore, in Indiana, selected
welfare responsibilities are supported by townships. By 1992 almost 12
percent of Center Township's taxes went for poor-relief services, a rate
six times larger than the effort required by any other township in the
City of Indianapolis (see figure 2). Finally, Center Township was also
burdened by high rates of tax-exempt and tax-abated property. Tax-
exempt property includes facilities owned by the state government and
federal government, as well as facilities owned by religious organizations. Tax abatements for economic development encourage businesses
to locate in Center Township. However, the combination of tax-exempt
and tax-abated properties meant, by 1992, that more than one-third of
the entire tax base of Center Township was tax-exempt (see figure 3).
That not only shifted the tax burden to lower-income families but
gave Center Township the highest tax rate in the county. By 1992 the

Figure 1
The Distribution of Low Income People
in Metropolitan Indianapolis

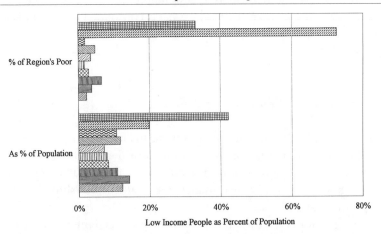

Low Income People as Percent of Population

| ⊞Center Tsp(Marion Cty) | ▧Marion County | ⊠Boone County | ▨Johnson County | ▩Hamilton County |
| ▥Hancock County | | ⊠Hendricks County | ▦Madison County | ▰Morgan County | ▨Shelby County |

Source: 1990 Census Low Income Defined as 149% of Proverty Level or Less As Measured by the Federal Government

Figure 2
Poor Relief Expenditures as a
Percent of Township Taxes

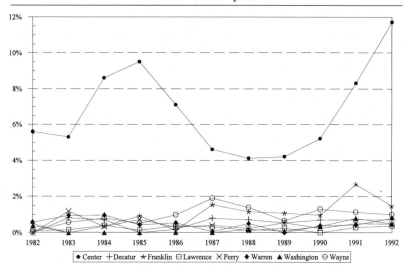

Source: State Tax Commission

Figure 3
A Comparison of Township Tax Rates

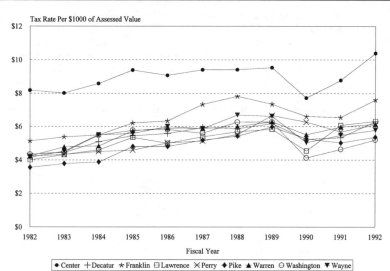

Source: State Tax Commission

property tax rate in Center Township was more than 30 percent greater than the tax rate in any other part of the City of Indianapolis.

We began by asking if Indianapolis was a fiscally healthy city at the end of Hudnut's term as mayor. If one looks only at the city's bond rating, Hudnut's administration did indeed leave Indianapolis fiscally sound. However, behind that Aaa bond rating is a tale of two cities. Within Indianapolis's Center Township there are substantial financial problems further complicated by the financial arrangements made to support Circle Centre Mall and other economic development projects. Indianapolis does have the capacity to support its commitments, but that capacity is not present within the boundaries of the old city of Indianapolis, the area largely encompassed by Center Township.

REFERENCES

Roy Bahl, "The Fiscal Health of State and Local Governments: 1982 and Beyond," *Crisis and Constraint in Municipal Finance,* ed. James H. Carr (New Brunswick, N.J.: Center for Urban Policy Research, 1984).

Katherine L. Bradbury, "Fiscal Distress in Large U.S. Cities," *New England Economic Review* (January–February 1982): 33–44.

"The City Report: Top 50 Cities 6th Annual Financial Report," *City & State,* December 2, 1991, 9.

James M. Howell and Charles F. Stamm, *Urban Fiscal Stress* (Lexington, Mass.: Lexington Books, 1979).

Helen F. Ladd and John Yinger, *America's Ailing Cities: Fiscal Health and the Design of Urban Policy* (Baltimore: Johns Hopkins University Press, 1989).

Daniel R. Mullins and Mark S. Rosentraub, "Fiscal Pressure? The Impact of Elder Recruitment on Local Expenditures," *Urban Affairs Quarterly* 28 (1992): 337–54.

Mark S. Rosentraub, Karen Harlow, and Michael Harris, "Uncompensated Costs and Indigent Health Care: Volunteers and a Community Services Budget," *Nonprofit and Voluntary Sector Quarterly* 21 (1992): 351–66.

The Amateur
Sports Strategy

DAVID W. SWINDELL, MARK S. ROSENTRAUB,
DANIEL R. MULLINS, AND
MICHAEL PRZYBYLSKI

I ndianapolis, during the Hudnut years, could have been described as sports crazy. The city's leadership had decided to change the image of Indianapolis through an extensive amateur sports emphasis that was joined with a downtown revitalization program. Together, sports and a new downtown were going to change Indianapolis's image and improve economic development. Did it work?

Indianapolis's emphasis, which began in the early 1980s, is particularly interesting because several analysts have tried to alert elected officials about the potential dangers of allocating excessive amounts of public funds to attract or retain sports teams and develop specialized facilities. Since 1988 alone, Baade and Dye (1988, 1990), Baim (1990, 1992), Euchner (1993), Rosentraub and Swindell (1991), and Zimbalist (1992, 1993) have all demonstrated the small or unlikely economic growth to be expected from stadium investments or the attraction and retention of a sports team. In that same period, numerous governments have collectively invested more than a billion dollars in sports facilities: the State of Illinois and the City of Chicago spent $185 million to build a new Comiskey Park, St. Petersburg spent $130 million on a still-empty facility, Baltimore spent $275 million on a new home for the Orioles, Arlington spent approximately $200 million to keep the Texas Rangers in town, Philadelphia has agreed to help the private sector build new facilities for the 76ers and Flyers (basketball and hockey), Atlanta's Falcons now play in a new facility (the Georgia Dome), and the Braves will soon have a new home (Olympic Stadium). By 1995, Cleveland's baseball and basketball teams both will be playing in new facilities, which are being funded with significant investments by local government. To secure one of the two National Football League expansion teams, Jacksonville was willing to commit $150 million in public funds (some at the expense of improving its local port facility) (Norton, 1993).

With this level of continuing interest in relying on sports for economic development, it is valuable to consider whether Indianapolis's approach, as implemented by the Hudnut Administration, led to enhanced development. The history of Indianapolis's economic revitalization strategy clearly shows that amateur and professional sports were integral to an overall investment emphasis on the downtown core for the community's economic development strategy; public and community officials tried to portray Indianapolis as the "amateur sports capital." As a result, Indianapolis's efforts provide an opportunity to assess the impact of sports as a tool for economic development for the first time.

Rebuilding Indianapolis

During the 1970s, Indianapolis had a limited national image, a deteriorating job base, and a declining downtown core. With sports as a central component, a $2.76-billion construction program changed the physical character of downtown Indianapolis. In 1974, Market Square Arena opened as the new home for the Indiana Pacers (basketball), across the street from the City-County Building. The city's former City Hall, two blocks to the north of the current building, became the site of the Indiana State Museum. From 1974 through 1992, more than 30 major capital development projects for the downtown area were begun (see table).

As the table shows, the State of Indiana also completed the new State Government Center at a cost of $264 million while Indiana University invested more than $231 million in its Indianapolis campus. Though these facilities are exempt from local property taxes, they clearly have enhanced the appearance of downtown Indianapolis and have become significant aspects of the overall strategy to cast a "new

Sources of Funds for Economic Development Projects in Indianapolis
(in Millions of Dollars)

Project	Year	Federal	State	City	Private	Philanthropic	Total
				Source of Funds			
Market Square Arena	1974	0	0	16	0	0	16
Children's Museum	1976	0	0	0	0	25	25
Hyatt Hotel/ Bank	1977	0	0	0	55	0	55
Sports Center	1979	0	0	4	1.5	1.5	7
Indiana Theater	1980	1.5	0	0	4.5	0	6
Capitol Tunnel	1982	1.4	0	0	0	0	1.4
IU Track and Field Stadium	1982	0	1.9	0	0	4	5.9
IU Natatorium	1982	1.5	7	0	0	13	21.5
Velodrome	1982	0.48	0	1.1	0	1.1	2.68
2 W. Washington Offices	1982	1.2	0	0	11.8	0	13
1 N. Capitol Offices	1982	3.2	0	0	10.41	0	13.61
Hoosier Dome	1984	0	0	48	0	30	78
Lower Canal Apartments	1985	7.9	0	10.3	0	2	20.2
Heliport	1985	2.5	0.12	0.6	2.36	0	5.58
Walker Building	1985	2	0	0	0	1.4	3.4
Embassy Suites Hotel	1985	6.45	0	0	25.05	0	31.5
Lockerbie Market	1986	1.8	0	0	14	0	15.8
Union Station	1986	16.3	0	1	36.01	0	53.31
City Market	1986	0	0	0	0	4.7	4.7

**Sources of Funds for Economic Development Projects in Indianapolis
(in Millions of Dollars)** *(Cont.)*

Project	Year	Source of Funds					
		Federal	State	City	Private	Philanthropic	Total
Pan Am Plaza	1987	0	0	5.7	25	4.5	35.2
Lockefield Apartments	1987	0	0	0.62	24.6	0	25.22
Canal Overlook Apartments	1988	0	0	0	11	0	11
Zoo	1988	0	0	0	0	37.5	37.5
Natl. Institute for Sports	1988	0	3	3	0	3	9
Eiteljorg Museum	1989	0	0	0	0	60	60
Westin Hotel	1989	0.5	0	0	65	0	65.5
Indiana University	1990	0	231	0	0	0	231
Farm Bureau	1992	0	0	0	0	36	36
State Government Center	1992	0	264	0	0	0	264
Lilly Corporate Expansion	1992	0	0	0	242	0	242
Circle Centre Mall	1995	0	0	290	0	10	300
Other Projects	'74–'92	0	0	0	1008.53	0	1008.53
Property Tax Abatements	'74–'92	0	0	55.8	0	0	55.8
Total		46.7	507.0	436.1	1536.8	233.7	2760.33
Percent		1.7	18.4	15.8	55.7	8.5	100

Source: Department of Metropolitan Development, City of Indianapolis.

look" for the downtown area. Also included in the table is the funding for the Circle Centre Mall (1995).

Over the 18 years of the capital development program, eight of the projects were specifically targeted toward expanding the image of Indianapolis as a sports city. In 1984 Indianapolis opened the 61,000-seat Hoosier Dome, which became the home for the Indianapolis Colts and hosts several additional events, such as the NCAA men's basketball Final Four, which will be in Indianapolis for the third time in 1997. Other sports-related investments included the Sports Center, a tennis stadium for the annual hard-court championships, the Indiana University Natatorium, the Indiana University Track and Field Stadium, the Velodrome (bicycle racing), and the National Institute for Fitness and Sports. Many amateur sports organizations relocated their national headquarters to the city with the financial assistance of private and nonprofit organizations in the area. By 1989, seven national organizations (Athletics Congress of the USA, U.S. Canoe and Kayak Team, U.S. Diving, U.S. Gymnastics Federation, U.S. Rowing, U.S. Synchronized Swimming, and U.S. Water Polo) and two international organizations (International Baseball Association and the International Hockey League) had relocated their main offices to Indianapolis.

The sports-related investments amounted to $172.6 million, (less than 10 percent of the capital spending in the downtown strategy). By including the investments in three hotels which were constructed in anticipation of attendance at sporting events, the sports focus of the downtown development would be approximately 12 percent of the total capital investment. Another 15 percent of the total, for Circle Centre Mall and Union Station, could also be added to this sum, as their success also assumes that people will frequent them while visiting the city for a sporting event. Sports, then, was clearly a significant element of the overall development strategy for downtown Indianapolis, but it was intertwined with other investments as well.

Not all of the projects that took place during this period are included in the table, since they were not part of the downtown sports strategy. For instance, the refurbishing of the city's monuments and a large park area, the state's revitalization of the Capitol building, and new fire stations were not included, since these projects would have occurred regardless of the city's strategy. Although there is clearly a level of subjectivity as to which projects are included on the list, interviews with local leaders helped identify which were part of the strategy.

The table, beyond simply showing the extent of the downtown development and the underlying role of sports, also identifies several other points that characterize the nature of Mayor Hudnut's vision for the city. Through a series of public-private partnerships in which the mayor played a significant leadership role, the city was able to leverage a considerably larger investment from the private and nonprofit sectors than the investment capital put up by the city. More specifically, the city spent $436.1 million in public money and, through the partnerships, leveraged a total investment of $2.76 billion. Through the entrepreneurial skills of Hudnut and his staff, the city managed to get the private and nonprofit sectors (along with the state's resources) to invest $5.33 for every dollar invested by Indianapolis. More than 55 percent of the total downtown investments came from the private sector. In a time when many cities are spending vast amounts of their limited public dollars on their downtowns, Indianapolis clearly did well in encouraging additional support from other sectors.

Did the Strategy Work?

Have the expected returns from these investments actually been realized? To analyze success we looked at four measures. The first measure was sports-related jobs and payrolls. While the formal sports strategy began in 1977, many of the programs were not fully operational until 1983. Therefore this analysis focuses on changes in this industry from 1983 to 1989 and compares Indianapolis against all other cities' sports-related employment growth. During this period, Indianapolis had the second-largest growth in terms of employment of all U.S. urban areas (exceeded only by Prince Georges County, Maryland). Furthermore, no city had a larger increase in sports-related payroll. While this is real growth, sports jobs represented only 0.32 percent of all jobs in Indianapolis by 1989. This small proportion is an increase of 0.03 percent over the 1977 levels. All sports-related payroll represented less that one-half of one percent of the aggregate Indianapolis payroll, an increase of one-quarter of one percent over the 1977 aggregate payroll.

A second measure examined the "multiplier" effects of the sports-related jobs and payroll. The idea behind a multiplier effect is that growth in these jobs will lead to growth in jobs in other sectors of the local economy. As people from outside the city come and spend money for a game, they also spend money for other services, such as a hotel room, which they would not have spent were the games unavailable. When compared with 29 other metropolitan areas across the nation, there was no relationship in Indianapolis between an increase in sports-related jobs and changes in the number of jobs in the economy as a whole. When examined by economic sector, however, we found a positive relationship between these jobs and increased jobs in Indianapolis's service sector and its hotel and lodging sector. In other words, as more jobs developed in the sports-related sector, there were also increases in the number of jobs in restaurants and hotels, for example.

A recent study sponsored by the Indianapolis Chamber of Commerce attempted to measure the actual dollar value of these "spillover" jobs (Schaffer et al., 1993). The study concluded that the city's investment in sports was a good one because of the rates of return the city and the residents received. It calculated an annual rate of return of approximately $120 million. Even accepting the assumptions used in this study, this rate of return amounted to only 1.15 percent of the annual economy of the Indianapolis area. Sports is a very small portion of the city's economy.

A third measure compared Indianapolis's growth versus that of the cities in the Midwest against which Indianapolis traditionally competes for economic development. While the effects of the sports strategy may be very small as a proportion of the local economy, the strategy may have enhanced the city's identity and helped it grow more than its competitors. Through a series of discussions with public- and private-sector local leaders, nine regional cities were identified as those with which Indianapolis competes: Columbus (Ohio), Minneapolis, St. Paul, St. Louis, Dayton, Cincinnati, Louisville, Milwaukee, and Fort Wayne. Indianapolis increased its overall number of jobs by 32.9 percent from 1977 to 1989. But Columbus and Minneapolis both increased their number of jobs over 50 percent.

When looking at all ten of the counties in which these cities are located and examining the number of jobs each has as a proportion of the total across all ten, Indianapolis increased it share by 0.2 percent from 1977 to 1989. Columbus and Minneapolis both realized larger increases. Indianapolis lost jobs in the manufacturing and finance sectors and gained in the service sector. Unfortunately, there are significant differences in the salaries paid in these sectors, and service-sector jobs frequently pay less. In fact, comparing Indianapolis against these other cities in terms of share of total payroll for all these areas, Indianapolis dropped 0.2 percent against these other cities. In 1977 Indianapolis had the second-highest average income of these ten cities. By 1989 the city ranked fifth. In other words, while Indianapolis's economic development efforts appear to have created more jobs, these jobs were lower-paying service sector jobs. While the sports strategy might have enhanced the city's image, the new image did not translate into a substantial increase in the number of jobs or into a higher average salary for Marion County residents when compared with the cities against which Indianapolis traditionally competes for such development.

The last measure to evaluate the sports and downtown development strategy is to assess how well the effort did in keeping jobs located in the downtown area. Maintaining a number of strong businesses downtown is necessary for the continued viability of the tax bases used by the several local governments that tax in Center Township. Once again, however, the evidence does not fully support the argument that the strategy was a success. In 1970, for instance, 95,562 persons were working in the downtown area. By 1990 this number had climbed to 105,500, a net increase of almost 10,000 jobs. However, the county was growing faster than the downtown in terms of jobs. As a result, the 30 percent of Marion County's workforce employed downtown in 1970 actually declined to only 21.2 percent downtown by 1990. Only two of the comparison cities (Cincinnati and Milwaukee) saw more jobs and payroll dollars seep out of their downtowns into their suburbs than did Indianapolis.

Conclusions

Indianapolis, more than any other city, developed a clearly stated economic development strategy for its downtown core using amateur and professional sports as the unifying theme to gather support for the program. This policy was designed to rebuild the core area and avoid the emergence of a "doughnut" pattern of prospering areas along an outer beltway surrounding a deteriorating center city, a pattern found in many of today's urban areas. Did it work?

While there were important accomplishments which clearly resulted from Indianapolis's sports strategy, the evidence suggests that overall there were no significant or substantial shifts in economic development. Without minimizing the favorable publicity that Indianapolis has enjoyed (e.g., public leveraging of private dollars, a stabilization of jobs in the downtown area, and an increase in higher-salary service-sector jobs downtown), outcomes of this size are so small that it is reasonable to ask whether, if Indianapolis's leaders had focused on alternative investment opportunities and strategies, a larger economic impact might have been realized. Indianapolis was successful with its amateur sports strategy if one measures success only with regard to rate of return on the investment (as the Chamber of Commerce concluded).

If one chooses to measure success in terms of increased employment opportunities and growth in aggregate payroll, however, then the city was not as successful as several of its competitor cities throughout the Midwest which realized greater increases on these measures of economic development. Simply put, the sports strategy unifying the downtown development did not attract significant amounts of other types of economic activity in industries with higher-paying and more numerous job opportunities. This outcome is somewhat disappointing, since the city was so successful in pursuing such a wide variety of public-private partnerships that led to substantial investments from the private and nonprofit sectors. While the evidence shown here suggests that the anticipated outcomes of the development strategy went unrealized, one can also argue that had the city not put together the efforts at revitalizing the downtown core, the local economy might have become much worse than it did during this same period. Sports may not have been the best strategy Bill Hudnut and other city leaders might have pursued, but it may have been better than many others or none at all, since sports became the glue that held many of the public-private partnerships together in the vision of a new downtown.

The experience of Indianapolis suggests that sports as a development tool simply cannot create the economic growth or overall economic impacts that its boosters and supporters (and franchise owners) frequently herald. This appears to be true even when considering the enhanced national image of Indianapolis as a major league city and as the amateur sports capital of America. An economic development strategy based solely on sports that encourages significant numbers of out-of-town attendees (e.g., the NCAA men's Final Four) can be a successful investment strategy if the measures of that success are based solely on the growth in sports-related employment. Given that sports (as an industry) is a very small component of the local economy and that jobs associated with this industry (excluding professional players and owners) are low-pay service-sector jobs and many times are only seasonal, sports cannot be considered the strongest base on which to build an economic development or redevelopment strategy. A sports strategy—even one as well-designed as Indianapolis's with its focus on leveraging additional downtown development—will not be a major stimulus for the economy of a community or region. Rather, public decision makers should learn from Indianapolis's successes and failures and realize that general economic development strategies and public policies might have more success if tailored to the natural economic advantages inherent in a region. A strategy that relies upon sports will not generate the economic outcomes for which it was designed. The economic value of sports is simply too small to change a region's general economic patterns.

REFERENCES

Robert A. Baade and Richard F. Dye, "Sports Stadiums and Area Development: A Critical Review," *Economic Development Quarterly* 2 (1988): 265–75.

Robert A. Baade and Richard F. Dye, "The Impact of Stadiums and Professional Sport on Metropolitan Area Development," working paper, Lake Forest College, Lake Forest, Ill., February 1990.

Dean Baim, "Sports Stadiums as Wise Investments: An Evaluation—Number 32," Heartland Institute Policy Study, Detroit, November 1990.

Dean Baim, *The Sports Stadium as a Municipal Investment* (Westport, Conn.: Greenwood Press, 1992).

Charles C. Euchner, *Playing the Field: Why Sports Teams Move and Cities Fight to Keep Them* (Baltimore: Johns Hopkins University Press, 1993).

Erle Norton, "Football at Any Cost: One City's Mad Chase for an NFL Franchise," *Wall Street Journal*, October 13, 1993, 1.

Mark S. Rosentraub and David W. Swindell, "Just Say No? The Economic and Political Realities of a Small City's Investment in Minor League Baseball," *Economic Development Quarterly* 5 (May 1991): 152–67.

William Schaffer, Bruce L. Jaffee, and Lawrence S. Davidson, "Beyond the Games: The Economic Impact of Amateur Sports" (Indianapolis: Chamber of Commerce, 1993).

Andrew Zimbalist, *Baseball and Billions* (New York: Basic Books, 1992).

Andrew Zimbalist, Testimony before the Committee on Tourism, Recreation, and Sports Development, New York State Senate, Oversight Hearings on Public Policy towards Minor League Baseball, February 9, 1993.

Neighborhoods and Unigov

DAVID W. SWINDELL AND ROGER PARKS

Indianapolis presents a rare opportunity to pursue a case study on the relationship between an individual and the governmental institution within which he is operating. Normally, once a person wins the mayor's office, he or she enters an institutional context defined by years of administrative practice. When William Hudnut assumed office in 1976 as the consolidated city-county's second mayor, however, he entered a governmental institution with very little historical baggage due to the youth of the Unigov reforms. He was in a position to do much of the defining—an opportunity not usually available to mayors of large urban areas.

Local governing organizations operate jointly to produce a complex web of interactions in all urban areas. Studies in urban governance cannot ignore such complexities by analyzing management in a vacuum. Thus this critique focuses on two general themes. The first focus addresses Mayor Hudnut's administrative style. The structural characteristics of Unigov presented the mayor with constraints that affected his ability to interact with other public and private officials at various levels of government (above, among, and below). The second focus concentrates on Hudnut's interactions with governance levels below that of the city-county, namely the neighborhoods. Given the large area of Marion County and the many diverse interests within its boundaries, a basic problem exists in how citizen preferences become revealed. Countywide voting aggregates the otherwise rich array of diverse tastes and preferences. Taxpaying citizens want the quality and quantity of their public services tailored to their desires. How does the county's top administrator recognize and pursue such differences across a large geographic area while trying to satisfy as many citizens as possible?

Administration under Unigov

The establishment of the Unigov system clearly created a strong mayor form of local government. The lines of authority and accountability made governing Indianapolis more feasible than did the prior structure, according to former Mayor Richard Lugar (NACO Roundtable, 1970). Lugar suggested that Unigov restructured local government in such a way that the mayor became the equivalent of the president of a corporation, with a deputy mayor and six "vicepresidents" (the directors of the six departments). Mayor Hudnut clearly agreed with this approach to government, and it illustrates his emphasis on administrative efficiency.

But a mayor is more than simply a powerful bureaucrat. He or she also must be a strong leader with a vision of where the city can and should go. Indianapolis has acquired a reputation for having weathered the late 1970s and 1980s better than other cities in the midwestern states. Hudnut's emphasis on economic development in and around the downtown area was a result of his vision for the city. To attract development he acted as the city's ambassador and promoted the city as a good area for investment. At the same time he had to be sure that this was the direction that the city wanted to go. Thus he also served as a salesperson for his own programs and initiatives.

All that was part of the mayor's philosophy of trying to bring harmony out of the urban cacophony. While he defines management as the art of getting things done through people, he defines leadership as the art of communicating to people what needs to be done. These definitions illustrate a major characteristic of Hudnut's style of governing: do not micromanage. Unigov facilitates such an approach. Hudnut identified the goals and left the details for the individual departments. Stuart Reller, a former administrator in the Division of Planning at the Department of Metropolitan Development (DMD), noted that the mayor was consistent in handing down clearly stated goals but expected staff to generate alternatives to implement the goals, alternatives which the mayor would either endorse or reject (Reller, 1991). There appeared to be a general belief that it was simply not the job of the mayor to formulate the particulars of a policy. This sentiment is echoed by Carson Soule, former executive director of the Greater Indianapolis Progress Committee, and by Paul Annee, chief of police under Hudnut. Both leaders noted the mayor's hands-off approach when it came to "detail work" while they applauded his ability to clearly specify the goals that he wanted accomplished (Soule, 1991; Annee, 1991).

To accomplish the leadership and management requirements Hudnut saw as necessary for Indianapolis, he always worked for consensus. This entailed bringing potentially diverse groups into line with his vision or program and helping them to see the value in it as well as take part in it in some way. Through consensus building he managed to maintain his prolonged interest in economic development in the downtown area. Consensus building was the foundation to Indianapolis's trademark public-private partnerships and a fairly well-followed growth strategy for the outlying areas (Hudnut, 1980).

His general rule for addressing entities or interests not under his authority (for instance, the excluded municipalities or county officials) was one of accommodation. The mayor has noted that he always tried "to avoid the acute angle. I don't want to be the kind of guy that has to have a fight every time you turn around. . . . " (Hudnut, 1991). Such an accommodation tactic is imperative for building consensus and forging partnerships in both the public and the private sectors. Obviously this approach is not going to function in every situation, particularly in highly controversial areas. In Indianapolis the probability of highly charged conflict is greatly reduced due to the fact that the Republican party is thoroughly woven into the fabric of local government. Almost all of the main players are in the same party, and that facilitates accommodation more often than not. Given the strength of the Republicans in Indianapolis (and Marion County more broadly), Hudnut was able to vigorously pursue numerous partnerships to accomplish his goals for local economic development while avoiding the two extreme positions of "open warfare and coalitionary paralysis" among members of the same team (Hudnut, 1987).

The View from the Neighborhoods

Hudnut placed a significant emphasis on the development of a vibrant downtown core as the economic engine to propel the county and did so through a series of public-private partnerships under the general strategy of making Indianapolis the amateur sports capital of

America. This strategy clearly enhanced the image of the city throughout the nation and resulted in more economic activity downtown. But the accomplishments were realized at a cost. Neighborhoods and community development programs were frequently overlooked in favor of the downtown development opportunities.

Many of the public and private political actors who participated in the design and passage of the Unigov reforms in the years before Hudnut was elected mayor saw it as an opportunity for investments in the downtown area. Many of these same individuals believed, however, that such investments would help prevent the slide of the old city neighborhoods into disrepair. But as many other cities following similar strategies have learned, it is not the quantity of the investments in an area that will or will not save it but the types of investments. Sports and hotels in the downtown core did very little to help the nearby inner-city neighborhoods of Center Township.

From 1960 through 1990 the population of Center Township declined by 45 percent, from 333,351 to 182,140 (DMD, 1985; U.S. Bureau of the Census, 1990). Many of the residents who left were those who could afford to leave. In general, it was the wealthier white residents who relocated to the outer townships. As a result, less well-off residents became more concentrated, much of the local housing stock was destroyed without replacement (DMD, 1989), home ownership began to decline sharply, poverty rose in Center Township, and many parts of the old city's infrastructure began literally to collapse. Many U.S. cities have witnessed this same phenomenon. As poverty becomes more concentrated, crime rates rise. The costs of providing police, fire, and school services go up.

The increase in these costs probably would have been less drastic if Unigov had more completely consolidated the tax base for provision of these services. However, the Unigov reforms left the financing of these basic urban services essentially unchanged. As a result, citizens living within the boundaries of the old city, especially those in Center Township, were (and still are) paying a larger proportion of their wealth to the taxes used to pay for these services.

In addition to this situation, Center Township is home to the downtown core where the vast majority of the mayor's economic development activities were being targeted. For many of these developments the city government offered various incentive packages to firms to locate in the downtown area. For instance, several hundred million dollars in tax abatements were granted in the downtown area. To cover this lost revenue, taxes on other businesses and citizens in Center Township had to be raised. This policy makes logical sense in a program of economic development designed to save inner-city neighborhoods through the creation of new jobs. But the types of jobs created were either low-paying service or retail jobs for individuals with little training or education or specialized service jobs such as insurance or banking that frequently require a skill and training level beyond that of residents whom such developments were supposed to help. These high-paying jobs went instead to suburban residents who lived outside the taxing districts created to pay for the incentive packages used to attract the jobs to Center Township. Some of the city's poorest residents thus are subsidizing jobs for outer township residents and receiving little in return.

The problems that have accompanied the deterioration of many Center Township neighborhoods are no longer limited to the township. In several instances, crime problems are spilling over to other neighborhoods. The quality of public education is a serious problem for the financially strapped Indianapolis Public School system, which must draw on the same overburdened taxpayers of Center Township who are already heavily supporting downtown development. The concerns of suburban neighborhoods are different from those of inner-city neighborhoods. Many times, conflicts arise as new developments emerge in undeveloped areas or alternative land uses are desired by neighborhood residents than the uses envisioned by property owners. Just as inner-city residents became increasingly frustrated with certain structural characteristics of Unigov, suburban residents also began to realize the problems that arise when government decision making is so far removed from them.

Other characteristics of Unigov that played a role in the rising frustrations of neighborhood residents are the structure and role of the City-County Council. Indianapolis possesses one of the largest councils in the nation, with 29 seats; 25 are elected from councilmanic districts covering the entire county and four are elected at-large. In the consolidated structure, the councillors represent the level of government closest to the citizenry. Currently, each district encompasses approximately 32,000 residents.

Indianapolis's average council district population is larger than that of most U.S. cities and towns yet the smallest among large cities nationwide. The relatively small districts might be expected to engender close relations between councillors and neighborhoods, but that has not been the case in many parts of the city. Many neighborhood leaders complain that their district councillor is not responsive to neighborhood organization concerns—"I don't do neighborhood meetings" was a councillor statement quoted by a variety of neighborhood leaders.

One source of frustration for neighborhood residents (and for councillors) is the power reserved to the City-County Council in the Unigov system. Given the strong mayor–weak council system, there are relatively few responsibilities for the councillors beyond budgetary matters and confirmation of the mayor's appointments. As a result, councillors have very limited ability to influence service bureaucracies to respond to neighborhood concerns.

A second source of frustration for neighborhoods is political. In very partisan Indianapolis, councilmanic districts are organized in such a way that the Republican party is in a position to maintain majority control of the council indefinitely. Democrats are elected from districts in the old city, but the number of these districts is well short of a majority. As a result of this design and traditionally low turnout for local elections, being responsive to local party officials is more essential to reelection than is response to neighborhood leaders' concerns. Councillors can do relatively little in their district's neighborhoods and still win easy reelection through the party system. There are, therefore, few strong incentives for councillors to be responsive to neighborhoods.

While those councillors who do try to be responsive to neighborhood constituents face the potentially daunting task of trying to represent multiple interests in their districts, the mayor of almost 800,000 citizens faces far more divergence over the geographic area of the city. The difficulties associated with trying to match services to the preferences of taxpayers is made more difficult at higher levels of government. When governmental decision makers are closer to their constituents, better communication and accountability are facilitated (Advisory Commission on Intergovernmental Relations, 1987).

Unigov effectively pushed politics and government further from the people. Early efforts at formalizing a voice for neighborhoods to complement the city-county bodies, but for smaller-scale problems—the "minigov" proposals—were defeated by the City-County Council even though Mayor Lugar and his staff had supported the idea. With no such formal voice, neighborhood residents were left with the only other voice they had: the voting booth. However, as David Mathews notes in his recent book *Politics for People*, "voting doesn't allow citizens to express all they feel about political issues. At its best, voting is restrictive because choices are limited to 'yes' or 'no.' Voting is confined to options that already exist; it does not allow for full political expression" (1994).

Mayor Hudnut did not stress or encourage neighborhood self-governance during his administration as he focused more specifically on the redevelopment of the downtown core and the revitalization of the city's national image. Though he did not stress citizen involvement, he did not totally ignore it either. During one point of his tenure, Hudnut held regular quarterly meetings with neighborhood leaders to hear their comments, criticisms, and suggestions. The mayor met with frustrations, however, and he perceived an inconsistent commitment from these community leaders because attendance rose and fell and finally tapered to nothing. The advisory group was discontinued.

Discussions with participants in this group suggest that the intermittent support was the result of a perceived lack of responsiveness on the part of the city. These participants indicated that meeting with the mayor was a good idea but that they felt that it was rare that any actions followed. This may be one of the side effects of the mayor's style of not micromanaging. Neighborhood issues tend to be microissues, and the mayor may not have been the appropriate person to solve them. At the same time, the city-county bureaucracy had difficulty maintaining an awareness of such small-scale problems. As Hudnut concedes, "I think that probably one of the criticisms of the Hudnut administration that will be made when the history books are written is that we did not concentrate enough on neighborhoods, that we were more interested in economic development and downtown development than we were neighborhood revitalization" (1991).

Action in the Neighborhoods

With the lack of focus on neighborhood concerns by public-sector interests, there was a clear response on the part of nongovernmental groups to come together and attempt to address the problems of neighborhoods. Several grassroots neighborhood organizations began emerging after Unigov's passage, even more so after 1978. In addition, several nonprofit groups joined in neighborhood efforts to address such issues as crime, housing revitalization, and clean-up.

One of the best-known neighborhood groups in Indianapolis is the Near Eastside Community Organization (NESCO). This is an organization "of citizens who work together to improve the quality of life in Indianapolis's Near Eastside . . . [striving] to bring citizens together to find their common voice and unified strength" (NESCO, 1991). Since its creation, NESCO has assisted in setting up several service organizations, such as the Near Eastside Multi-Service Center, People's Health Center, Eastside Community Investments (the local CDC), and the Near Eastside Community Federal Credit Union. The area is its own miniature ecosystem of several neighborhood organizations and block clubs complete with their own conflicts as well as numerous successes.

One of the area's main concerns was housing and land use; it was fighting the effects of decline. On occasion the residents' views on the development of the area ran counter to the city's views and that gave rise to conflicts, some of which ended in legal proceedings. Mayor Hudnut, avoiding the micromanagement of his policy directives, maintained a hands-off approach while NESCO and the Department of Metropolitan Development fought out their differences, draining the neighborhood of its very limited monetary and human resources in an effort to have a say in how their community would evolve.

Despite these conflicts, the Near Eastside experience indicates that with little governmental assistance (and some hostility), neighborhoods within a metropolitan area are capable of working for the interests of area residents with resident cooperation. Leaders trained through activities in NESCO have moved to other parts of the city to begin new activities and address new problems specific to those areas.

The experience of another part of the inner city, the northwest corner of the downtown area known as Midtown, was somewhat different. The area had a unique and "long history of serving as the social, cultural, and economic center of the black community" (Downtown Development Research Committee, 1980). Unfortunately, the area was located between downtown to the east and the White River to the west, the Indiana University–Purdue University campus to the south and a new interstate highway cutting the area in half. The highway was placed in the neighborhood after its economic decline was well under way.

Many residents in the area have continually feared the continued growth of the university, since the university has few choices of direction to expand. Dealings among the university, the neighborhood's community development corporation (Midtown Economic Development Industrial Corporation, or MEDIC), local residents, and city agents have not always been on good terms as a result. One of the most contentious periods resulted from a city plan made with the university to demolish the Lockefield Garden apartments (arguably the city's only successful public housing venture, located between the university and the neighborhood), acquire the land, and make it available to the university.

The city's plan galvanized the African-American community so much so that the Greater Indianapolis Progress Committee (the lead agency in the city's Midtown redevelopment strategy) funded a new plan and helped acquire additional funding for integrating more of the neighborhood residents' concerns in the planning. As a result, much of Lockefield Gardens was saved. Only the less structurally sound buildings were demolished to create open space, while other buildings were renovated. But Lockefield's character as public housing changed greatly. The complex now houses students as well as low-income families who receive housing assistance from the federal government.

The partial success of MEDIC in the 1970s led to a working arrangement with the city and the Health and Hospital Corporation for the continued redevelopment of the Midtown area. While this partnership was born out of protest, MEDIC accomplished several projects in the 1980s, including restoration of the Madame Walker Building and the Walker Theater, construction of the Goodwin Plaza elderly housing project and another public housing project for the elderly, completion of the Lockefield Gardens project and the Walker Plaza office complex, and establishment of Business Opportunities Systems (BOS) as a financing arm for MEDIC's projects.

The president of BOS noted Hudnut's support of this series of partnership projects but also noted that rarely did the mayor involve himself in the specifics, leaving the details to his staff (Morgan, 1991). The lack of clear support during the difficult Lockefield Gardens episode again illustrates the potential problems associated with a hands-off approach: less direct responsibility for the details but greater potential for the implementation of policies to cause additional problems or to further alienate a segment of the community.

On the northeast corner of downtown are several gentrifying neighborhoods in the Riley area. Three neighborhood associations were organized in the 1970s in response to the deterioration of the area's housing stock. Over time the area developed a community development corporation (the Riley Area Revitalization Program, or RARP). RARP assisted the area in addressing social concerns that arose in response to the process of gentrification and assisted in the process itself through acquiring Community Development Block Grant money for housing rehabilitation projects (DeLong, 1991). The neighborhood groups played a strong role in the election of their city-county councillor, who has been a strong advocate for the community and its projects.

As with the BOS experience, RARP's director, Valery DeLong, noted that the role of the mayor tended to be one of general support for the effort, but the city staff did the detail work and many times that follow-through by the staff was mediocre. While RARP realized several successes, it is surprising to note that the city did not support these projects actively as they were in line with the mayor's goal of more upscale housing units close to the downtown area. The implementation of the mayor's policy objectives might have been better realized had he played a more significant role.

REFERENCES

Advisory Commission on Intergovernmental Relations, *The Organization of Local Public Economies* (Washington, D.C.: ACIR, 1987).

Paul Annee (Chief of Police), interview with David Swindell, Indianapolis, October 14, 1991.

Valerie DeLong (Director, Riley Area Revitalization Program), interview with David Swindell, Indianapolis, October 11, 1991.

Department of Metropolitan Development, *Development Data for Indianapolis–Marion County Indiana, 1985* (Indianapolis: Division of Planning, 1985).

Department of Metropolitan Development, *Development Data for Indianapolis–Marion County, Indiana, 1989* (Indianapolis: Division of Planning, 1989).

Downtown Development Research Committee, *Indianapolis: Downtown Development for Whom?* (Indianapolis: Indiana Christian Leadership Conference, 1980).

William Hudnut, *A Growth Strategy for Indianapolis* (Indianapolis: Department of Metropolitan Development, 1980).

William Hudnut, *Indianapolis: Past, Present, and Future* (New York: Newcomen Society of the United States, 1987).

William Hudnut, interview with Roger Parks and David Swindell, Indianapolis, August 12, 1991.

David Mathews, *Politics for People: Finding a Responsible Public Voice* (Chicago: University of Illinois Press, 1994).

Kenneth Morgan (Director, Business Opportunities Systems), interview with David Swindell, Indianapolis, October 8, 1991.

NACO Roundtable, "City-County Consolidations, Separations, and Federations," *American County* 35 (1970): 12–31.

NESCO, *NESCO: Neighborhood Directory* (Indianapolis: NESCO, 1991).

Stuart Reller (Senior Planner, Department of Metropolitan Development), interview with David Swindell, Indianapolis, October 11, 1991.

Carson Soule (Director, Greater Indianapolis Progress Committee), interview with David Swindell, Indianapolis, October 11, 1991.

United States Bureau of the Census, *1990 Census of Population and Housing* (Washington, D.C.: U.S. Government Printing Office, 1990).

The Police Department

DAVID J. BODENHAMER AND
WILLIAM DOHERTY

On January 1, 1976, newly elected Mayor William H. Hudnut inherited a police force in disarray. Two years earlier the *Indianapolis Star*, in a Pulitzer prize-winning series, had exposed pervasive police corruption: brutality, widespread political influence, shakedowns, ghost payments, and unsavory connections with known criminals, among other illegalities. The impression was of a department rife with corruption, scandal, and malfeasance.

Hudnut's predecessor, Richard Lugar, had been unable to reform the department. Its adherence to a "code of silence"—the unwillingness to inform on a fellow officer—and the refusal of ranking officers to resign frustrated his best efforts. The *Star's* series prompted Lugar to appoint an experienced outsider to head the force in March 1974, but by summer 1975 the new chief was a figure of ridicule. Many officers met his efforts at reform by slowing the rate of arrests and failing to appear as witnesses in municipal courts, an action that led to the dismissal of hundreds of cases.

Judged by other big-city departments, the Indianapolis Police Department (IPD) in 1976 was not unusually corrupt, but it was unruly and beyond the mayor's control. Lugar admitted as much in a valedictory interview: "Even if I had a very good idea of precisely who was dark and evil as could be, my chances of making much difference about that are close to nil." The chief culprit in Lugar's view was the Fraternal Order of Police (FOP) and its success in gaining protective state legislation that frustrated efforts to discipline police officers (*Indianapolis News*, December 29, 1975).

Beyond the comment that the department was the "Achilles' heel" of the city administration, a statement that infuriated Lugar, Hudnut's campaign platform strongly supported the police and pledged to be tough on crime. Hudnut finessed the corruption issue by shifting attention to the crime rate. Crime was his "first priority," and police inefficiency, not police corruption, hampered its control (*Star*, September 4, 1975; *News*, August 1, 1975). The new mayor, Hudnut said, should rally the community behind "the men who are doing a good job—and I think most of them are" (*Star*, September 23, 1975; see also *News*, October 15, 1975). Hudnut's 11-point program to fight crime, announced during the campaign, included support for good police work, more uniformed officers, better training and equipment, closer police contact with neighborhoods through a Crime Watch program, nonsuspensive sentences for violent criminals, and a citizens' task force on crime (*Star*, August 7, 1975).

Hudnut also promised to remove politics from the Police Department. As a Lugar appointee to the Board of Public Safety in 1970, serving briefly as its chairman, Hudnut became aware of the political interference that existed in the department. To get promoted, he later recalled, a candidate needed to demonstrate "political clout" by having ward chairmen, vice-committeemen, and precinct officials write letters of endorsement. The department in 1975 reflected this pattern of political influence: the GOP county chairman was "heavily involved" in personnel decisions, the eight majors "were all very close to [him] and [all were] card-carrying Republicans, and the head of the civilian personnel office was a Republican ward chairwoman" (Hudnut interview, September 13, 1991).

Significantly, many police officers supported the depoliticization of IPD. Few officers enjoyed finding a political sponsor or gambling on which party affiliation would best advance their career. All of them resented the required contribution of 2 percent of their pay to the party in power. Sensing public and police dissatisfaction with the existing system, Hudnut pledged to separate policing from politics, even though no reform in this area had succeeded since the Merit Law of 1935. In retrospect, this decision was not as bold as it seemed. Traditional patronage practices were under attack everywhere, and campaign advisers had alerted Hudnut to a case then on federal appeal, *Bums v. Elrod*, that outlawed political firings for persons in non-policy-making positions (*Bums v. Elrod*, 509 F. 2d 1133 [7th Cir. 1975]; January 8, 1987, memorandum and draft of a Hudnut law review article, Mayor's Office Files).

Although determined to address problems in the department, Hudnut assumed that it was futile to confront the police. Corruption aside, police officers still drew upon a reservoir of good will that made them difficult to attack. The belief that an open clash would embroil the new administration in endless debate and alienate voters led to a set of related strategies. First, Hudnut would publicly praise the police and deflect criticism of them by emphasizing their difficult and dangerous job. Second, he would professionalize the department, his primary objective, by removing it from politics, an action that many officers supported. Third, he would cement this support by promoting from within the department, raising salaries and pension benefits, improving the work environment and morale, and enhancing the public image of the department. Finally, he would make the department more representative of the city's population by hiring and promoting more African-Americans and women. An affirmative-action plan would broaden community support for his goal of professionalization. In short, Hudnut approached the issue of public safety with a far more sophisticated and coherent strategy than his campaign rhetoric implied.

Even before taking office, Hudnut signaled a new beginning by naming a 37-member committee to interview and recommend candidates for the position of chief, stipulating only that the chief come from the department and that no questions be asked about the candidates' political or religious affiliations (*Star*, December 20, 1975; Hudnut interview, September 13, 1991). He followed these actions in January by directing the police and fire chiefs and respective merit boards to hire and promote solely on merit, which he defined as technical competence, experience, knowledge, and leadership. He also ended political clearances for all city jobs (memorandum to public safety director, "Guidelines for Promotions of Policemen and Firefighters," January 28, 1976; see also State of the City address, December 8, 1976, Mayor's Office Files).

The rule against political interference also applied to the mayor's office: Hudnut pledged "not [to] intrude in promotions" nor "dictate to the chief" (*Star*, May 2, 1976). It was a pledge he kept, according to chiefs who served under him (*Star*, January 8, 1978; interview with Paul A. Annee, August 5, 1992). Hudnut disavowed the role of "super chief," choosing instead to appoint the top officials and set broad policies for them to follow. Only during budget hearings, negotiations with the FOP, or crises did his regular Friday meetings extend beyond the scheduled half-hour briefing (Hudnut interview, September 13, 1991).

In his annual State of the City address and budget messages to the City-County Council, Hudnut never tired of repeating that public safety was the city's "first priority." And public safety, in fact, always had first claim on available funds: as much as 80 percent of the property tax revenues, all general revenue sharing funds, and a portion of the county option income tax went for police and fire equipment, capital projects, and salaries and pensions. From 1977 to 1992, transportation's share of the budget declined by a third and parks and recreation by almost 30 percent, but public safety's share remained a steady one-third of the budget, growing from $181.7 to $481.3 million, or 265 percent, over Hudnut's four terms.

Hudnut carried out his pledge to improve police salaries and pensions. From 1976 to 1992, the pay for a patrol officer at the beginning of the third year, the pension base year, rose from $12,173.25 to $32,099, outpacing inflation (IPD Planning and Research Office). The base salary, moreover, understated the compensation of police officers: at the end of the Hudnut era, they received an annual clothing allowance, longevity pay, hazard and technical pay, stipends for field and field training duty, education incentives, and a shift differential. Additionally, officers drew overtime pay under a standard more favorable than the one mandated by law. Improved salary and benefits brought a more highly educated and better-qualified force. By early 1988, 47 percent of the patrol officers, 55 percent of sergeants, and 68 percent of lieutenants and above had some college education (IPD interdepartmental memoranda, July 18, 1988, and February 1988, Mayor's Office Files).

Increased pay and benefits naturally brought higher costs. The overtime bill in 1981 was $856,000; by 1990 it had risen to $1.87 million. A far more significant expense was police and fire pensions. Mandated by state law but with no state funding, pension benefits were part of the city's annual operating budget. By 1976 Indianapolis had an enormous unfunded liability for these retirement plans.

Hudnut appointed a bipartisan task force on intergovernmental relations to address the issue, with the goal of seeking state aid. Chaired by former Democratic governor Matthew E. Welsh and future Republican lieutenant governor John M. Mutz, the committee urged the Greater Indianapolis Progress Committee, a quasi-governmental group that linked public and private interests, to press for legislation to gain state contributions and create a single state agency to administer all local public-safety funds. In 1977 the Indiana General Assembly accepted this recommendation and others, including using the county option income tax to underwrite pension costs. State action led to the creation of a new plan in 1978 that was more advantageous to retirees and to the city. Pension fund problems did not disappear, but the nearly $1-billion unfunded liability projected by 2016 declined to an estimated shortfall of only $86 million by 1990 (budget message, August 2, 1982, Mayor's Office Files).

The increasing cost of salaries and benefits and the disappearance by the mid-1980s of federal revenue-sharing and Law Enforcement Administration Assistance funds necessarily affected the size and structure of the department. During the Hudnut years (1976–91), the number of employees of the Police Department grew by only one percent and sworn officers declined by 11.7 percent. The administration touted the advantages of a leaner, more efficient department. It also adopted the strategy of shifting sworn officers from administrative support to law enforcement. The number of administrators declined from 34.8 percent in 1977 to 20 percent in 1992, while the percentage of officers correspondingly rose from 65.2 to 80 percent. Less expensive civilian employees took over support functions (IPD, "Staffing Statistics, 1976–1991").

Addressing the internal problems of the department made it easier for Hudnut to move IPD to hire a more racially diverse force. During the 1975 campaign he had signaled his intention to increase the number of blacks and women in the city administration, especially in the Police and Fire departments (*News*, September 24, 1975). He did not believe in "quotas," he told the Indianapolis chapter of Indiana's Black Republican Council, but "obviously more minority members are needed" since blacks constituted fewer than 10 percent of the city police and only 6 percent of the firefighters. His administration, he pledged, would be "representative of all members [of the community]—blacks, whites, men, women, or whatever" (*Star,* September 30, 1975).

Hudnut's desire for greater minority participation in government was genuine, yet he was also aware of the 1975 lawsuit filed by seven African-American policemen alleging discrimination in the department. He knew as well that the U.S. Department of Justice was considering a suit against the city (William H. Hudnut and Judy Keene,

Minister/Mayor, 152, 153). Thus both principle and necessity led to a directive during his first month as mayor for all city departments to increase black and female employment until it more closely mirrored the city's population. The Police and Fire departments received a more specific order: include 25 percent blacks and women in all future recruit classes (State of the City address, 1976, Mayor's Office Files).

Hudnut's voluntary affirmative-action program did not satisfy the Justice Department, which filed suit against the city in June 1978 and again in January 1979. Without admitting wrongdoing, the city in federal district court entered into separate consent decrees on race, July 19, 1978, and sex, January 9, 1979, that made the voluntary hiring goals legally binding. The city pledged to hire blacks and women in a percentage "reasonably representative" of their number in the county's workforce and to promote them in percentages that corresponded to their number and rank in the department. Pending promotions were canceled and qualifying tests and performance evaluations were recast to reflect true "job related standards and criteria." The decrees were to run five years, with elaborate monitoring established to ensure substantial compliance ("Summary of Consent . . . for Management Personnel of Indianapolis Police Department," Affirmative Action folder, Mayor's Office Files).

The shift from a voluntary to a legally mandated program, if not welcomed by Hudnut, certainly made the mayor's goals in affirmative action much easier. But in October 1984 a U.S. Supreme Court decision, *Firefighters Local Union No. 1784 v. Stotts,* called into question the constitutionality of consent decrees, like the one in Indianapolis, in which there was no explicit finding of racial discrimination. The implications for Indianapolis—and the mayor's goal—were obvious.

Hudnut reacted swiftly: he made public a memo to all city departments reaffirming his commitment to nondiscrimination and affirmative action (news release, October 19, 1984, Affirmative Action folder, Mayor's Office Files). But *Stotts* suited the Reagan Administration's conservative agenda, and in April 1985 the Justice Department filed a motion in the U.S. District Court for Southern Indiana to set aside the hiring goals of the Indianapolis decrees and substitute an "enhanced recruitment program" (*United States v. City of Indianapolis,* April 26, 1985, "Motion for . . . Modification of Consent Decrees, 9, 10, 17–19, Mayor's Office Files).

Hudnut was not willing to give up the program he had established. At a press conference on April 30 he announced the city's intention "voluntarily" to continue affirmative action in the Police and Fire departments "even if it loses a court battle" because Indianapolis had come "too far along the road of minority involvement to turn back now" (*Minister/Mayor*, 153; *Star*, May 1, 1985). Six weeks later the city modified its plan to promote minority hiring even more aggressively by increasing the number of qualified minority slots from five to six of every 25 recruits (*News*, June 17, 1985).

Despite positive attention from the national media, including appearances on "The MacNeil-Lehrer News Hour" and "Face the Nation," Hudnut received mixed support back home. But he held to his position because he believed that affirmative action was constitutional, morally right, and necessary. Affirmative action, Hudnut believed, did not involve hiring or promoting less-qualified applicants on the basis of race or gender. The candidate list represented "a pool of equally well qualified applicants [from which] we are going to pull some out [by using] race and sex conscious policies and guidelines . . . so we don't have an all white class . . . or all white people promoted, or all white males." Minorities, he concluded, faced too many obstacles in the appointment and review process to ensure equitable representation: the department operated "a good old boy network . . . they tend to go with their own" (Hudnut interview, September 13, 1991).

The Justice Department's motion divided the police along racial lines: Fraternal Order of Police Lodge 86 voted to file a "friend of the court" brief on the side of the Reagan Administration, an action which prompted the highest-ranking African-American in IPD, Assistant Chief Joseph J. Shelton, to resign from the FOP in protest. Complaints from whites also greeted Chief Joseph G. McAtee's decision to promote a black sergeant over ten whites who stood higher on the list (*News*, July 11, 1985; *Star*, July 12, 1985). The rift was only partially healed when the FOP, in a special meeting and by a close margin, 140–126, withdrew its amicus brief before black officers resigned from the union en masse (*Star*, August 1, 1985).

With the racial tensions in IPD much in mind, on September 20 Hudnut met with Assistant U.S. Attorney General Bradford Reynolds in Washington, carrying a letter addressed to Attorney General Edwin Meese III. The Justice Department's actions, the mayor wrote, had "sown seeds of discord and contributed to . . . racial tension and strife" in the Police and Fire departments "where none existed before." Hudnut noted that since April other federal courts had rejected the department's broad interpretation of *Stotts* and that the city's affirmative-action program had inspired "virtually no litigation" claiming reverse discrimination. The letter cited the unanimous support of the 29-member City-County Council and expressed hope that the Justice Department would withdraw its motion and "allow us to return to our stable and peaceful existence" (September 18, 1985, Affirmative Action folder, Mayor's Office Files).

The meeting ended in an impasse, with Hudnut promising to see Reynolds in court, but within the year the U.S. Supreme Court in *Local 28, Sheet Metal Workers v. EEOC* (1986) and *Local 93 Firefighters v. Cleveland* (1986) upheld "hiring goals" for minority workers, the heart of the Hudnut plan, proclaiming these voluntary initiatives to be "the preferred means of achieving Title VII goals." With obvious reluctance, the Justice Department dropped its litigation against the city on August 4, 1986. But for the admittedly thin-skinned Hudnut, the department's action still rankled: it had "created unnecessary turmoil [and increased] tensions between black and white officers" (*Washington Post,* August 18, 1986).

If the purpose of affirmative action was to show results, what was its effect on the Indianapolis Police Department? Although Hudnut labeled the gains "modest," statistically the consequences were significant. Small annual increases in minority hiring over Hudnut's four terms brought substantial change. When he became mayor in 1976, 9.8 percent of the police were black and 6.9 percent female; when he left office in January 1992, black officers constituted 17.8 percent and women 14.7 percent of the force. During this period, females and black males totaled 122 of the 315 recruits, or 38.7 percent (80 blacks [25.4 percent] and 42 white women [13.3 percent]). Total minority representation rose from 18 percent in 1978 to 28.6 percent in 1992. A police force that was 83.3 percent white male when Hudnut entered office was only 70.7 percent white male when he left it (IPD, interdepartmental memoranda, October 9, 1991, Office of Planning and Research).

Gains were not as impressive in the area of promotions, at least not for blacks. From July 1978 to June 30, 1991, blacks and women as a group were not promoted in numbers consistent with their presence on the force, a circumstance that may be explained in part by their shorter time in rank. As late as April 1989, only 13 of 98 officers lieutenant and above were blacks and women, or 13.3 percent compared to their 25.8 percent presence in IPD. White females fared far better than did black males or black females, receiving promotions in proportion to their representation on the force. This result corresponds to findings elsewhere that affirmative-action programs benefit white females most (see Andrew Hacker, *Two Nations: Black and White, Separate, Hostile, Unequal,* New York, 1992, 132). Minorities fared better in the highest, most publicly visible ranks of the department. By December 1991, 12 of 33 section heads from commander to chief were held by minorities (eight black males, four white females), an overrepresentation of their presence on the force. Among the four division heads, one, the assistant chief, was a black male; of the six majors, two were black males and one a white female (IPD Annual Report, 1991).

The real test of affirmative action is whether the percentage of blacks and females on the police force corresponds to their presence in the total population. Here the results show the same trend toward proportional representation. No matter how compared—whether to the population of Indianapolis or Marion County, the area labor force, or even the population in the IPD service district—the trend was toward proportional representation of blacks. Measured against 17 other cities, Indianapolis ranked fifth in the percentage of blacks on the police force compared with the black percentage of the total population. By this standard, Hudnut's record in affirmative action, far from modest, was exceptional.

For Hudnut success in affirmative action meant success in policing the community. Credibility in law enforcement required a diverse police force that mirrored the racial composition of the citizenry it served. Another benefit was that a racially and gender-balanced department had a variety of experiences and skills not otherwise available to a white-male-only force, especially in using verbal tactics to defuse a volatile situation. Thus, beyond the arguments for equal opportunity, affirmative action strengthened Indianapolis law enforcement.

Hudnut's success in affirmative action did not happen without significant commitment from the department's senior leadership. And this internal support came, in large measure, because the mayor gave the director of public safety and the police chief wide latitude to run the department. He stayed out of the department's internal affairs. He also demonstrated his loyalty to top officials by keeping them in their jobs: Hudnut had only three directors of public safety in 16 years—one died in service—and three chiefs. Hudnut regarded Paul A. Annee, chief from August 1987 through December 1991, as his best appointment in this position. With a degree in criminal justice, Annee was more open to change, more supportive of the mayor's policies, more attuned to public relations, more willing to exercise authority in the face of resistance, and more distant from the FOP than his predecessors. Upon taking office he immediately made chemical repellents and nightsticks mandatory as alternatives to lethal force, moves Hudnut had long wanted but that Chiefs Gallagher and McAtee had resisted. In line with the mayor's thinking, Annee sought to distance supervisory officers from the ranks, improve training with emphasis on better human relations, promote younger and better-educated officers, and support reorganization and the use of new technologies (*Star*, October 27, 1986). He reinforced the managerial role of supervisors by excluding them from the merit system, a signal that the FOP would no longer negotiate for the entire force. Ranking officers, Annee hoped, would begin to look to the administration, not the union, for leadership (Annee interview, August 5, 1992).

Hudnut and Annee placed great importance on the psychological evaluation of recruits in order to weed out unsatisfactory candidates. They also promoted better police-community relations by doubling the number of police academy hours devoted to problems of poverty, gender, and ethnic diversity. Training focused first on the need to exercise judgment and discretion, with armed force used only as a last resort. Always the emphasis was on anticipating and preventing a problem rather than merely reacting to it (Annee interview, August 5, 1992).

Reorganizing the department and investing in new police technologies were other priorities for Hudnut and Annee. Quadrant headquarters moved from the City-County Building to the neighborhoods. To the mayor and his police chief, this move was a first step in mapping a new direction toward "community policing." It represented a fundamental reconceptualization of police work, with an emphasis, in Annee's words, on "service, not . . . battle" (Annee interview, August 5, 1992). New technologies complemented this strategy. An automated fingerprint-identification system, a video "mugshot" capability, computer-aided dispatch, and an enhanced 911 system linked to a countywide radio network of police, fire, and emergency services would, Hudnut and Annee argued, bring IPD into the 21st century (*News*, November 23, 1991).

To improve community relations, Hudnut and Annee established an advisory group of 12 citizens representing professional, minority, and neighborhood groups. The council even included the executive director of the Indiana Civil Liberties Union, a traditional antagonist of Indianapolis police (*News*, September 2 and December 5, 1986). But here the mayor and his chief ran into a problem that has plagued numerous big-city administrations: how to permit civilian review of police actions, especially police shootings, without alienating the rank and file.

In the mid-1980s IPD came under attack for a string of police-action shootings, some of which occurred in questionable circumstances. The most extreme example, but one deemed emblematic by many members of the city's African-American community, was the fatal shooting of a black youth in the back seat of the police car transporting him to the station after his arrest. Even though the 17-year-old's hands were cuffed behind him, the policeman involved claimed the wound was self-inflicted, a claim the department accepted after an internal review conducted by a black ex-IPD officer.

Public concerns about the adequacy of police review intensified following several shootings over the next two years. There were numerous calls for a civilian review board with the power to investigate the incidents and discipline offending officers. The resulting public pressure placed Hudnut in an especially uncomfortable position. From his first campaign and throughout his four terms, he held fast to the position that public criticism of the police was an ineffective method of reform. He was also aware that police officers opposed a civilian review board, and he knew firsthand their power to engage in tactics, such as a work slowdown or strike, that would threaten his primary objective as mayor, maintaining Indianapolis's reputation as a city that worked (Hudnut interview, July 30, 1992). In 1977, for example, the FOP had fostered a protest of Hudnut's policy rescinding the practice of permitting officers to take patrol cars home for off-duty use. Hudnut considered this action, which resulted in police cars parked in front of City Hall with lights on and sirens wailing, one of the most stressful events of his four terms.

Despite the adverse publicity over police-action shootings, the city's record improved markedly during Hudnut's administration. The average number of shootings during the last years of the Lugar Administration was 20.5, compared to 12 for Hudnut's first term and slightly more than 9 over his 16-year tenure (1991 IPD Annual Report). This trend tracked almost precisely the experience of other big cities, which from 1971 to 1984 witnessed an average decline of 51 percent in such incidents (Sherman et al., "Citizens Killed by Big-City Police, 1970–1984," Washington, D.C.: Crime Control Institute, 1986). Several factors explain the decrease: tighter policies on the use of deadly force, more progressive police administrations, increased liability to civil suits, and greater public scrutiny of police activity.

In Indianapolis, police shootings in the mid-1980s commanded much greater attention than had been true previously, in large measure because the most prominent incidents involved white officers shooting black suspects. The African-American community, divided internally but increasingly disaffected by the Hudnut Administration's focus on downtown revitalization, presented a solid front of protest, not only over the shootings but over what it saw as a broader problem of racism in the urban society. One demand attracted support outside the black community: the call for a civilian review board with disciplinary authority. Yet despite its potential to distance the mayor from criticism of police actions, Hudnut and the City-County Council stoutly resisted this reform.

Hudnut recognized that racism existed on the force, and he acknowledged the disillusionment among blacks over the shootings, some of which he later termed "bizarre" in their circumstances (see, for example, the budget message of August 6, 1989, Mayor's Office Files, in which Hudnut digressed from fiscal issues to address the problems; the characterization as bizarre comes from Hudnut interview, September 13, 1991). He also bowed to pressure in 1986 with the creation of the Civilian Complaint Review Board, although the board had no effective disciplinary power. But Hudnut would go no further in pressing for reform, even though his refusal soured a previously amicable relationship with the African-American community.

The mayor's reasons were complex and contradictory. In defending his policies after he left office, Hudnut claimed that sufficient controls existed without an external review board. The prosecutor and grand jury, coroner, police merit boards, the Board of Public Safety, and Justice Department all had authority to review, expose, and discipline or prosecute officers guilty of wrongdoing. Yet he also acknowledged that the police, and especially FOP lawyers, "quickly co-opted" the merit board and persuaded it to reverse internal discipline, that the Marion County prosecutor, a political opponent who eventually succeeded him as mayor, refused to carry cases to the grand jury, and that the department often acted to defeat his and Annee's efforts to sanction or get rid of bad officers (Hudnut interview, July 30, 1992).

For Hudnut the ultimate issue concerned something far more fundamental than civilian control over the police: it involved instead the basic questions of who would protect citizens, if not the police, and how the police could promote a well-ordered society under the supervisory system that his critics demanded. The mayor recognized the ills of the Police Department, but he chose to work internally to rid the force of its "bad apples," as he characterized them. He hesitated to interfere with IPD's ability to do its job, which he defined as the maintenance of law and order. This view came through vividly in 1989 when Hudnut was caught between public pressure to propose a civilian review board and internal pressure to resist one. Earlier he had seen his job as "keep[ing] peace in the larger family" of Indianapolis, a balancing act that required him simultaneously to shield and discipline the police or, as he put it, to come down "on both sides of the fence." Yet in the digression in his annual budget message, after pledging to prosecute actual police misconduct, he placed himself squarely on the side of the police. Adopting apocalyptic clichés, he pledged not to "handcuff" IPD officers: "It's a thin blue line," he wrote, "that separates civilization from barbarism, and law and order from chaos" (budget message, August 6, 1989, Mayor's Office Files).

In large measure, Hudnut placed great faith in the reforms he had already instituted and in the police chief he had charged with implementing them. This strategy might have worked, if not for the police shootings, the killing of an officer, and a storm of allegations about police brutality and harassment of blacks. These incidents and charges put IPD on the defensive and at times led Annee to resist the mayor's pressure for strict disciplinary action. Time, circumstance, and the mayor's reluctance to jeopardize his goal of a well-run city combined to frustrate Hudnut's best intentions.

All organizations resist change, and police departments are among the most resistant to reform efforts. So it is not surprising that Hudnut's efforts were, at best, only partly successful. The accomplishments were significant: his administration eliminated the most blatant forms of political interference; IPD was more professional, better trained, and better paid in 1991 than it had been in 1976; the chief had more authority to manage and discipline the department; police shootings and fatalities declined; and, most important, the force reflected the racial and gender diversity of the community. Some problems remained unsolved, especially relations between the African-American community and IPD, which were at their nadir during Hudnut's last term. It is also debatable whether the departmental culture had changed sufficiently to enable reforms to bring about permanent change.

Upon leaving office, Hudnut appeared to recognize the limits of his success, although perhaps not the reasons for it. He continued to believe that with the right chief "you can make some progress," yet ultimately his and Annee's efforts yielded a department that fell short of where either of them intended for it to be. As Hudnut put it, he left the department a seven on a scale of ten as opposed to the three he had inherited (Hudnut interview, September 13, 1991). The assessment was probably accurate. What was missing was the recognition that Hudnut unwittingly may have limited his efforts by placing the concept of a well-run city above all other goals for his administration. By placing emphasis on the police rather than the community to maintain the order that makes a city work, the mayor made himself hostage to the department. And as he discovered, a department that operated ulti-mately on its own sense of right and wrong could upset much of the progress and good will upon which a well-run city depends.

The Politics of Health

KAREN S. HARLOW, KATHRYN
DIEFENTHALER, AND AMY DILLOW

F ew areas of public service better exemplify the complexities of intergovernmental relations and leadership than does that of the provision of public health.
The monitoring of safety hazards, water quality,
drainage, and insects that spread disease are responsibilities of local
government and controlled through regulation. The indicators most
often associated with perceptions of good health and quality of life—
i.e., infant mortality, low birth weight, teenage pregnancy, suicide
rates—may be more closely tied to federal and state policies or to a
medical delivery system with little or no connection with city hall.

The type of leadership in cities also varies from strong mayors with
weak councils to city manager type governments. Some mayors have
only a ceremonial role, with little impact on local public policies, while
others act as chief legislators, chief ambassadors, or opinion leaders for
their cities (Pohlmann, 1993). The political culture of an area, defined
as "the propensity to engage in the production of public services and
the manner in which problems are approached by the political leadership" (Millman, 1981: 47), can encourage productive leadership or can
act as a barrier to governmental involvement in the solution of problems. Mayors may have strong commitments to the idea of high-quality
health services within a community, but the complexity of organizational arrangements and interrelationships of public and private providers, the lack of jurisdictional control over the health care sector, and
a political cultural environment that devalues public involvement in

provision of services may mediate against opportunities for policy impact.

In searching through Mayor William Hudnut's speeches during his 16-year administration, it may be telling that only one was found that focused on the subject of public health and the role of the city government. Relatively late in his administration, 1988, he delivered a speech in which he identified health problems as a core concern of economic development in the city and defined his role in dealing with those problems as that of a facilitator who could bring together members of the public and private sectors to address concerns.

An analysis of the provision of public health services in the City of Indianapolis provides a challenge for students of urban governance. Indiana historically has a form of health-service governance identified as "shared organizational control" (DeFriese et al., 1981). In shared organizational control, local health departments are operated by local government either directly or through a local board of health. In certain circumstances, these same health departments also fall under the authority of the state health department.

The organizational structure of local health for Indianapolis is unique among most of its midwestern counterparts of comparable size and racial or ethnic diversity. In 1951 the Indiana General Assembly enacted legislation creating a health and hospital district covering all of Marion County with power to conduct its own affairs of city and county governmental control. In 1954 the Health and Hospital Corporation of Marion County was constitutionally confirmed as an independent unit of government with five board members (Buell and Robbins, 1984). The mayor's direct role involves selection of three board members, two of whom may be from the same political party, to the now-expanded, seven-member board. The City-County Council selects two board members, and county commissioners are responsible for the final two. Thus the city government and mayor have little direct control over the policy directions or decisions of the health sector except through the selection of board members who serve four-year terms, which may be repeated.

Nonetheless the quality of health in a city is viewed by many as a major indicator of quality of life and, as such, is a central component of economic development. This critique focuses on health policy in the city as it evolved during the Hudnut Administration. While admittedly the mayor's office may have little direct control over the corporation responsible for developing public health services, the image of the city government as a partner in provision of leadership is a legitimate focus.

In determining the role that the mayor and his staff played in major health policy directions, interviews with 25 leaders were conducted and written records of health programs and health corporation budgets were analyzed.

To understand the patterns that are identified in Indianapolis and the level of impact Mayor Hudnut might have had on those patterns, it is important first to place the Hudnut Administration and the Indianapolis experience in a national context. Perhaps the most far-reaching national health-policy change during the Hudnut Administration was the introduction of a prospective payment system (PPS) based on diagnosis-related groupings (DRGs) in 1983. Under PPS, hospitals were reimbursed depending upon the diagnosis of the patient regardless of what specific services were offered or how long the patient was hospitalized.

In addition to this major shift in public policy and the associated implications for local health, two crises in the health care sector also created challenges for administrators and health providers at all levels. Spiraling health care costs caused many companies to rethink and retool their health benefit packages, limiting access and eligibility for many previously covered individuals and services. Bad debt, charitable care, and indigent care became increasingly difficult challenges for local health care providers during the Hudnut Administration. In the early 1980s, a new health risk, acquired immunodeficiency syndrome, appeared on the horizon.

To understand policy decisions made by any administration, one must identify the contextual environment in which these decisions are made. Lammers and Klingman (1984) have identified several indicators that influence the perception of need for various social/health policy responses in any area and the associated innovativeness of state and local governments to respond to the perceived needs. These characteristics include the percent of the population who are minority, elderly, or poor; the growth or decline of an area; the average household size; and the per capita income.

To couch discussions in a comparative framework, ten cities including Indianapolis were studied for this discussion. Criteria for selection as a comparison site included geographic proximity to Indianapolis (Chicago/Cook County; Louisville/Jefferson County; Cincinnati/Hamilton County; Cleveland/Cuyahoga County; St. Louis/St. Louis County), comparable involvement in major rebuilding or renovation in downtown areas (Detroit/Wayne County; Baltimore/Baltimore

County; Pittsburgh/Allegheny County), and combined city/county governing structure (Nashville/Davidson County). Cities/counties selected are ranked by 1990 populations in the table.

Population Comparison of Cities/Counties, 1990

City/County	1990 Population
Chicago/Cook County	5,105,067
Detroit/Wayne County	2,111,687
Baltimore County	1,428,148
Cleveland/Cuyahoga County	1,412,140
St. Louis County	1,390,214
Pittsburgh/Allegheny County	1,336,449
Cincinnati/Hamilton County	866,228
Indianapolis/Marion County	797,159
Louisville/Jefferson County	664,937
Nashville/Davidson County	510,784

Conventional wisdom would predict greater concentrations of health problems in the counties with the largest central cities with higher poverty rates and larger proportions of minority residents. Comparison data provide an empirical basis for examination of this perception.

Examining the comparison cities/counties on several of the need indicators identified by Lammers and Klingman (1984), Indianapolis/Marion County exhibits growth patterns for the African-American population similar to those found in the reference counties. All ten areas experienced a small growth in this population between 1980 and 1985. The large, central city counties in the reference group all had substantially higher percentages of black residents, with Detroit/Wayne County and Baltimore reporting the highest concentrations. Indianapolis ranked fourth from the bottom among the ten. Indianapolis reported the lowest percentage of elderly population and Pittsburgh the highest.

Indiana's poverty rate at the beginning of the 1980s was the lowest of the comparison states at 9.7 percent for individuals and 7.3 percent for families. Indianapolis/Marion County reported a rate of 11.1 percent during that same time. By the 1990 census, the poverty rate for individuals was 12.1 percent in Indianapolis/Marion County and 9.3 percent for families. For the state, the rate had increased to 10.7 percent for individuals and 7.9 percent for families.

Rapid population growth and decline present different policy/service challenges for a mayor. St. Louis (city) experienced the most rapid rate of decline from 1980 to 1990, while the remainder of the county experienced a small growth. Only Indianapolis and Nashville grew during the decade of the 1980s. The growth in Nashville has been consistent across both decades ('70s and '80s), but Indianapolis/Marion County experienced decline in the 1970s.

The average number of persons per household was largest in Detroit/Wayne County at the midpoint of the Hudnut Administration. Indianapolis/Marion County actually ranked next to last, with Nashville reporting a lower ratio of persons per household.

Per capita money income was highest in Nashville/Davidson County when considering total counties. Nashville/Davidson County fell midrange on per capita personal income. Indianapolis/Marion County ranked in the middle to lower range among the ten, with Chicago/Cook County reporting the highest per capita personal income and Cleveland ranking second.

Unemployment in Indianapolis declined from 6.1 percent in 1988 to 4.3 percent in 1989. Only Pittsburgh and Baltimore experienced greater declines in the unemployment rate. Louisville and St. Louis experienced increases. Detroit/Wayne County declined only 0.1 percent and maintained the highest rate, 8.2 percent, among the sites. Nashville/Davidson County maintained the lowest rate across the 12-year span.

Using these indicators of social need, Indianapolis/Marion County would not be considered a city with a high level of problems or a high "hardship" index. Compared to officials of the nine other reference cities, Mayor Hudnut's administration faced lower percentages of black and elderly residents, lower poverty rate, and declining rates of unemployment. Indianapolis experienced economic decline in the early part of his administration, then growth during the 1980s; the city reported a modest growth, 59.1 percent, in per capita money income from 1979 to 1987.

These positive conditions may generate a more philanthropic attitude of concern for the less fortunate and frequently are associated with substantial investment in social and health programs and expenditures. But an examination of expenditures does not confirm that pattern for Indianapolis/Marion County. Perhaps reflecting the prevailing political culture of the state, Indianapolis reported a comparatively low rate of combined city-county health expenditures per capita. The health expenditure patterns in Indianapolis for the period 1978–90 are most comparable to Nashville, Louisville, and Chicago in terms of absolute numbers. Detroit, Cleveland, and Baltimore were spending substantially more per resident at the beginning of the Hudnut Administration, and the differences in investment widened. St. Louis also dramatically increased the rate of health spending from 1984 to 1990. Louisville is the only one of the reference counties where per capita spending declined since its midpoint high in 1984.

One major difficulty in the use of demographic indicators as measures of need is that the populations, such as minority or elderly, who are used to estimate need are not homogeneous and consistently in need. In fact, some areas may cater to wealthy, retired elderly in retirement communities who are generally less impaired or in need of service than smaller groups in other areas who are not wealthy enough to move. Some counties may attract upper- and middle-income black families at a greater rate than poor, inner-city blacks. In other words, membership in a demographic category does not necessarily predict need or problems.

Thus, to examine how well Indianapolis fares on actual measures of health, several widely accepted indicators were chosen. The first type are process indicators that compare rates of health resource availability as a reflection of access or potential for health care. Indianapolis/Marion County is at the midpoint of reference cities/counties in supply of physicians. It reported a substantial increase from 1976 to 1985 and continued at a slower rate of increase to 1989. St. Louis, Cleveland, Pittsburgh, Nashville, and Baltimore all reported more active MDs per 100,000. Detroit/Wayne County reported the highest rates of full-time registered nurses per 100,000 in the 1981–88 period. Indianapolis/Marion County ranked second in registered nurse ratios among the comparison sites.

Bed-supply variations over time reflect the national trend of expansion of health facilities in the 1970s and the constriction of these facilities throughout the 1980s. All the comparison locations experienced cuts in the number of community hospital beds per thousand. Total hospital beds per 100,000 residents in the counties also reflect the emphasis on declining supply to control costs associated with national policies. Nashville/Davidson County reported the highest rate, with Pittsburgh second and St. Louis third. Indianapolis/Marion County was at the midpoint, and Chicago/Cook County reported the lowest rate.

The second type of measure relies on social indicators of outcomes against which the health of the cities is judged. Most health policy analysts agree that these outcome indicators are those against which health care providers and community organizations will be judged in the future in terms of achieving a healthy environment. Rather than looking at process measures that identify the *potential* to provide care through health care resources or expenditures, these outcome indicators measure actual health status. Infant-mortality rates are one leading type of indicator. The comparison rate chosen for this study calculates the death rates of infants one year old or less per 1,000 infants born during a five-year cohort. All counties except Baltimore report decreasing levels of infant mortality during this period. Chicago/Cook County posted the largest decline. St. Louis, Cleveland, and Pittsburgh also reported declines greater than 20 percent. Although Indianapolis ranked in the middle of the counties in terms of absolute rate, it ranked at the bottom of the comparison counties when declines were reported. In Indiana, the mortality rate for white infants has fallen steadily since 1976. However, Indiana is the only state in the comparison group where black infant mortality increased from the early to the late '80s.

Low birth weight is an outcome measure that is used as a proxy for identifying poor nutritional status in a community as well as poor prenatal care. For low birth weight, the states and the nation as a whole experienced a slight decrease from 1976 to 1981 and a small increase from 1981 to 1988. Although the net change is a decrease in low birth weights, the change has not been substantial, and lower birth weights are again on the rise. Indiana ranks at the bottom of the comparison states in low birth weights of all races. However, throughout the states, the rate for low birth weight of black infants has gradually increased. Although Indiana is still ranked among the lowest of the states, the direction of change is not encouraging. While other states in 1976 were substantially higher than Indiana, several have decreased their rates and Kentucky has achieved a lower rate than Indiana. City-specific data show Indianapolis/Marion County with an increasing rate until 1985, then decreasing in 1987. Five comparison sites were lower by 1987.

Late in the Hudnut Administration a campaign to address continuing concerns with Indianapolis's dismal rankings in black infant mortality was mounted. The city joined with private foundations to fund a two-year project to improve the health and survivability of all babies in the city but especially black infants. The 1991 annual report of the Indianapolis Campaign for Healthy Babies cited a neighborhood-based team of health care professionals and lay health care workers as the "heart of the campaign." This group was responsible for problem solving, program modification based on surveillance reports, idea sharing, and needs identification. The teams were funded almost entirely by city government funds (Keener, 1991). Despite some early successes in the program, the city failed to continue its part of the funding.

Indianapolis also ranks among the highest in the comparison sites for births to mothers under age 20. Only the rates in the central cities of St. Louis and Baltimore are higher. The children born to these mothers are often associated with family situations where the family lives at or below poverty level. If an early pregnancy interrupts a young woman's education, she is more likely to access poverty programs and less likely to rise above poverty lines than her counterparts who postpone child bearing until later years. Higher levels of parental education are also associated with positive health promotion and disease prevention activities, which lower many of the health risks outlined here. Leaders from the public school system interviewed concerning the role of city government in dealing with the problems of teen pregnancy were unable to cite examples of projects where the city cooperated with the schools to provide funding or leadership for educational or service programs related to the problem.

AIDS deaths reported at the state level since 1983 indicate a steady, cumulative increase in the states. Illinois deaths surpass the other states, with Pennsylvania ranked second. Both Tennessee and Kentucky have experienced fewer deaths and slow rates of growth of this problem. More than one-fifth of the AIDS deaths in Indiana occur in Indianapolis/Marion County.

Toward the end of the Hudnut Administration, one large experiment was attempted for the elderly. Room and board assistance housing was jointly sponsored as a public-private partnership of the type Hudnut identified as his style or mandate. This experiment involved refurbishing a deteriorating school building into an assisted living facility for low- to moderate-income elders as an alternative to intermediate care facilities in nursing homes. Neighborhood residents (minorities) participated in interior demolition of the old building, for a savings of $25,000. Central Indiana Building Trades, Jungclaus-Campbell, Lilly

Endowment contributions and the city's community development funds assisted in the development of the project, and the AFL-CIO Housing Trust Fund provided a $2.1-million federally insured, low-interest mortgage (*Indianapolis Star,* May 23, 1990). Unfortunately, as with the healthy babies program, city funding was short-term and no long-term commitments to this type of service or activity was demonstrated or continued into the next administration. Evaluation funds were never allocated to determine whether this approach improved the quality of life of elders over that experienced in intermediate care facilities.

As a measure of mental health in an area, suicide rates are the most frequently referenced indicator. At the beginning of the Hudnut Administration, Illinois reported the lowest rate among the comparison states. Indiana's rate was next lowest, but by 1988, Maryland and Ohio had lowered their rates below that of Indiana, and Illinois had maintained its position even though the rate had steadily increased.

Other death rates are reported that many argue can be more directly attributed to city policies, i.e., accidental death (drownings, fires, etc.), motor vehicle deaths, and homicide. Each of these rates may reflect the level of investment in corresponding enforcement activities or emergency rescue services. During the decade from 1979 to 1989, accidental death rates in Indianapolis dropped rather precipitously from 1979 to 1982, experienced a small increase and another decline by 1986, and rose again by 1989. The 1989 rate remained well under that reported in 1979. Motor vehicle deaths also dropped substantially by 1982, rose until 1986, and ended the decade in a downward trend. Homicide rates rose to a peak in 1988, falling off sharply in 1989. Thus there was improvement in these three areas of health indicators over which Mayor Hudnut had jurisdiction.

Indianapolis has fared better in terms of these outcomes, which can be associated with safety and protection services, than in the more traditional health services, and these are service areas over which the mayor has more direct control. Though individuals interviewed concerning the mayor's role in health during this period were supportive of his involvement in these more global activities, they hastened to add that these activities were dedicated to improving the business environment and the competitiveness of Indianapolis as a safe place to live. Their role as health indicators was described as coincidental or at best, not a primary concern.

In comparison to the midwestern counterparts and to counties where strong economic development programs have been in existence during periods comparable to the Hudnut Administration, Indianapolis/Marion County has failed to address some of the problems generally considered as benchmark indicators of good health outcomes as successfully as have other sites. While the economy improved, unemployment declined, and the city gained in population rather than declined during the 1980s, black infant mortality was on the upswing as were low birth weights among blacks. Other cities and their corresponding states were generally able to decrease their rates at a much faster rate for all races and for blacks in particular. Baltimore was the only city among the comparison groups where the rate for black birth weights rose rather dramatically.

One successful and comprehensive health program begun during the Hudnut Administration involved mayoral participation in committing Indianapolis as a test city in the Healthy Indiana Cities project. Six cities in Indiana were selected to participate in the project, and a critical component for each selection involved working agreements with the mayors and city governments. It is still early in the evolution of the project, but Indianapolis remains active under Hudnut's successor.

An examination of health department budgets and annual reports from the Health and Hospital Corporation illustrates a broadly developed, interagency network of projects, but few that could be linked with city funding. The largest and ongoing financial transfer from city funds entailed contracts from the city to local providers for primary medical and dental services for medically indigent populations. For some local clinics, the city/county contribution represents almost one-third of the operating budget, although statewide less than 10 percent of the primary health care clinics' budgets come from this source. Other examples included cooperative projects with the city for testing and surveillance of lead poisoning, revitalization of deteriorating neighborhoods to make them viable again, and planning for response capability to emergency incidents. Mayor Hudnut cited additional examples of assistance in obtaining a federal grant through the U.S. Conference of Mayors for funding an AIDS hotline, negotiating a fitness center as a health promotion incentive and a method of lowering the health insurance bills for city employees, a ban on smoking in the city buildings, and movement of funds away from other municipal areas when regulations of community development funds would have required cutbacks in community centers and multiservice centers.

Comparison of budgets across sites can be deceiving, since much variation exists in how items are categorized. For example, an examination of Indianapolis/Marion County's budget from 1976 to 1988 would support the notion that health had become a major priority. However, much of the change can be accounted for by a shift in categories for reporting from nonspecified to a specified category.

Although community residents and leaders interviewed for this critique described Mayor Hudnut as a "bricks and mortar" man concerned with building the downtown area so people would have a decent place to work and live, they were often perplexed or appeared to be struggling to identify health-related projects that could be associated with the administration. Most indicated that since the provision of health was structurally outside the realm of the city government, it was simply not part of the role that the mayor defined for himself and his administration. Mayor Hudnut indicated that at several times during his administration the possibility of folding the public health services into city administration was explored. The proposed modification would have placed public health under the domain of the mayor's office with a deputy mayoral position assigned to administer it. Interviews with public health officials indicated mixed reaction to the appropriateness of such a move, since public health projects would then be bound by city statutes concerning tax increases. Under the current separation, the Health and Hospital Corporation can raise taxes separately from the city as long as it falls within the guidelines of the state tax board. Thus, although health services do not have a readily identifiable and accountable proponent in the mayor, the organizational structure is considered by many health providers to be an advantage.

The lack of an innovative, committed, and highly visible leader may mitigate against much movement forward in public policy. For example, two states have actually made health a central focus of their economic development programs, largely as the result of interest from a governor. Hawaii is capitalizing on its extremely positive health indicators to identify itself as the "health state." Massachusetts also made considerable strides forward in expanding coverage prior to the recent election of a conservative governor. Other states to a lesser degree have focused on health issues and elders as a source of economic growth, competing to attract young and wealthy retirees to areas to boost spending and improve the economic base of communities.

Therefore, many of the indicators which would lead to a successful linkage of economic development and health may be lacking in Indianapolis. What is not lacking is the obligation of the city government to address basic quality-of-life issues for its citizens. To date, partly because of the structural separation and jurisdiction of public health outside the mayor's office, city government has been only marginally involved in programs that address the health needs of the community.

Given the complex interrelationships of federal, state, and local dollars in the provision of health care, it would be presumptuous and inappropriate to lay all the ills at the foot of any mayor. Indeed, at this point no data exist to substantiate whether systems perform better when structurally located within or separate from a city government agency. Reorganization cannot create a policy commitment where none exists. Whether structural reorganization is needed in Indianapolis/Marion County is clearly a controversial question. When a mayor has little interest or commitment to health and social issues, the separation of jurisdictions may be beneficial to the health environment of the city. When a city is led by a committed health policy entrepreneur, then location under the city/county government umbrella might be beneficial.

What is evident from this analysis is that given the current structure, local health officials must take the initiative to involve, educate, and sensitize local elected officials to become partners in the quest for a healthy city environment. Although a strong or charismatic leadership style from a mayor who is interested in health issues would surely enhance the city's position and strengths, involving both the public and private sectors in coordinated projects to achieve health goals is imperative if the city is to remain competitive in comparison with other cities. As more corporations become concerned with the costs of health care provision for employees and their families, knowing the health score card for potential business sites will become more important.

REFERENCES

L. Buell and C. Robbins, 1984, Comprehensive Annual Financial Report, Health and Hospital Corporation, Indianapolis.

G. DeFriese et al., "The Program Implications of Administrative Relationships between Local Health Departments and State and Local Government," *American Journal of Public Health* 71, 1109–1115.

Indianapolis Star, May 23, 1990, "Cogburn Place Provides Room and Board Alternatives for Elders."

P. Keener, 1991, Annual Report: Indianapolis Campaign for Healthy Babies.

W. Lammers and D. Klingman, 1984, *State Policies and the Aging: Sources, Trends and Options* (Lexington, Mass.: Lexington Books).

M. Millman, 1981, "The Role of City Government in Personal Health Services," *American Journal of Public Health* 71, 47–57.

M. Pohlmann, 1993, *Governing the Postindustrial City* (New York: Longman).

Education

CAROL D'AMICO AND LESLIE LENKOWSKY

I n the seven months since its announcement, the United Airlines decision to locate the facility in Indianapolis had been big news. The city had competed with 92 others for the project, which was expected to create more than 6,000 high-skilled and high-paying jobs directly, and many more indirectly. Along with Governor Evan Bayh, Mayor Bill Hudnut had received much of the credit for fashioning the deal that convinced United to choose Indianapolis. It was vintage Hudnut, a complex package of public and private money and other incentives, tied together with more than a little effective salesmanship. It promised not only to bring significant economic benefits to the city but also to reinforce the image of Indianapolis as a place where globally minded dynamic companies were going. For Hudnut it was a triumphant capstone for his 16 years as mayor.

At a July briefing, however, what should have been a fairly upbeat report unexpectedly took on a somber tone when a United official casually revealed that the company was having difficulty persuading its current employees to move to Indianapolis because of the poor performance record of the city's public schools. In comparing the finalists among the cities competing for the maintenance hub, United had discovered that Indianapolis was spending more money on elementary and secondary education but getting worse results than any of the other

The authors greatly appreciate the assistance of Joey Merrill and O. Adam Kimberly in preparing this critique.

places. Indeed, according to the official, that had been the biggest weakness in the city's campaign to obtain the project. Although it had ultimately proved not to be decisive, the quality of education in Indianapolis was still causing the company to worry about relocating its employees, as well as about finding new ones with the skills needed for servicing its high-tech aircraft.

Virtually all the members of the Corporate Community Council had heard about the problems of the Indianapolis schools before. Many had experienced difficulty in finding well-trained workers for their own businesses. But the revelation that poor schools had perhaps come close to torpedoing the largest economic development project in the city's recent history had a stunning effect. Despite the years of work all of them had put into making Indianapolis attractive to growing companies, the city still had a major disadvantage: its schools.

As in other parts of the country, the problems of the city's schools grew out of a complex mixture of demographic and cultural trends, court orders, educational philosophies, and much more. But what happened to education in Indianapolis during the Hudnut years is also a story of the limits of mayoral power over an area of public policy that is increasingly crucial to mayoral success.

Even though education is the most costly local service, mayors in most of the United States have little authority over it. As a result of high-minded efforts to separate education from "politics," schools are generally governed by citizen boards, elected separately from other political offices and frequently on a nonpartisan basis. Moreover, an intricate web of state and federal rules, judicial mandates, and collective bargaining agreements further serves to insulate education from other activities of local government. These arrangements have not, in fact, taken politics out of schooling. But they have ensured that the politics—and priorities—that drive a city's schools need not correspond to the objectives of a city's mayor or other municipal leaders.

The creation of Unigov never included jurisdiction over the city's schools. Indeed, the 11 school districts in Marion County were not consolidated, as other public services were when Unigov was established. They remained independent, with their own governing boards, schools, and teachers. As a result, while the city's leaders pursued an ambitious plan to make Indianapolis more attractive to industry, the city's schools—especially those in the most populous district, Indianapolis Public Schools (IPS), located in Center Township—became embroiled in a bitter controversy over racial desegregation. By the end of the

Hudnut years, little progress had been made toward integration of IPS, but the quality of education had declined to the point that it posed a serious threat to the city's economic vitality. Under the existing arrangements for school governance, Hudnut could have done little to prevent this, even though what occurred in the schools jeopardized virtually everything else he had sought to accomplish for Indianapolis.

Education in Indianapolis, 1970–90

In Indianapolis, as in most other places, measures of school performance are hard to come by. From the limited and scattered information that is available, however, education in Indianapolis has clearly deteriorated during the past two decades, even though public spending on schooling has risen sharply. On scores from the Scholastic Aptitude Test, the principal college admissions test in the United States, the Indianapolis Public School system ranks far below the nation as a whole and the state of Indiana as well. Although SAT scores are not the only way to measure educational quality, they are one of the few that provide a basis for comparing student performance over a two-decade period.

Other evidence reinforces the conclusion that "quality" of IPS schools has declined over the past 20 years. In 1971, IPS's high school graduation rate was 64.8 percent, Marion County's was 73.8 percent, and the state of Indiana posted an 80.7 percent rate. Eight years later, IPS's graduation rate had fallen to 50.6 percent, Marion County's to 64.6 percent, and the state's to 74.7 percent. A decade after that, the IPS graduation rate remained the same, while both the county and the state rates had increased about four percentage points. By 1990, although Indiana's graduation rate exceeded the national average of 71.2 percent and Marion County's was almost equal to it, IPS's was substantially below it. Indeed, at some IPS high schools, as few as one in five students who entered were leaving with their diplomas.

The opposite side of this coin, dropout rates, presents the same picture. Despite changing definitions of "dropout" and the migration of inner-city families from Center Township to the suburban parts of the county, the dropout rate for IPS in 1990 was, at 49 percent, extraordinarily high. Not only was this nearly twice the U.S. average, but since 1971, the IPS dropout rate had grown almost three times as fast as that of the nation as a whole.

Throughout this period, public spending for IPS schools steadily increased. Since 1971, operating expenditures in IPS (unadjusted for inflation) have risen by 229 percent and between 1980 and 1990 alone, they nearly doubled. Because the district's enrollment declined by slightly more than one-half during the same time, unadjusted per pupil spending in IPS grew by 591 percent between 1971 and 1990, significantly more than the growth in Marion County as a whole (514 percent), Indiana (442 percent), or the United States (395 percent). As the Hudnut era was about to begin, IPS spent about the same amount per pupil as Marion County did—and about 17 percent less than the national average. By 1990, it was spending over $5,600 per pupil, approximately 15 percent more than either Marion County or the United States average. Nonetheless, whether measured by student test scores, dropout and graduation rates, or even daily attendance, performance in IPS schools had taken a sharp turn for the worse.

To be sure, IPS is not the only school district in Marion County. And its school-age population—composed heavily of minorities and children from low-income families—is not typical of the county as a whole. In the suburban districts, the schools were generally doing better (although by national norms, they too lagged). Even so, more than 40 percent of the students in the county—and of the tax dollars spent on education—are to be found in IPS. Consequently, for employers trying to gauge the local labor force or the effectiveness of school expenditures, concentrating on IPS is not unreasonable. Moreover, during the Hudnut years, the most important issue affecting education in Marion County originated in IPS and involved most of the other districts as well.

The Busing Case

Like Indiana Senator Richard Lugar, noted philosopher Allan Bloom, and many current leaders of Indianapolis's business and professional community, novelist Kurt Vonnegut attended Shortridge High School. Attracting pupils from a variety of backgrounds, it flourished until late in the 1960s; and while it was the nationally known jewel in the crown of public education in Indianapolis, the district also had other well-regarded schools at every level, including a predominantly black high school, Crispus Attucks. No one set out deliberately to destroy these schools, but that is more or less what happened as the focus of the educational debate in Indianapolis, as in many other cities during the 1970s, shifted toward a lengthy, contentious and ultimately futile quest to achieve racial integration in the schools. As Vonnegut has stated, "I went to a wonderful high school—an elite high school—in Indianapolis. Such schools don't exist any more, because they're considered undemocratic."

In 1968, the U.S. Justice Department filed a petition against the Indianapolis Public Schools, claiming the city was operating a "de jure" segregated school system. (This meant that the school system was accused of explicitly making administrative decisions on the basis of race that resulted in segregated schools, not merely failing to compensate for changes in housing patterns or other circumstances that "de facto" led to segregated schools.) The charges resulted from a complaint by Andrew Ramsey, a Shortridge High School teacher and local NAACP leader, acting on behalf of an African-American parent who objected to the treatment her child was receiving at an elementary school. Although then-Mayor Lugar responded that Indianapolis had nothing to fear from a federal investigation because it was not operating a constitutionally impermissible dual public school system based on racial factors, the real issue was not so much the law but rather different notions of educational policy.

The investigation that followed focused exclusively on the racial composition of the city's schools. The Justice Department further charged school officials with "conscientiously" administering policies, drawing attendance boundaries, setting up transportation routes, and assigning students and faculty with the intent of perpetuating segregation after it had been declared illegal by state law in 1949 and federal law in 1954.

School officials acknowledged official segregation prior to 1949. After that, they claimed, both black and white students were offered options to enroll at schools regardless of their previous designation as "white" or "black" schools. Few students exercised their options and most continued to go to the schools they had been attending.

On August 18, 1971, Federal Judge S. Hugh Dillin shocked the city by declaring the Indianapolis public schools guilty of practicing de jure segregation: "a segregated school system wherein segregation was imposed and enforced by operation of law." He went on to rule that the IPS board had "the affirmative duty to take whatever steps might be necessary to convert to a unity system in which racial discrimination will be eliminated root and branch."

To that end, Judge Dillin ordered the district to take several actions before the start of the school year in September. The first was to develop plans to integrate its schools, including Crispus Attucks High School, and to assign teachers without respect to race. In addition, IPS was to prevent schools that had a "reasonable" racial mix from reaching the "tipping" point toward segregation. (While not specified in the order, that was generally considered to be 40 percent black, since the makeup of the school district was about 37.4 percent black at the time.) Finally, the district was told to begin negotiations with suburban school corporations—both within and outside of Marion County—to permit black students to transfer voluntarily outside IPS.

In his order, Judge Dillin also raised the possibility of a longer-term solution. To avoid the possibility that IPS could become an all-black school system if white families moved to Marion County's suburban townships, he suggested that consolidating schools within the boundaries of Unigov might be required. While he noted that accomplishing this might be beyond the court's authority and require action by the state legislature, the clear implication of the judge's opinion was that an integration plan could not succeed if it were confined to IPS alone.

Thus, in one decision, the federal court placed its weight behind two controversial propositions. The first was that racial balance was the key to improving education in the city's schools. The second was the need to revisit the delicate set of compromises that enabled Unigov to come into being. The suburban school districts had been left out of the consolidation largely as a gesture toward preserving local identities, which, Judge Dillin and others felt, included their racial composition.

Implementing the Court's Ruling

In the summer of 1973, after the Supreme Court's denial of a motion to review his initial ruling, Judge Dillin issued a desegregation plan calling for the compulsory busing of black students from IPS to 18 suburban school systems, including several outside of Marion County. The judge also ordered the city school system to alter attendance zones for its elementary schools so that every school would have a minimum black enrollment of 15 percent. Students from the suburbs, however, were not to be bused to IPS, nor were any school district boundaries to be abolished.

In April 1979, following an appeals court ruling upholding his authority to do so, Judge Dillin ordered IPS to prepare plans to reassign involuntarily 6,125 black city students to eight suburban school systems in Marion County. Three hundred IPS teachers were also told that because of changes in enrollment, they were likely to lose their jobs.

In August of 1979, however, to the consternation of those getting ready to shift schools, the latest busing plan was suspended. Pending further review, the Seventh Circuit Court of Appeals issued a new stay and all the teachers were rehired. A year later, another stay was granted to permit Supreme Court action. In the meantime, IPS announced that it would require an additional 6,000 students to be bused, but only within the district. Finally, in October of 1980, the Supreme Court refused to hear the appeal of Judge Dillin's order, permitting the plan for compulsory, one-way busing of Indianapolis students, which had originated in 1973, at last to be implemented.

On August 16, 1981, 5,600 IPS school children were transferred to six Marion County school districts. (Another 17,000 were being bused within IPS.) As a direct result, at least ten elementary schools and one high school in IPS were closed, and over 500 teachers laid off. Because of population shifts from the inner city to the suburban townships in Marion County, the reduction in IPS enrollment was greater than that due to busing alone. At the time of the original complaint of segregation in 1968, the district operated 110 grade schools and 11 high schools; after the desegregation plan had gone into effect, 79 grade and nine high schools remained open. Perhaps as many as 20 elementary schools and three high schools operated at less than half-capacity and were scheduled to be closed in the future. Among them was once-famous Shortridge High School.

The Mayor as Peacemaker

Although the desegregation case had begun eight years before Hudnut became mayor in 1976, it was his principal concern in education for virtually the full 16 years of his tenure in office. Passions over the case ran high. Within IPS, some favored the busing plan, others did not, and their competing views dominated school board elections and meetings. In the county's other districts, fears of eventual consolidation with IPS were rampant, as were practical concerns, such as how to pay for teaching the thousands of new students who were to be bused into their schools.

A committee to impeach Judge Dillin had been created in 1973. It later became the Committee for Constitutional Government and was dedicated to bringing an end to court-ordered busing. At the same time, many felt that the city's political and community leaders were not doing enough to bring about peaceful compliance with the court's order.

Once Unigov had been absolved of complicity in creating the city's segregated schools, the mayor of Indianapolis was not—at least in a legal sense—a party to the case. Nor did he have the authority to control the actions of the county's school districts, which were independent of the city's government and run by politically autonomous boards. Mostly, his responsibility consisted of raising the revenue necessary to pay for whatever plan was finally adopted. Yet Hudnut felt he had to become more involved.

Hudnut was determined to prevent Judge Dillin's decision from having a negative effect on Indianapolis. Shortly after taking office, he and Indiana Governor Otis Bowen issued a joint statement promising full cooperation in integrating the schools, once all appeals had been resolved. The main vehicle for accomplishing this was to be a task force, formed in 1979, that was known as PRIDE (Peaceful Response to Indianapolis Desegregated Education).

Operating under the aegis of a civic group, the Greater Indianapolis Progress Committee (GIPC), and consisting of leaders from government, business, churches, and community agencies, PRIDE sought to prepare the public to meet the requirements of the law, peacefully and effectively. Using volunteer networks, it served as a channel of information about how the busing plan would actually work, maintained a telephone hotline to answer questions, and distributed a weekly newsletter. Visits to suburban schools were scheduled for IPS parents whose children were required to be bused, while administrators from the outlying districts came in to IPS to talk about their schools' programs and curricula.

As the busing plan got under way in 1981, a survey of Indianapolis residents found that almost two-thirds expected a peaceful response. While law enforcement agencies admitted to having a contingency plan in the event of violence, they did not have to use it. Although the design of the desegregation plan, especially the fact that it called only for one-way busing (and not the transfer of suburban children to inner-city schools), undoubtedly helped, many agree that PRIDE also played a key role in reducing apprehension and rumors in the community. The image Indianapolis conveyed to the rest of the nation as it began desegregation was encapsulated by a *New York Times* photograph of an IPS youngster boarding a bus for a peaceful trip to a suburban school district.

The Aftermath of Busing

For the most part, this picture remained undisturbed throughout the 1980s. Although not necessarily with enthusiasm (especially within portions of the black community), Indianapolis accepted desegregation and busing proceeded more or less uneventfully. Some of the suburban districts even came to like Judge Dillin's plan. Yet, ironically, though the effort to achieve desegregation has occurred peacefully, little improvement seemed to be occurring among the students or in IPS, the school district that was supposed to benefit.

Having done its work, PRIDE evolved into a monitoring group, the Community Desegregation Advisory Council (CDAC), to see that the busing order continued to be carried out as intended by the court. Made up of business and community leaders and paid for largely by the mayor's office, CDAC sought to "assure that children and parents involved in the school desegregation process are provided with equitable educational opportunities and access to educational opportunities without overt and covert discrimination of any type." Since the court has not appointed a watchdog, CDAC wound up with the responsibility for producing reports on how IPS students were faring in the township schools and responding to questions and complaints from students and parents involved in busing.

How well the students involved were doing was much less clear. The information CDAC had been collecting pertained largely to enrollment and conduct, not student achievement. As one GIPC staff member put it, "A real shortcoming of CDAC was that they didn't evaluate whether the program was actually working—whether the students who were bused were actually getting better, or equivalent education, than the students who remained in IPS and were not bused." The school districts participating in the desegregation plan also did not gather—or chose not to report—such information. Although CDAC repeatedly examined how to improve its own work and to promote racial balance in the Indianapolis schools, neither it nor anyone else looked closely at the effects of the desegregation plan on students or their families.

The limited evidence that was available was not encouraging. CDAC reports showed that black students in the suburban schools were disproportionately being disciplined, retained, suspended, and expelled. A higher percentage of blacks were assigned to special education classes and few were in gifted and talented programs. Parents of the students being bused complained about treatment their children received (although many also acknowledged that their children had been worse off in IPS).

Due to transportation problems, black students in the suburban schools were less likely to participate in clubs, theater, student councils, and sports than their classmates. Many also felt unwelcome in the suburbs and thought they were viewed as "outsiders" by school administrators and the other parents in the community. In addition, most of them had no way to influence school policy since, lacking residence in the district, they could neither run nor vote for seats on the suburban school boards.

When the court handed down the busing order, it required the State of Indiana to pay for the costs incurred by the schools receiving students. In the decade after the plan went into effect, this came to about $151 million. Part paid for tuition and was tied to the number of students transferred from IPS to the township schools. Part also covered the cost of transporting the students to their new districts. And part went for "other" expenses.

The last was the fastest-growing category, increasing, according to the *Indianapolis News,* by 183 percent, even after adjusting for inflation, from the 1981–82 to the 1989–90 school years, despite the fact that the number of students bused had remained steady. (The total is now nearly $58 million, or more than a third of the cost of the desegregation plan.) The money was used for desegregation coordinators, counselors, teacher aides, secretaries, bus monitors, administrators, psychologists, training for staff, and curriculum-related materials.

In 1987, James Adams, then IPS superintendent, charged that the suburban school districts were employing these funds for general operating expenses that went beyond the requirements of the desegregation plan. One township, for instance, used them to support six assistant principals; another district had bought telephones. With this subsidy, the suburban schools were able to allocate more of their own revenues to teachers' salaries. Yet, as long as they could show justification to the State Budget Agency, the townships could request as much as they needed for "other" desegregation expenses and ran little risk of being denied.

By contrast, IPS received practically nothing for its efforts. Even though more students were involved, no extra money was provided for the busing that occurred within the district. IPS did receive financial aid from Indiana to help it adjust to losing students bused to the townships. But under court order, that support ended after five years.

In 1990, IPS petitioned Judge Dillin for state money to pay for extra teachers, counselors, reading and math specialists, staff training, medical assistants, bus monitors, home/school liaisons, and other items that the township schools were using desegregation funds to purchase. However, the court turned down the request and in so doing was highly critical of IPS. Judge Dillin placed the blame for the dismal performance of IPS on its administrators and said it was up to IPS to find ways to improve.

By that time, how far behind IPS had fallen was beginning to be documented. In 1987, as part of the nationwide effort at education reform, Indiana enacted legislation that required school districts to report performance measures and instituted a statewide achievement test (ISTEP) as well. Since no common standard had previously existed for the state's schools, the release of the first set of results in 1988 was, for many, an eye-opener. Although it was not surprising that IPS did worse than the other school districts in Marion County, the distance between it and the rest—despite the fact that it spent more on its students—indicated that integrating the schools had not been sufficient to ensure a quality education for those remaining in the district.

After nearly two decades of effort, an IPS administrator claimed, while "racial integration has been achieved, the challenge is to bring about equity in educational achievement of all students." Some CDAC members also began to comment on the lack of information about how the students being bused were doing academically and raised questions about their graduation rates and college enrollment levels. While IPS had by no means been an exemplary school district before the desegregation controversy began, the idea that achieving racial balance would improve it seemed to be wrong and, at least some believed, had made the condition of the city's schools worse.

Desegregation Reconsidered

In 1991, the IPS School Board hired its first African-American superintendent, Shirl E. Gilbert II. He talked candidly and passionately about the problems facing IPS and the need to make dramatic improvements in its schools. Within months of taking office, he was also calling for a major change in the court-ordered desegregation plan. This reflected not only the IPS experience, but also a growing disillusionment throughout the United States with busing as a tool for achieving equal educational opportunity. One reason is that it coincided with—and perhaps precipitated—an exodus of children from public schools that were to be involved in the desegregation plan. Rather than have their young offspring bused to distant neighborhoods, parents chose to put them in private schools or move to another district.

In Indianapolis, census data indicated that Center Township lost 65,000 residents during the 1970s, or nearly 25 percent of the township's population. How much of this was due to what Hudnut called the "instability" surrounding school desegregation cannot be known for certain. However, as the court battles dragged on, parents often could not be sure where their children would go from one year to the next. This "continual readjustment of the 'interim' plans," the *Indianapolis Star* suggested, "could have done more damage to IPS than fears of desegregation itself." IPS administrators agreed.

The out-migration of higher- and middle-income black families—no less than of white ones—produced a district in which low-income blacks and low-income whites were largely all that remained, a combination not likely to do much for the scholastic achievement of either group. Although Judge Dillin tried to offset this by busing black IPS students into the suburbs, the numbers were always small. Meanwhile, many more black students were bused within the IPS district to schools that were little better (if that) than the ones they had left.

While not the only obstacle to achievement, busing added to the difficulty. By enlarging the distance between where families lived and where their children were to be educated, by imposing additional rules and regulations upon administrators and teachers, and by placing racial balance ahead of parental choice of (and commitment to) schools, the desegregation plan in Indianapolis—and similar ones elsewhere—may have unwittingly reduced educational opportunity rather than enhanced it.

A Mayor without Standing

By this time, Hudnut had retired from office. The previous fall, his successor, Stephen Goldsmith, had campaigned on behalf of eliminating busing and allowing children to attend neighborhood schools. After his election, he tried to join with IPS officials in petitioning the federal court to change the desegregation plan. However, Judge Dillin ruled that the legal standing of the mayor of Indianapolis in the case was unclear and, pending further consideration, refused to allow him to be heard.

Throughout his terms in office, Hudnut had faced this same problem. Whether or not he favored the plan, he could not have stopped the court from adopting it. On the most important issue concerning education in Indianapolis during his tenure as mayor, he had neither the power nor the authority—despite his position as the city's chief executive—to influence the outcome. At best he could have taken the lead in producing a different kind of desegregation plan, perhaps one that redrew boundaries to create more heterogeneous districts within Marion County (as Charlotte, North Carolina, did). However, apart from the political feasibility of doing so, the acceptability of such an alternative would have rested entirely with a federal judge, empowered to adopt whatever remedy for the city's "segregated" schools he chose, no matter how "administratively awkward, inconvenient, and even bizarre."

Not surprisingly, in light of his inability to affect this decision, Hudnut saw his job principally as ensuring that the court's order was peacefully obeyed. As the protests in Boston and other cities demonstrated, this was no small task. But both Hudnut's personal skills and the scope of his office enabled him to perform it successfully.

Since Marion County included all the school districts that were involved in the busing plan, Hudnut represented the people and neighborhoods affected, worked regularly with their leaders, and could enlist their assistance relatively easily. His long-standing ties to Indianapolis religious and civil rights officials, as well as his reputation as a moderate Republican, also helped him in building coalitions to support the desegregation effort. Even though the educational results left much to be desired, the city avoided a divisive racial conflict and kept its focus on economic growth, in no small measure because of Hudnut's ability to keep communications going among groups that elsewhere had taken to yelling at one another, hurling stones, or worse.

Hudnut's relationship to other education issues that arose during his period as mayor was similar to his response to the busing order. Since Marion County's school boards were constituted as independent and nonpartisan bodies, Hudnut viewed his proper role as being supportive when he could but not becoming involved in making or influencing policy. He treated school board members as he did other elected officials, recognizing that they had their own agendas and mandates from the voters in their districts. (If the school boards had been appointed by the mayor, Hudnut acknowledged after leaving office, it would have been "a different story.") In any event, he had enough on his plate without adding problems which he had no legal authority or responsibility to solve.

This hands-off approach occasionally caused Hudnut to be criticized. In 1985, for example, he refused to become involved in a referendum, initiated by IPS, to raise additional revenue for the district by increasing property taxes. Hudnut feared that his support for the IPS referendum might actually hurt its chances for passage. However, many backers of the initiative urged him to campaign for it and when he declined to do so, they were outwardly critical of his failure to take a stand.

On the other hand, Hudnut's independence from school district politics also enabled him to serve as an honest broker for issues other than those related to the desegregation plan. For example, during the 1970s, teacher unions gained strength within Marion County and on two occasions, in 1979 and 1990, Hudnut was called upon to mediate labor disputes in IPS. Had he been a party to school district policy making, his ability to do so would undoubtedly have been diminished.

The mayor's lack of legal authority over education in Marion County was not the only factor responsible for the nature of Hudnut's relationship with the schools. In addition, other than in the context of the desegregation controversy, few of his constituents demanded that he do anything about education. Although Hudnut himself had a sense that it was a problem, for most of his period as mayor, neither business and civic leaders nor ordinary citizens appeared to be much concerned about the quality of education in Indianapolis.

Looking back, Hudnut blames the state of the Indianapolis schools on the fact that the "aspiration toward excellence doesn't exist here" and faults himself for not having done more to raise consciousness of the community about the importance of quality education. Nonetheless, even if he had tried to rally support for school reform, the likelihood is slim that even his great abilities at building coalitions and mobilizing resources would have been enough. For important as they were, neither the apathy of the public nor the limited influence the mayor's office had in education were crucial. Rather, what mattered most was that for Hudnut's 16 years in office, the Indianapolis public schools—like many others in the United States—were in the grip of an educational theory that gave top priority to achieving racial balance. For over two decades, instead of pursuing more promising paths toward excellence, those who were concerned about the city's schools devoted most of their time and energy to debating, implementing, and adjusting to an oversimplified, even mistaken, idea. Until it changed, not even a strong mayor with impressive political skills could have done much to reverse the path of decline on to which the city's schools had fallen.

Epilogue

On February 9, 1993, Judge Dillin approved an IPS motion to change his desegregation order to permit a "select schools" program. The claim of those defending the busing plan that it is "working well," he wrote, "is . . . not correct, insofar as desegregation is concerned." While IPS was not required to adjust its school assignment plans, the judge acknowledged that it "has every right to do so."

An era in educational policy in Indianapolis had come to an end. Although several thousand students would continue to be bused to the suburbs, the court had agreed to let parents whose children remained within IPS choose their schools, provided that their choices did not lead to egregious racial imbalances. Symbolically, if not legally, a large part of the busing order had been lifted and the notion that desegregation was the key to improving the city's schools laid to rest. Educators and parents would henceforth have to focus—as many had already begun to do—on making schools more effective, not on mixing students to fulfill a court's vision of equal opportunity.

So too for the city's leadership. No longer will the politics of education in Indianapolis be dominated by the issue of busing. Instead, it will—as it has already begun to do—revolve around how to achieve better performance from the schools. And that, in turn, may call for an end to the arm's length relationship between the mayor of Indianapolis and the schools.

If they want to be successful in attracting people and businesses, mayors throughout the United States are learning that they cannot avoid paying attention to the quality of education in their cities. They may even have to take the lead in crafting educational policies, perhaps including radical changes in how schools are governed, financed, and organized. In Baltimore, for example, the mayor was instrumental in arranging for a private company to manage several of the city's schools and has proposed eliminating the independent school board, thus bringing education under the control of the city's government. Similarly, the mayors of Milwaukee and Jersey City have supported efforts to give low-income parents the choice of public or private schools for their children.

Although the political obstacles facing them are formidable, these kinds of changes reflect a desire by mayors to overcome the limits of their power in an area of public activity that is central to much else they wish to accomplish. Whether such steps will be possible in Indianapolis remains to be seen. But the ending of the desegregation controversy has at last given the mayor of Indianapolis a window of opportunity to take them.

The Urban Environment

DAVID McSWANE AND JERRY SMILEY

W hen William H. Hudnut, III became mayor of Indianapolis in 1976, the National Environmental Policy Act was less than a decade old and many of the federal laws that would shape the United States environmental policy agenda did not exist. At that time, *environment* was still a relatively new and unrefined term. Analysts were more concerned with the problems stemming from environmental degradation, and the literature "did not address the question regarding whether present institutional structures and political processes are inherently incapable of producing a satisfactory response to the accelerating deterioration of the environment" (Lester, 5).

Like many northern industrial centers of the day, Indianapolis was experiencing air, land, and water pollution problems that required immediate attention. "The city's wastewater treatment plant was old and undersized, the sludge incinerator was inadequate, and there was no place to dispose of the dried sludge. The county's primary sanitary landfill was nearing capacity, and Indianapolis was the largest city in the United States that was in nonattainment for four criterion air pollutants" (Hudnut, 1992). In addition, Indianapolis had embarked upon the largest public works project in the country, the construction of a multi-million-dollar advanced wastewater treatment plant, with a Public Works Department that was floundering.

Hudnut, like many other mayors at that time, faced a new frontier of unprecedented municipal problems. However, according to Barbara Gole, a former director of the Indianapolis Department of Public Works, Hudnut "worked to make Indianapolis better than the law." He wanted "the best that could be bought, based on the best research and findings of fact available." This use of the best available technology is evident in many of the major projects that came to fruition during the Hudnut Administration. Mayor Hudnut had an understanding that technology was only one side of the coin. "The city had to put its house in order if it was to gain credibility" (Hudnut, 1991). His unique management style and knowledge of decision-making processes brought Indianapolis from "India-no-place" to a model city on the leading edge of environmental awareness and accomplishment.

Whether due to the previous administration's lack of regard for the environment or ignorance of the damage that was being done, Hudnut inherited a difficult situation that was typical of most Rust Belt cities in regard to the environment. In 1976 there were many environmental problems that required satisfactory solutions. Initially, environmental improvement activities were prompted by the U.S. Environmental Protection Agency's directives and state mandates to reduce pollution produced by the city. Early on, Hudnut and city officials were forced to target environmental problems that the city had the authority to address.

However, as early as 1979 Hudnut became fully aware of the potential environmental problems facing Indianapolis. In a speech given to the Kiwanis Club, the mayor talked about the importance of proper decision making regarding the future management of the water treatment plant and the future disposal of trash and sludge. He noted that primary concern for the maintenance and expansion of a city's infrastructure is always cost. Tackling the tough environmental questions of clean air, clean water, and resource recovery, as well as augmenting the county's economic development, would be controversial and expensive issues facing the community in the 1980s.

Water Quality

Water quality problems have plagued Indianapolis for decades. In the early 1950s through the 1960s, the city designed and built combined sanitary and storm sewers. The combined sewers carried waste from homes and industries in addition to runoff from the streets. During peak times, the system would overflow. To prevent the wastewater treatment plant from overloading, combined sewers were designed so that overflows would discharge directly into Fall Creek,

White River, and its tributaries. The concept was that the raw sewage would be diluted by the storm sewer flow to safe levels, then further diluted by the increased flow of the creeks and rivers due to the heavy rainfall. However, the concept did not match reality. As many as 20 overflows per day would occur, even during the dry season, dumping raw sewage into the river. By the late 1970s it became obvious that the water quality in White River was deteriorating and much of the river had become anaerobic, limiting the viability of fish life and waterfowl. Mechanical failure of the pumps in the lift stations of the combined sewers contributed to the overflow problem, and this was further compounded by the amount of untreated industrial discharge.

The first environmental problem faced by the Hudnut Administration involved the construction of an EPA-mandated tertiary wastewater treatment plant. The EPA mandate called for Indianapolis to build a $250-million plant that would be able to significantly reduce the amount of water pollution that was being produced by Indianapolis and Greenwood, a suburban city to the south. This process began during Hudnut's predecessor's last term as mayor and was left to the next administration. Little had been done to correct the situation by the time Hudnut took office.

At the time of the mandate, the city was land-applying the sludge from the wastewater treatment plant to local landfills. The EPA maintained that Indianapolis was not properly disposing of waste sludge from the facility and that the treatment plant was allowing large quantities of untreated sewage to be discharged into White River. The planning, development, and implementation of the mandate was protracted over the early part of the Hudnut Administration and by 1978 the design for the advanced wastewater treatment plant had been completed and was approved, with a target completion date of 1981.

Construction difficulties, litigation, and mismanagement of the project led to a confrontational relationship between the EPA and the city. Many public officials did not support the environmental improvement effort, and the EPA threatened to withdraw funds for the tertiary treatment plant because of the lack of proper management. Hudnut said, "It is our problem, not someone else's," and responded by hiring Barbara Gole as director of the Department of Public Works (DPW) in 1984.

Gole was the city's third director of public works under the Hudnut Administration and was perhaps most influential in terms of accomplishing the goals set by the administration. Gole helped to complete what was at the time the largest municipal construction project of its kind in the United States. Of the $250 million needed to complete the proposed project, 75 percent was paid by the federal government, 10 percent by the state of Indiana, and 15 percent by the city. Gole was influential in directing the project and a force in bringing management issues to the mayor.

Hudnut was required to make staffing decisions at the treatment facility. Was it better to hire experienced individuals to efficiently operate the pollution control facilities or hire turn-key operators to build and operate the facility? The public works director approached the mayor with this dilemma, informing him that the market value of an experienced, qualified professional to run the plant was more than what the mayor was being paid. Hudnut made the decision to hire Tom Quinn, an experienced, professional operator, to operate and manage the wastewater treatment facility. This decision paid handsome dividends. Over the years, Quinn saved Indianapolis millions of dollars through creative management and decision making. For example, the treatment facility is the largest user of electricity from Indiana Power & Light. Quinn installed a main control system, a computerized system that helped the plant handle peak loading efficiently and paid for itself in two years.

Prior to the completion of the wastewater treatment plant, Dick Ripple, Indianapolis's second director of the Department of Public Works under the Hudnut Administration, provided an extra million dollars per year (via the Health and Hospital Corporation) for sewer maintenance. In three years, the combined sewer system went from 20 overflows per day to three overflows per year. However, the combined sewer problems for the city were far from over. It has been estimated that the city may be facing a billion-dollar infrastructure problem in the downtown sewers. Much of the system beneath the city is wooden, some of it built more than 100 years ago.

Because Indianapolis is a large city sitting on a relatively small body of water, clean water was an issue throughout the Hudnut Administration. Even 16 years later, City Councilman Ray Irvin is leading a push for the "greening" of White River, the beautification of a once "dead" river into a place where people can enjoy landscaped trails and canoeing.

Another water quality concern that still plagues the city is the 270 high-density housing areas within the county that are served by private septic systems. Indianapolis is the largest city in the United States with the greatest percentage of households on septic systems. Extending sewers to these areas is critical, but to date the cost is prohibitive to home owners.

Solid Waste Management

In 1976 a Solid Waste Task Force, formed by Mayor Lugar, was comprised of community leaders, City-County Council members, and waste haulers. They studied solid waste disposal alternatives and technologies from around the world and concluded that mass-burn, waste-to-energy technology was best suited to deal with the large quantity of waste produced in Indianapolis. However, there were many considerations which the task force recognized as being crucial to the feasibility of such a project. To ensure economic feasibility of a waste-to-energy plant, state legislation was passed giving the county flow-control over the waste stream. To this day, Marion County is the only public entity in Indiana that maintains flow control over its solid waste. Also, the task force requested and received passage of a City-County Council special resolution that allowed the county to implement the best available technology to solve the longterm solid waste problem (Gole, 1990).

With the changing of administrations came a change in agendas as well as public works directors. The first director of DPW appointed by Hudnut did not take an active role to advance or limit solutions to the solid waste problem. The second director worked hard to promote environmental issues and the mayor supported those efforts. However, the director chose not to pursue the waste-to-energy facility because of the controversy surrounding it. In early 1984, when Gole replaced Ripple as head of DPW, she provided the impetus. She and Hudnut developed a rapport that led to the successful completion of the waste-to-energy plant.

Hudnut and Gole agreed that the time was right, politically and economically, to site a landfill and resource recovery facility. Politically, it was the beginning of Hudnut's third term, and as Gole stated at the Fourth National Conference on Environmental Issues, "It is a rule in government that all controversial projects should be undertaken in the first or second year of any administration so the wounds can heal before the next election" (Gole, 1990). Economically, the city had to take advantage of low interest rates and significant tax breaks for industrial revenue bonds before the tax reform of 1986. The stage was set and Mayor Hudnut promoted the project to the hilt.

The Solid Waste Task Force was resurrected while the DPW went through the arduous task of reevaluating much of the old information and hiring external consultants to explore alternatives for financing a facility of this sort. Next, Mayor Hudnut focused on the task of public relations along with Gole and the DPW. The inclusion of the public and all involved groups in the decision-making process was perhaps the single most important factor in bringing the resource recovery facility to reality. In the summer of 1984, the DPW invited the environmental community to evaluate all of the environmental risks associated with the facility and accepted all recommendations with regard to facility environmental controls. Throughout the rest of 1984, public hearings regarding landfill sitings took place while the task force examined and evaluated criteria for the siting of the resource recovery facility and a 200-acre landfill. Requests for qualifications were released in November and 12 companies responded. In early 1985, members of the City-County Council went to Pinellas County, Florida, to inspect and observe a resource recovery facility as part of the decision-making process.

According to former deputy mayor John Krauss, the mayor met strong opposition to the landfill siting alternatives, much of it due to the "NIMBY (not-in-my-backyard) syndrome." With this, the City-County Council agreed to cease all attempts to find a suitable landfill site in the county. But Hudnut guided the council, the environmental groups, the anti-landfill activists, and the community toward the resource recovery facility as the only viable option left for the Solid Waste Task Force to pursue. In the end, the mayor spent $2 million for public education, technical planning, and research. The gamble paid off. All involved groups publicly supported the proposed facility as the most environmentally sound waste-disposal technique for the future.

Gregory K. Silver, who was president of the local chapter of the Sierra Club at that time and sat on the Resource Recovery Steering Committee, said, "Mayor Hudnut used his personality to bring different factions together to participate in the decision-making process. He wanted all factions involved provided that one, they were willing to participate, and two, they were willing to work within the government to get things done."

The DPW began accepting bids for the resource recovery facility from private companies in May 1985. Several factors added a sense of urgency to the solid waste situation. First, the Indiana Department of Environmental Management charged the city's only private landfill with violation of its permitted trash height limit. The situation was further exacerbated when the commissioner of the Indiana State Board of Health wrote a letter to Hudnut stating that the landfill "technically" had no space left for trash. At the same time, the DPW was threatening that trash collection could occur only every two weeks because of the rising costs of disposal. By August, four firms had submitted bids to burn 1,800 tons per day of solid waste and 150 dry tons per day of municipal sludge.

The Resource Recovery Steering Committee recommended Ogden Martin Systems as the vendor to build and operate a 2,362 ton-per-day waste-to-energy facility at a cost of $83.8 million. The committee also accepted the request of the environmental subcommittee that the environmental controls be upgraded from an electrostatic precipitator to a baghouse and dry acid gas scrubber. This further demonstrated the mayor's commitment to fulfilling the public's requests and solving concerns that the air quality standards would be met beyond standards set by the EPA. In mid-November the Board of Public Works guaranteed flow to the resource recovery facility and the City-County Council, by a 27–1 vote, authorized Ogden Martin to build and operate the plant. The city was to sell $120 million in revenue bonds to finance the project.

The completion of these two projects reveals only one facet of how the city of Indianapolis was on the road to credibility. Hudnut also created timely policies and programs relating to other environmental issues. While Hudnut's administration was reactive to the water and solid waste problems, it has been proactive in other areas.

Air Quality and Other Problems

Air quality problems have been a point of contention for the city in many aspects. When Hudnut took office, Indianapolis was the largest city in the United States to be in nonattainment in four air-pollutant criteria—carbon monoxide, sulfur dioxide, particulates, and ozone. In the late '70s and early '80s the administration's philosophy was one of protecting local industry from the EPA. The Air Quality Control

Department was trying to warn industry of impending pollution problems before EPA was forced to take action. Even though federal mandates required the city to reach attainment through pollution cut backs, there were arguments regarding the value of clean air.

It was not until the middle '80s that the administration realized that the city's poor air quality was not good for the community environmentally or economically. Two events led to this realization. Ford Motor Company was interested in expansion in Marion County. When asked what the city's "environmental scan" was, Mayor Hudnut responded, "nonattainment." The Ford executives said, "We have nothing to talk about." Later Chrysler considered using the abandoned Western Electric plant to build minivans but did not do so in part because of the city's air pollution problems.

With new industry avoiding Indianapolis because of its nonattainment status, the city was forced to attract nonpolluting industry such as amateur sports. While fighting the EPA served some business interests, it did not serve the city as a whole and other business interests. Hudnut gave focus to the problem when he said, "There is a connection between clean air and jobs, but people don't understand that. I used to try to make that point many times in speeches and so forth. It's a tough point to make—it's easier to build the argument on the basis of public health and safety."

Since these incidents, the Chamber of Commerce has become much more aware of the relationship between air quality and economic growth. The mayor was able to sell business leaders on the proposition that "what's good for the environment is good for the city." Since 1984, the Air Pollution Control Agency has managed to bring Indianapolis into attainment with the national ambient air quality standards for carbon monoxide, particulates, and sulfur dioxide. The waste-to-energy incinerator has helped to bring sulfur dioxide levels down by 52 percent because its air pollution control units use the best available technology. The plant also saved 374,000 tons of coal in 1990. Ozone was the only pollutant that remained a problem for the city.

In 1978 Hudnut and Tom Hasbrook set up the Indianapolis Clean Cities Committee (CCC). This committee was funded primarily through private enterprise and was established to mount an antilitter campaign as a participant in the Keep America Beautiful Program. Under the leadership of Betty Stanford and with the cooperation of the Department of Transportation, the Health and Hospital Corporation, and the Department of Public Works, Indianapolis was designated the cleanest city in the United States for populations greater than 500,000 in 1978 and again in 1980. In 1977 a 29.7 percent reduction in litter accumulation was observed when compared with baseline measurements taken in December 1976 (State of the City address, 1978).

Much of this effort was forged by the mayor's commitment to and participation in the Clean Cities Program. For example, during the time of Woodsy the Owl's "Give a Hoot, Don't Pollute" campaign, Hudnut created a public service commercial that depicted the mayor "sky-hooking" a piece of trash into a garbage receptacle. The ad campaign was extremely successful as an environmental education program. The CCC is currently advocating community recycling efforts, although, in terms of popularity, nothing has attained the success of the Hudnut hook.

Another program that began in 1978 was the creation of the first full-time municipal environmental court in the United States. Betty Stanford, while chairing the Indianapolis Clean Cities Committee, helped convince Hudnut that an environmental court was needed. The Marion County Health and Hospital Corporation provides environmental health services for the area. The agency, on issuance of environmental warnings, had a voluntary compliance rate of 60 percent. Due to an overcrowded court system, environmental litigation was being pushed further down on the court dockets, and higher enforcement was not possible without a special court to handle code enforcement. In two years, under Judges David Jester and Harold Kohlmeyer, compliance rates rose from 60 percent to 96 percent of the cases that went through the environmental court.

Under the passage of a comprehensive litter ordinance that set down strict penalties for violators, the administration, Clean Cities Committee, and the environmental court surveyed abandoned service stations in the city. Nearly 70 of them were cited for code violations, and they were given a deadline for compliance. Failure to comply landed the service station owners in environmental court.

In 1991 Indianapolis was voted as having the best environmental health of any city its size in the country. The environmental health of the city was based on a five-point "environmental stress index" by the nationally recognized organization Zero Population Growth. The index incorporated population change, air quality, water quality and availability, sewage, disposal, and toxic releases.

REFERENCES

Barbara S. Gole, 1990, "Achieving Public Confidence in the Siting of Environmentally Sensitive Facilities," in Proceedings of the Fourth National Conference on Environmental Issues, 247–63.

William H. Hudnut III, 1991, personal interview at School of Public and Environmental Affairs, Indiana University–Purdue University at Indianapolis, May.

William H. Hudnut III, 1992, personal interview at Hudson Institute, Indianapolis, July.

James P. Lester, 1989, *Environmental Politics and Policy: Theories and Evidence* (Durham, N.C.: Duke University Press).

Affirmative Action

DAVID A. CAPUTO

"In government, the tendency of 'bureaucrats' is to tell you why something cannot be done, why it won't work. In fact, what we need are positive thinkers who can achieve breakthroughs. . . . Government needs positive thinkers to help make positive decisions." This statement probably epitomizes the underlying leadership philosophy of William H. Hudnut III.[1] Mayor Hudnut maintains that positive decisions are needed when one is confronted with the specifics of many local issues, but the outlook is perhaps best illustrated by a review of his leadership on affirmative action when Indianapolis's plan was attacked by a Republican presidential administration.

By the early 1970s, Indianapolis was beginning to emerge as a major transportation and economic center as the interstate highway system and the nation's strong postwar economy complemented each other. With the advent of a partial city-county governmental consolidation in the late 1960s, Indianapolis had been transformed from a somnolent capital to a thriving one with a considerable economic base just waiting to be developed.

Related to this advantageous economic situation was a unique political factor. Under the Unigov legislation, one mayor served all of Indianapolis and most of Marion County, but because of the consolidation's nature, this individual had an expanded role to play in a variety of economic and political decisions. The practical political result of Unigov, passed when Richard Lugar was mayor, was to change the political boundaries of the city so that it became one of the nation's largest cities while at the same time shifting its underlying political distribution from a ratio of approximately three-to-two Democratic voters to three-to-two Republican voters. While the political impact was important, the long-term impact Unigov had on the governmental process was more significant for the economic development of the "new" city and for its residents.[2]

Coupled with these local developments was a broader set of events taking place nationally by the late 1960s and into the 1970s—the emergence of New Federalism, which served as the cornerstone of President Nixon's domestic policy and was left relatively untouched by the Carter Administration. Under Nixon's New Federalism, the main emphasis was on providing local governments and their agencies with the financial resources and the authority needed to deal with a wide variety of local problems. New Federalism advocated avoiding the more narrow and focused approach of the categorical grants characteristic of President Johnson's Great Society and instead, through general and special revenue-sharing programs, attempted to support political leadership at the local level with the resources needed to deal with problems in an innovative and autonomous way. The emphasis was on reducing the red tape and bureaucratic delays long associated with the categorical grant programs. At the same time, federal monies increased dramatically as the nation provided significant resources in an attempt to deal with a variety of urban problems.[3]

Local leaders needed fiscal resources if they were to deal with local problems in a local way. It was not a question of whether such governmental action was needed but rather which level of government had the responsibility and ability to best address the problem. New Federalism, as advocated by the Nixon Administration, prided itself on redirecting both effort and control away from the federal government and emphasizing both the right and responsibility of local governments to act to resolve the problems facing them.[4]

Another useful way of viewing New Federalism was as a form of empowerment for local officials. No longer looking to Washington for specific programs to deal with particular problems but rather utilizing the resources and flexibility granted by the new programs, these local officials were to begin the "second American revolution," which would lead to greater participation and problem solving at the local level by local government officials.[5] This distinction is important—New Federalism wanted to return power to local governmental decision makers and not private groups. Through this return of power to governmental officials at the local level, local citizens would have both greater opportunity and incentive to become more involved with local political decision making. New Federalism, simply put, argued that decisions were best made at the local level by elected leaders from that level.

This was a fertile setting for political leaders who defined their role as activist. In his book *Minister/Mayor,* William Hudnut describes what a mayor should be, and it is clear that this New Federalism environment was ideal for a person of his talents and energy. He stressed four main characteristics for a mayor to be successful: consensus builder, cheerleader, facilitator, and packager.[6] Each is spelled out in some depth, but the important point is that each represents an activist orientation toward governance. None of the characteristics is passive and all four require a wide degree of action and activity on the part of the mayor and those working in the mayor's office. This definition of leadership sees the mayor as "in charge" and the leader in all matters relating to the city. It is not a matter of city government reducing its role, but rather extending it.

It is exactly this personal leadership philosophy coupled with the growing dynamism of the Indianapolis economy and the prevailing New Federalism philosophy of the 1970s that helped propel Hudnut to the forefront of urban leaders. He was seen as the Republican mayor responsible for the continued growth and development of one of the nation's largest cities and as an individual who dealt with problems in a decisive and positive way. He brought a faith and an optimism to the job; these characteristics often resulted in his being sought after by the national press as a spokesperson who maintained that there was hope for American cities and their future. In a chapter on building the city in *Minister/Mayor,* Hudnut comments:

> Our lives, our business and professional and social and educational and religious worlds, are grounded in the city. The city is the hub of communication and transportation networks, the cockpit where crucial commercial and political decisions are made, the arena where conflicting communities of interest are battling it out.[7]

In sum, here was an individual who held the activist leadership philosophy at the time both local and national conditions called for activist leadership. The timing could not have been better for his first term in office (1976–80), but after the Reagan Administration took office and proposed its version of the "new New Federalism" the mayor and other activist urban leaders found themselves confronted with a changing set of political conditions at the national level.

By the mid-1980s and beyond, the definition of and the political agenda for New Federalism were quite different than those of the mid- to late 1970s. The Carter Administration had already been successful in reducing the increase in federal intergovernmental expenditures,[8] and with the new Reagan Administration in 1981 there was a frontal assault on government programs. The emphasis was on reducing the role of government at all levels. Candidates and office holders argued not only for limiting but actually for reducing the scope and number of governmental programs with the justification being that such programs were not only ineffective but in many cases were exacerbating the very problems they were intended to alleviate.[9] To properly understand the political maelstrom Mayor Hudnut found himself in regarding affirmative action, one has to fully appreciate how the changed national political environment would influence his political capability.

For a variety of reasons (including formal complaints and litigation), the City of Indianapolis had decided to enter into a series of initially voluntary and then legally binding consent agreements with the U.S. Justice Department to resolve allegations of discrimination and underutilization of minorities and women in the city's Police and Fire departments. These consent agreements, critics contended, were really preferential treatment for the individuals involved in the form of quotas determining who would be hired. They were seen by others as a way to reach a longer-term solution by assisting the city in increasing its recruitment of minorities and women. The agreements focused on recruiting and on increasing the number of minorities and women at the upper levels through the promotion process.

What makes this case so interesting from an intergovernmental perspective is that even though the city, for whatever reasons, had entered into the agreements with the Justice Department, the same Justice Department, under new political leadership, decided that the Indianapolis plan was objectionable and that the city should modify it. The debate and controversy that occupied Indianapolis in the mid-1980s thus resulted from a federal system that permits the development of new intergovernmental policies from one presidential administration to another. In this case, the activist intergovernmental policies of the 1970s were now being changed to policies that discouraged both national and local action to address a variety of problems. Thus the mayor and the city had to decide how to react—their decisions were part of an important and interesting intergovernmental debate.

The Justice Department's contention that the Indianapolis plan was illegal was based on the decisions reached by a frequent but often ignored participant in the intergovernmental process, the courts. In this case, the U.S. Supreme Court had ruled in 1984 that a bona fide seniority system could only be changed if it could be shown that such a system actually had resulted in individuals being victimized because of their racial or gender status. The Justice Department quickly decided that the *Stotts* decision ruled out the establishment of numerical goals as a way to deal with underrepresentation of various groups or classes.[10] Specifically, the Justice Department agreed that *Stotts* "renders unlawful and beyond the Court's [U.S. District Court for Southern Indiana] remedial authority employment preferences based on race/sex to persons who are not victims of the defendants' unlawful employment practices."[11]

Now the intergovernmental battle was joined. Hudnut and the city had to decide if they were going to agree to amend the consent decrees they had entered into with the Justice Department. It was an interesting dilemma. On the one hand, the city had been working with some success to resolve the concerns represented in the consent decrees, and modifying them was seen as a potential setback in achieving the city's ultimate goal—a public safety workforce that was more nearly representative of the underlying population demographics in the city. On the other hand, did a Republican mayor really want to take on the federal government and a Republican-led administration with their significant resources over an issue that had limited political popularity and clearly had important implications for the nature of intergovernmental relationships in the United States?

Hudnut and the city responded in a very decisive way. The mayor waged his battle legally and politically while at the same time retaining a position that was consistent with an activist's view of local intergovernmental decision-making. In a letter dated September 18, 1985, to Attorney General Edwin Meese, Hudnut argued that the Justice Department's action "seeks to totally eliminate hiring goals for minorities and females in the Indianapolis Police and Fire Departments. I was disturbed by this and instructed our legal counsel to oppose this action vigorously."[12]

In addition to the legal reasons Hudnut cited, he went on to consider the "practical" reasons why the Justice Department should cease its attempts to modify the consent decrees. Hudnut maintained that "the affirmative action goals have been good business for the City of Indianapolis and its citizens" and contended that there was increased cooperation, a greater sense of community, and "relative racial harmony" since the city began to implement the policy.[13]

Hudnut then cited an interesting intergovernmental perspective contending that the Republican party had long espoused a need to get the federal government "off of the backs" of the state and local governments. Actions such as these, challenging a duly constituted local decision, according to Hudnut was seen as undermining public morale and confidence.[14]

The mayor waged a vigorous public campaign to thwart the Justice Department's request and to build public support. He used his leadership role in various national urban groups to rally support, and he made sure his message was well covered by the media. At the same time, he unsuccessfully attempted to reach an agreement with the Justice Department.

What is significant is not the specific points raised but that they reflect a general intergovernmental perspective that is locally and activist oriented. The Indianapolis community, not well known as the center of liberal thought, was taking on the federal government and, in doing so, arguing that the Justice Department had both legally and politically overstepped its prescribed bounds. The irony was that a local Republican leader was accusing his party of ignoring the ability of local decision makers to creatively solve their problems. This was exactly the same argument the proponents of Nixon's New Federalism had used when citing the difficulties and problems associated with the Great Society.

The end result was again largely a factor of the judicial system's subsequent decisions regarding other affirmative-action cases. When the courts failed to uphold the earlier more restricted rulings, the Justice Department abandoned its request to change the consent decrees. The City of Indianapolis, although its overall success under the various aspects of the plan could best be described as moderate, was free to continue its recruitment and promotion plans.

So what are the lessons to be learned from this particular case that may apply to other intergovernmental issues and mayoral leadership?

First, as the table indicates, there was significant change in the city's public safety workforce. By 1990 the percentage of blacks and women employed in the Police Department had increased substantially. Even more dramatic gains were evident in the Fire Department, where the percentage of black males doubled and there was a steadily increasing percentage of women on the force. Black women continued to be the most underrepresented of the groups included in the table. Clearly the Indianapolis plan was producing results; the often-debated question was whether it was producing them fast enough and at what costs.

Composition of City of Indianapolis Police and Fire Departments, 1978–90

Year	Police			
	White Males	**Black Males**	**White Females**	**Black Females**
1978	82%	9%	7%	2%
1980	81%	10%	7%	2%
1982	80%	11%	7%	2%
1984	79%	11%	8%	3%
1986	78%	12%	8%	3%
1988	74%	12%	10%	3%
1990	71%	13%	11%	4%

Year	Fire			
	White Males	**Black Males**	**White Females**	**Black Females**
1978	91%	9%	—	0.1%
1980	88%	12%	0.1%	—
1982	88%	12%	0.1%	—
1984	87%	13%	0.5%	—
1986	85%	13%	1.3%	0.2%
1988	80%	17%	2.5%	0.2%
1990	78%	18%	3.0%	0.3%

Source: Data prepared for consent decree compliance and provided by Gregory J. Utken. Rounding errors are the reason totals do not equal 100 percent.

Second, it is clear that Mayor Hudnut's positive, assertive leadership style had an important role to play both in the city's success in thwarting the Justice Department's request and in assisting the city through the many changes taking place in the intergovernmental system. The lesson should be clear: organized, direct, and positive leadership is essential if well-conceived decisions are to be both reached and implemented at the local level.

Third—and an important point for students of U.S. intergovernmental relations—local decision makers can be successful when dealing with the federal government and in fact, despite two centuries of legal and often constitutional restraints limiting local power, local political leaders still have considerable political resources at their disposal. In addition, the energy and initiative of local decision makers constitute a potent force not to be ignored or taken lightly by the federal government. To do so could cause greater problems for federalism and result in less time and fewer resources being devoted to designing effective and efficient programs. Clearly the federal government's goal should be to foster a dynamic partnership with all the participants in the intergovernmental system. A partnership that will lead to greater cooperation and concerted efforts to deal with the complex and pressing problems facing the United States would be the desired nature of intergovernmental relationships.

Finally, analysts need to understand that individual leaders' successes often depend on the environment in which they find themselves. In this case, a rapidly changing set of intergovernmental conditions clearly influenced Hudnut's ability to lead. The changing nature of U.S. intergovernmental relations will continue to have a significant impact on all the participants in the federal system as they deal with complex problems and possible solutions. The case of Hudnut's leadership is instructive for others who wish to understand and forge new policies under a changing set of conditions. Decisive and positive leadership on the part of a particular leader can have considerable impact on the local community and beyond.

NOTES

1. William H. Hudnut III (with Judy Keene), *Minister/Mayor* (Philadelphia: Westminster Press, 1987), 130.

2. For a detailed discussion of the early history of Unigov, see C. James Owen and York Willbern, *Governing Metropolitan Indianapolis* (Berkeley: University of California Press, 1985).

3. David A. Caputo, "Richard M. Nixon General Revenue Sharing and American Federalism," in Leon Friedman and William F. Levantrosser, eds., *Richard M. Nixon: Politician, President, Administrator* (Greenwood Press, 1991), 59–76.

4. Richard L. Cole and David A. Caputo, *Urban Politics and Decentralization* (Lexington, Mass.: Lexington Books, 1974), 17–65.

5. Richard M. Nixon, 1971 State of the Union message.

6. Hudnut, 167–69.

7. Ibid., 162.

8. David A. Caputo, "Political, Social, and Economic Aspects of the 'Old' and the 'New' New Federalism," in Louis A. Picard and Raphael Zariski, eds., *Subnational Politics in the 1980s* (New York: Praeger, 1984), 21–34.

9. Caputo, "Political, Social, and Economic Aspects," 27–33.

10. United States District Court for the Southern District of Indiana, United States Department of Justice, Motion for Prospective Modification of Consent Decrees, April 29, 1985.

11. Ibid., 1.

12. William H. Hudnut III, 18 September 1985, letter to Attorney General Edwin Meese, 1.

13. Ibid., 1–2.

14. Ibid., 3.

ACADEMIC CONTRIBUTORS

David J. Bodenhamer is a Professor History and Director of the POLIS Research Center at IUPUI. He is the author or editor of six books and over 50 articles and papers, including *Fair Trial: Rights of the Accused in American History* (1992) and *The Bill of Rights in Modern America: After 200 Years* (1993, with James W. Ely, Jr.).

David A. Caputo is the Dean of the School of Liberal Arts and Professor of Political Science at Purdue University in West Lafayette, Indiana. His research emphasis includes extensive work on urban politics and urban fiscal management.

Carol D'Amico is the Deputy Director of the Educational Excellence Network at the Hudson Institute in Indianapolis. She is also a research fellow specializing in education issues.

Kathryn Diefenthaler is a fellow at the Washington Hospital Group in Washington, D.C. She received her Master of Health Administration degree from Indiana University's School of Public and Environmental Affairs at IUPUI. She has published papers on aging and forecasting needs for human resource personnel.

Amy Dillow is the Departmental Coordinator at Anderson Hospital, Anderson, Indiana. She received her Master of Health Administration degree from Indiana University's School of Public and Environmental Affairs at IUPUI. She received the Presidential Scholar award upon graduation in 1993 and has published a series of needs assessment analyses for South Carolina area agencies on aging.

William Doherty is a Professor of History at Marian College in Indianapolis. He has written widely on issues of public safety and crime.

Karen S. Harlow is an Assistant Professor jointly appointed with the Indiana University School of Public and Environmental Affairs and

Family Medicine at IUPUI. She has served as director of a national long-term care research center, and her publications focus on needs assessment, aging and health policy, and the impact of governance on agency outputs and community health outcomes.

Leslie Lenkowsky is the President of the Hudson Institute in Indianapolis. He is the author of "Politics, Economics, and Welfare Reform: The Failure of the Negative Income Tax in Britain and the United States," among numerous other publications. Lenkowsky is also a regular contributor to the *Chronicle of Philanthropy*.

Laura Littlepage is a Policy Analyst with the Indiana University School of Public and Environmental Affairs' Center for Urban Policy and the Environment at IUPUI. She is the principal author of several Center publications in the areas of fiscal impact and local government finances.

David McSwane is an Associate Professor and the Director of Undergraduate Programs for the Indiana University School of Public and Environmental Affairs at IUPUI. He has written extensively in the field of environmental health with a focus on the safety of food and drinking water.

Daniel R. Mullins is an Assistant Professor in the Indiana University School of Public and Environmental Affairs at Bloomington. His research focuses on issues of state and local government finance.

Roger Parks is a Professor in the Indiana University School of Public and Environmental Affairs at Bloomington. He has written extensively in the areas of urban governance and the delivery of public services.

Michael Przybylski is the Senior Research Scientist with the School of Public and Environmental Affairs' Center for Urban Policy and the Environment at IUPUI. He is an economist specializing in public finance and econometric modeling.

Mark S. Rosentraub is Professor and Associate Dean in the School of Public and Environmental Affairs and Director of the Center for Urban Policy and the Environment at IUPUI. He has written over 50 articles, book chapters, and monographs, and his interests in urban policy focus on economic development and issues related to financing, delivery, and governance.

Jerry Smiley is an Environmental Planner for Wendy Lopez and Associates, an architect engineering firm in Dallas, Texas, with experience in solid waste and environmental impact planning and analyses. He has written in the area of service delivery.

David W. Swindell is a Ph.D. candidate and an Assistant Professor of Urban Affairs at Wright State University. His research focuses on issues of urban governance and neighborhood development.

PART THREE

CITIZEN CRITICS

William Styring III

L et's get one thing straight at the outset. I voted for Bill Hudnut at every opportunity when I was a resident of Indianapolis. And that electoral support was more than simply registering a preference for Mayor Bill over the generally lackluster collection of opponents the opposition party staggered onto the ballot.

Hudnut's estimable qualities were many. He was a man of unquestioned integrity. As a cheerleader for Indianapolis, he was nonpareil. And, well, he just looked every inch a leader. Still, this essay is a critique of the Hudnut years. Critiques by definition emphasize negatives and disagreements, so the remainder of this essay will focus on what Bill Hudnut Did Wrong.

It is my contention that the philosophical and economic centerpiece of Hudnut's 16 years in office was state- (i.e., government-) driven downtown development. On the appropriateness and success of this policy, Hudnut should ultimately be judged. For all of the good will and good intentions Hudnut heaped upon the vision of a revitalized downtown Indianapolis, I believe history will adjudge this policy to have been a failure, in part because of the corrupting consequences state capitalism has on the traditional and proper role of government.

A native of Indianapolis, William Styring III is a 1967 magna cum laude graduate of Wabash College with an M.A. in economics from Harvard University. In August 1992 he became the director of the Benjamin Rogge Chair for Public Policy at the Indiana Policy Review Foundation, an Indianapolis-based think tank concentrating on state and local public policy issues. He is also a Senior Adjunct Fellow of the Hudson Institute.

The Nature of Downtown Development

An Indianapolis resident who left town in the late 1970s would be amazed by the appearance of downtown Indianapolis today. Clustered in a roughly ten-square-block area south and west of Monument Circle, he would find a domed stadium complete with NFL football, a downtown shopping mall under construction, a convention center in the midst of further work, new office buildings, and hotels and shops, including an old train station modernized as a shopping area. To the west, what was once essentially the Indiana University Medical School has become Indiana University–Purdue University at Indianapolis, an institution that has the trappings of an urban megaversity. To the east, a modern arena boasts NBA basketball plus the usual assorted circuses and rock concerts.

What happened to ol' Naptown? The answer is that Hudnut's Indianapolis embarked on a conscious policy of public-private development partnerships. The city's contribution to the deals were some combination of tax abatement, below-market loans or guarantees, favorable zoning rulings, and, in some cases, outright infusions of public cash. The explosion of downtown development was in one sense unremarkable. Governments have always been able to amass resources through taxation and/or borrowing for monumental capital projects. The pharaoh could build pyramids. Louis could build Versailles. Reagan could build submarines and B-1 bombers. But it is shallow analysis to simply admire the grandeur of Versailles and the pyramids, the destructive power of the B-1 . . . or the face-lifting of Indianapolis. To look about and say, "Gee, this is wonderful," misses the hidden costs.

The Downside

Few are aware of just how extensive the city's role was in bankrolling these projects. A partial listing would include the following:[1]

Project	City Commitment
Union Station	$4-million loan (renovation) (6%)
One North Capitol	$3.2-million construction loan (6%)
Embassy Suites	$6-million construction loan (interest free)

Merchants Plaza	$4.5-million bond issue for land acquisition/preparation
Two West Washington	$1.2-million renovation loan (6%)
Indiana Theater	fee owner/$1.5-million renovation loan (6%)

There are additional projects and provisions. For example, Union Station depended on $16.5 million in various federal grants. Twelve million dollars came from mass-transit funds, though it is unclear just what connection the retail center renovation of a train station that was a Civil War transportation hub has with transportation. Additionally, the city used its good offices to help obtain a 25 percent historic preservation tax credit for the developer. Thus, on a $65-million project, half of the funds were public.

Major league sports teams have also been the beneficiaries of city help. Market Square Arena (Indiana Pacers) has connections with the city which are substantial but which the author has not adequately researched (and which are pre-Hudnut, in any case). The Hoosier Dome (Indianapolis Colts) was built with the proceeds of a 1 percent food and beverage tax. The city has also contributed to the Colts training facility and has provided attendance guarantees whereby attendance below specified levels commits the city to make up the difference in ticket income.

The crown jewel is Circle Centre Mall, a multi-hundred-million-dollar downtown shopping mall. The city is heavily involved in land acquisition and site preparation. Despite fits and starts, the project is finally under way.

Tax abatements accompany most of these efforts. Abatements are particularly corrosive. They violate the most elementary notion of fairness, that equally situated taxpayers should be treated equally (some business ventures have their property taxes lowered; others do not). They also run the grave risk of starting what some call the "death spiral." The spiral works as follows: abatements are granted (and/or outright city ownership of property is undertaken), driving up tax rates on remaining property, prompting business flight, and/or demands for further abatements, driving rates even higher, etc., etc. Large hunks of downtown Indianapolis have been removed from the tax rolls by abatement or outright city ownership. Because of this (there are other reasons also) property tax rates in Center Township are 50 percent higher on average than in surrounding townships and more than double on average those in surrounding counties. Is this a death-spiral situation with horrendous long-term consequences for the very downtown Hudnut was trying to save? My own research using a methodology developed by the Federal Reserve Bank of Philadelphia is inconclusive. At best, Center Township is not far from that brink.

But to return to the central thesis of this essay: while the long-run economic consequences of the Hudnut state-sponsored downtown development strategy may turn out perversely, the social and political costs will likely prove even greater. Simply put, the line between public and private has been blurred beyond distinction.

These projects were largely the brainchild of a group known as the City Committee. The City Committee consisted of around 30 male executives. The members were real estate developers, contractors, bankers, lawyers, and Lilly Endowment officials who, perhaps coincidentally, also were either beneficiaries or managers of many of these projects. This is not necessarily to suggest sinister motives. It is perfectly possible that City Committee members genuinely believed in what they were recommending and happened to be those whose involvement with the projects was vital and necessary. Nonetheless, the very existence of the City Committee was not widely known, much less its creative advocacy of much of the downtown development agenda. What the citizens of Indianapolis mostly got from their local media was a dose of civic boosterism.

Several things happen when state and private entities sleep in the same bedroom . . . none of them good. Private power centers largely free of easy ways of government intimidation are a crucially necessary element in preserving individual liberty. Economist Milton Friedman once invited us to examine history to find even one example of a society in which substantial personal freedom existed for any period of time in which the bulk of economic activity was not also largely organized around relatively unfettered private enterprise.[2] He has found none; neither have I. State-sponsored downtown development co-opts the private sector in a manner inconsistent with the maintenance of classical liberal values. Any short-term gains in bricks and mortar are outweighed by the change in political discourse required. Use of state power and tax money to acquire a Nordstrom or a football team is at odds with what formerly was a culture more attuned to individualism.

Public/private "partnerships" corrupt not only the private partner but also the governmental partner. Once public funds are committed, not only does the city have an economic stake, but political leaders identified with the project have their own personal political futures at risk. Put bluntly, if the project goes down the tube, they may go with it. Most of these projects have been chronic money-losers (itself an indicator that creating special incentives for some private interests is a futile attempt to second-guess the market; any deal that requires a heavy dose of government finances to make it work is likely a bad deal). There is a temptation, once committed, to *make* these projects succeed. For example, when Union Station or the shops in the Embassy Suites were being discussed, I do not recall anyone saying, "Look, these things will go bust if we don't also pour hundreds of millions into an adjacent downtown shopping mall." (Maybe this was the thinking in the mind of some obscure urban planner ensconced in the bowels of the City-County Building; if so, he wasn't talking.) Now, faced with chronic red ink, an argument in favor of the downtown mall is that it's necessary to give the "critical mass" for success of prior city projects. If the mall also disappoints, what will be next?

Finally, there is the damage done to what might be termed the sociology of capitalism. Business has never been loved, only tolerated as necessary to material well-being. Its press has been terrible. The people Jesus evicted from the temple were foreign exchange dealers. Shylock was not someone you'd want your daughter to marry. J. R. Ewing was a louse. Even the kids watching Saturday morning TV get treated to Captain Planet battling some plutocrat who gets his jollies by polluting Mother Earth. I'm not sure that business people understand that when the state gets involved, when political leaders take credit at ribbon cuttings, we send a powerful message that the state has become the engine of economic progress. This used to be the province of business. If the electorate ever becomes convinced that business is perceived to be no longer discharging its sole redeeming function . . . it's over.

What Would Have Happened If . . .

The response to the foregoing may be yes, that's all true, but is it not also true that we do have a bright, shiny new downtown Indianapolis, and the fact of the matter is it wouldn't have happened without state capitalism and public/private partnerships. Of course downtown Indianapolis would today look much different had these projects not taken place, just as the Nile Valley would be much different without the pyramids. The question is not whether downtown is different than it would have been, but rather whether the quality of life for the average citizen is demonstrably better than it might otherwise have been. This is pure speculation. We cannot predict what would have transpired. However, the resources devoted to downtown development would have found a home somewhere; they would not have been locked away under a mattress. Moreover, those resources would likely have found uses that we would value more highly. Downtown projects as a group have generally failed the market test; the profit-and-loss statement is a marvelous test of whether resources are being put to their best use.

All in all, Mayor Hudnut, I salute you. Your devotion and energy made a lot of things possible. I just have a nagging doubt that they were the right things.

NOTES

1. This list omits the single largest commitment of the Hudnut Administration, the UAL maintenance hub at Indianapolis International Airport, because it is not "downtown." The total financial commitment of city, state, and Hendricks County governments, including up-front cash and the present value of forgiven future taxes—basically a no-taxes-on-anything-forever pledge—was in the vicinity of $630 million. In exchange the city received a somewhat tenuous pledge of 6,000 new jobs.

2. See Milton Friedman, *Capitalism and Freedom* (Chicago: University of Chicago Press, 1962).

William M. Schreiber

For Indianapolis Republicans, the New Age began in 1967 when Richard Lugar was elected mayor. A prominent businessman who had entered public life by winning a seat on the Indianapolis School Board earlier in the decade, Lugar was only the third Republican elected mayor of the Indiana capital in 40 years. His campaign portrayed him as the articulate, urbane challenger in brutal contrast with the Democratic incumbent, who was portrayed as a cigar-rolling, old-style politician more interested in doing favors for friends than in tending to the business of city government. Lugar's election set the stage for one of the most incredible displays of power politics in the history of Indiana, a state described by Theodore S. White in *The Making of the President, 1960*, as "one of the few states in the nation where cutthroat politics is still practiced."

The Republican victory in the general election of 1968 was no less important even if it was more predictable. Republicans gained majorities surpassing two-thirds in both chambers of the Indiana General Assembly. That allowed them to meet quorum requirements in both the Senate and the House, thus denying Democrats the usual minority party power to bring a halt to legislative business. The GOP legislative majorities

William M. Schreiber, a Democratic party activist and strategist at the local, state, and national levels, has taught American government and politics at Butler University, the University of Indianapolis, and Indiana University–Purdue University at Indianapolis. Known for his political commentary on several Indianapolis television stations, Schreiber is Executive Assistant to Indiana Lieutenant Governor Frank O'Bannon. He recently wrote Burgoo!!, *a one-man play about Harry S. Truman's vice-president, Alben Barkley.*

included a Marion County delegation of eight state senators and 15 state representatives. Ironically, the election of 1968 was the last election in which Marion County elected its legislators at-large countywide.

As if Marion County's political power was not enough, the governor elected in 1968 was also a Republican, one who had been nominated in the hotly contested Indiana Republican State Convention in which Marion County Republicans exercised the balance of power. In a three-way race that included Purdue dean of agriculture Earl Butz and Speaker of the House Otis Bowen, former Secretary of State Edgar Whitcomb received his party's nomination only after he received 294 of Marion County's 346 delegate votes.

In two consecutive elections held a year apart, Marion County Republicans put together the basic political elements that would be necessary to advance the concept of metropolitan or consolidated government in Indianapolis and Marion County:

1. the election of an articulate Republican mayor of Indianapolis;
2. the election of quorum-meeting Republican majorities in both chambers of the Indiana General Assembly;
3. the election of an all-Republican legislative delegation from Marion County;
4. the election of a Republican governor with a tremendous political debt to Marion County Republicans.

The Passage of Unigov

When the legislature convened on January 9, 1969, the public was already aware of Marion County Republican plans to consolidate Indianapolis and Marion County governments. The Task Force on Governmental Reorganization had announced its final recommendations just before Christmas. During the next month, a Lawyers Task Force comprised of highly skilled pro bono attorneys drafted the actual legislative proposal which came to be known generally as Unigov (from "unified government"). Realizing that the unique set of political circumstances might never recur, the draft was defused to the greatest extent possible of anything that might be politically controversial. These "anticipatory responses" included the exclusion of the 11 city and county school districts from consolidation; the exclusion of the cities of Beech Grove, Lawrence, and Speedway from full consolidation; the exclusion of city and county police from consolidation; the similar exclusion of city and suburban fire departments from consolidation; and the retention of the township system of administering poor relief.

Of greater significance, the drafters provided that Indianapolis and Marion County would be consolidated by legislative fiat. Not since the Honolulu–Honolulu County, Hawaii, merger of 1907 had a city-county consolidation been effected without a referendum. It is reasonable to inquire as to why in 1969 Indianapolis merged with Marion County on the sole basis of legislative action.

First, only seven of 29 consolidation referenda during the past 50 years had been successful. Of the eight held outside the South, none had been successful. The certainty of legislative action as opposed to a 25 percent chance (at best) by referendum was obviously an easy choice for Marion County Republican leaders.

Second, Indiana had no provision in its Constitution for a binding referendum. Instead, it had a tradition of advisory referenda, the results of which could be submitted to the next General Assembly for concurrence. Since the Indiana legislature would not meet again until January 1971 and since Democrats could be expected to control more than one-third of the seats in at least one legislative chamber and thereby regain the power to deny a quorum, final legislative action was required in 1969.

Finally, the only other alternative was a constitutional amendment, which Mayor Lugar described as "very hard to come by in Indiana and usually a six-year process."[1] Since the real thrust of Unigov was political and not governmental, no method of consolidation that could not be accomplished before 1971 and that year's mayoral election was acceptable.

In any event, the lopsided GOP majorities in the House and Senate eased Unigov's passage. Legislators were lobbied, Lugar said, "in groups of five or six. We saw 91 out of 127 of them in this way, and made fairly accurate head counts."[2] Of equal importance, the Marion County house delegation made peace with Speaker Bowen, who was still smarting from his loss of the gubernatorial nomination at the hands of Marion County Republicans. Bowen's support, or acquiescence at a minimum, was critical, since the speaker had life-or-death power over pending legislation.

On March 13, 1969, Governor Whitcomb signed the Unigov statute into law, less than three months after the consolidation proposal became public. Today, nearly a quarter of a century later, an inventory of Unigov shows little governmental change has occurred.

Unigov in Retrospect

Eleven separate public school systems continue to exist, disturbed only by a federal judge's order that African-American inner-city students be bused to six of the surrounding township school systems. This order resulted from the judge's finding that the specific exclusion of the schools from the consolidation constituted de jure segregation. (Four systems escaped the busing order. The Pike Township and Washington Township systems were found to have adequate indigenous black populations. Beech Grove and Speedway, as "excluded cities" in the Unigov statute, were found to have special legal standing. Lawrence, the other "excluded city," was not similarly situated since it shared a school system with its township.)

The township system of poor relief survives, freeing the affluent in suburbia from sharing the financial burden associated with this level of welfare. Townships themselves precede the Constitution of the United States, having been prescribed by the Northwest Ordinance that many believe to be the single greatest accomplishment of our fledgling nation under the Articles of Confederation during the 1780s.

Public safety—police and fire departments, specifically—continues to evade consolidation. Despite the claim of Mayor Lugar's successor, Bill Hudnut, that taxes are paid only for services actually received, property owners in the old city who pay for and receive police protection from the Indianapolis Police Department also pay for—shall we say subsidize?—the Marion County Sheriff's patrol, which covers only those areas outside the old city.

In fact, more taxing districts exist today than existed when consolidation originally occurred. This reality conflicts with the experience in Nashville, Tennessee, where a two-tiered tax system replaced the preconsolidation hodgepodge. It indicates that government in Indianapolis and Marion County has become increasingly fragmented despite the cosmetics of consolidation.

Metropolitan Politics

If Unigov is not, then, an example of consolidated government, what is it? Perhaps L. Keith Bulen, GOP power broker during the late 1960s and early 1970s, was correct when he characterized Unigov in an interview with the *Wall Street Journal* as "my greatest coup of all time, moving out there and taking in 85,000 Republicans."

Democrats, who had won seven of ten mayoralty contests prior to Unigov, have lost six consecutive mayor's races since 1969. Only in the 1975 election, held in the aftermath of the Watergate scandal, was the Democratic candidate even competitive. Upon inspection, Unigov may not qualify as metropolitan government, but it is clearly a premier example of metropolitan politics. While African-American representation on the City-County Council does approximate the black population for the first time, this phenomenon is more a tribute to single-member districts and the demise of at-large elections of the council than anything else. Equating the power of a minority (blacks) within a minority (Democrats) on a fragmented city council to that of a strong mayor who appoints all executive officials, has a line-item veto, and has unlimited tenure potential raises sophistry to unprecedented heights.

Even so, Hudnut's sensitivity to "the black question" requires a consideration of whether the passage of Unigov was racially motivated. At least one federal trial court judge, affirmed by numerous federal judges at the appellate level, concluded that Unigov was an example of de jure segregation.

That blacks were at the threshold of real political power in Indianapolis before Unigov is probable when power is defined as the ability to control nominations in the usual majority party. In 1970, blacks comprised 47 percent of a Democratic electorate in the old city that included a great but unknown number of independents. Based on black voting cohesion—a reality in Indianapolis—and the likelihood that the black percentage of the Democratic vote in a primary election would be higher than the black percentage of the Democratic vote in a general election because white independents would join the Democratic coalition only in the general election, blacks had acquired real political clout in Indianapolis. At minimum, they held the balance of power. At maximum, they were the dominant force. While blacks might not be able to ensure the election of a black mayor, they were in a position to elect a mayor who was sensitive to black interests.

Next, according to William R. Keech, there is a point at which government becomes responsive to black interests in a competitive two-party system.[3] This point may be called the threshold of governmental response and appears to lie somewhere between the 25 and 30 percent levels of the black electorate. In 1969, blacks comprised approximately 25 percent of the old city electorate but only about 14 percent of the expanded Unigov electorate. Governmental response, of course, may be positive or negative. Without ascribing racist motives, it is at least possible that the passage of Unigov can be interpreted as a negative governmental response in the context of Keech's theory.

Finally, the notion that Unigov was a result of racial malice gains credibility when related to the threshold of white hostility identified by Donald R. Matthews and James W. Prothro in their 1963 study of black voter registration and participation in the South. They concluded that "there would seem to be a critical point, at about 30 percent Negro, where white hostility to Negro political participation becomes severe."[4] Since the black population in pre-Unigov Indianapolis was 27 percent (and higher if it is true that the census undercounts inner-city, predominantly black residents), the passage of Unigov may be interpreted in Matthews-Prothro terms as an example of "white hostility."

What is clear is that consolidation diluted black voting power in Indianapolis. Whether it did so as a side effect or a primary purpose is difficult to determine, although there is strong circumstantial evidence that it may have been the latter, quite possibly at an unconscious level. Lee Sloan and Robert M. French reached a similar conclusion in their appraisal of local government mergers:

> Governmental consolidation may be emerging as a new means of dealing with the growing black threat to the existing political structure. . . . local political elites may be deceiving themselves as well as others in failing to face the racial realities behind governmental reorganization.[5]

If Unigov was an exercise in metropolitan politics rather than metropolitan government, which seems clear from the record, then Democrats were the primary victims of the consolidation of Indianapolis and Marion County governments. To the extent that blacks were and continue to be oriented toward the Democratic party, they may be seen as secondary victims. This is to suggest that blacks may have been victimized because of their partisan preferences rather than their race.

The Legacy of Unigov

Some urban scientists believe that the most important and necessary attribute that will allow local government to succeed is flexibility, since different services should be offered in different geographic areas that are determined by economy of scale. They argue that the greatest danger to urban government is the rigidity that arises from institutionalizing government and in an artificial geography.[6] Furthermore, they suggest that informal arrangements among local governments that can be altered as necessary provide the best opportunity for quality governance at the local level.

Consolidating Indianapolis and Marion County in order to perpetuate the political power of the Republican party was cynical beyond description. And since the right to vote for mayor was virtually the only thing that Unigov extended countywide, metropolitan politics should not be misinterpreted as metropolitan government.

NOTES

1. "Three Mayors Review Their Governments," *Nation's Cities*, November 1969.

2. Ibid.

3. William R. Keech, *The Impact of Negro Voting* (Chicago: Rand McNally, 1968), 101.

4. Donald R. Matthews and James W. Prothro, "Social and Economic Factors and Negro Voter Registration in the South," *American Political Science Review* 57, no. 1 (March 1963): 29.

5. Lee Sloan and Robert M. French, "Black Rule in the Urban South," *Transaction* (November–December 1971): 30.

6. Vincent Ostrom et al., "The Organization of Government in Metropolitan Areas," *American Political Science Review* 55, no. 4 (December 1961): 831–42.

Amos C. Brown III

I arrived in Indianapolis in April 1975, five years after the creation of Unigov, as the city was beginning to blossom. I was a 24-year-old native Chicagoan whose only knowledge of this city was that it was Indiana's capital and held an auto race in May, the Indianapolis 500.

My first impression of Indianapolis was that it was a sleepy city, with a small boring downtown of three tall buildings. While large in land area, in terms of people the city seemed small. I didn't learn till several months later that Indianapolis was home to some 790,000, including some 150,000 African-Americans.

There was a different feel to Indianapolis. It didn't seem midwestern; it seemed more southern. Language had something to do with that. Partly it was the twang many Hoosiers have in their voices, but there were other linguistic clues. For example, people didn't call buses "buses," they called them "coaches." When you went into a store, clerks asked, "Do you want a sack?" instead of "Do you want a bag?"

When it came to race, there were other contradictions. There were obviously segregated neighborhoods, yet there were neighborhoods, especially on the north and northwest sides of the city, where blacks and whites lived side by side in nice large houses on large lots or in apartment complexes.

Unlike Chicago, Indianapolis seemed to have no streets or neigh-

---

Amos C. Brown III, a 1972 graduate of the Northwestern University School of Speech, is Director of Strategic Research for three Indianapolis radio stations, a television station, and the country's third-oldest African-American newspaper. He is also a highly visible personality as host of WAV-TV's "Noon Show," an Indianapolis version of "Crossfire."

borhoods that blacks entered, or moved into, at their own peril. But my first week in the city, my boss, who was black, said, "You can live anywhere you want to in Indianapolis, except you don't want to live south of Washington Street. That's 'Kentucky.' "

While most neighborhoods appeared open, there were other signs of, if not closure, then creeping intolerance. Blacks were not visible in the pages of the city's two newspapers. The afternoon *News* seemed to showcase blacks only on the obituary pages. The morning *Star* rarely featured them at all. It even seemed that the papers rewrote AP and UPI wire service stories, changing the word *black* to *Negro*.

You rarely saw black faces on TV newscasts and never saw blacks in local TV commercials or on a billboard. A white police reporter on the number one radio station occasionally referred to black suspects as "colored."

But after spending more than 19 years in Indianapolis, I must say that in many respects our city has changed for the better. Still, many contradictions remain, especially as they concern the one out of four citizens who is part of the 178,000-strong African-American community. (The 1993 population estimate was made by ACB Data Consulting and Amos Brown.)

The period 1976 through 1991, the Hudnut years, did benefit many of the city's African-Americans, regardless of what some may write, say, or think. But the entrepreneurial spirit of the Hudnut years masked some serious problems and flaws in Indianapolis, especially in its African-American community. Hudnut's vaunted public-private partnership and both the black and the white communities must address these problems and flaws if the investments Indianapolis made in the Hudnut years are to be protected and enhanced.

To keep Indianapolis from remaining a backwater state capital, the city's public and private leadership took risks and chances to achieve the objective of building a successful new city. In the main, that entrepreneurial risk taking worked. I'm convinced that without unified government and without that risk taking, the old city (downtown) would be a financial cripple, nearly bankrupt, with high taxes on top of a deteriorated tax base and infrastructure. The growing businesses, both industrial and service, would be in the suburbs, which would have the low tax rates necessary for economic growth, at the old city's expense. Some 80 percent of the city's minorities would be living in the old city, but because of the crippled financial state, social services and assistance would be severely lacking.

While we've avoided that doomsday scenario, building a city on an entrepreneurial vision does have one major flaw: the entrepreneur, while worrying about the big picture, fails to notice cracks in the foundation and facade of the city. It happens to entrepreneurial businesses all the time. The business matures yet fails to keep pace with its growth and the problems that growth creates. The same happens to entrepreneurial cities, including Indianapolis. How has it affected Indianapolis's African-American community? During the Hudnut years, my community changed from a community some sociologists called "one of the nation's most segregated" into one with less rigid residential segregation patterns. When the Hudnut years began, 70 percent of blacks lived in the northern third of Center Township, the so-called inner city. Today, I estimate that just 42 percent of the city's black population live there.

Indianapolis's reputation as a rigidly segregated city isn't borne out by the facts. An analysis I did using 1990 census data at the political precinct level showed that only 57.1 percent of blacks lived in a segregated neighborhood (one 70 percent or more black). That same study found that more than a third of the city's blacks (34 percent) lived in majority white neighborhoods. The number of blacks moving into integrated areas continues to grow, while the number of blacks in rigidly segregated neighborhoods continues to decline.

The much-heralded public-private partnership, the city's emphasis on amateur sports, and its aggressive job-creation efforts paid off in increased employment opportunities for all citizens, including African-Americans.

Even though Indianapolis lost more than 20,000 manufacturing jobs during the Hudnut years, it experienced a net gain of some 70,000 jobs.

Employment in the black community has always been strong, buttressed by a strong black employee base in service and blue-collar occupations. However, the employment shifts in Indianapolis put that record to the test. Notwithstanding the sharp drop in manufacturing jobs in the '70s and '80s, an additional 15,367 African-Americans were employed during the Hudnut years, despite a loss of nearly 5,200 black manufacturing jobs.

During the Hudnut years the number of African-Americans holding executive, managerial, professional, and technical jobs rose by 47.8 percent; those in sales, clerical, and administrative support jobs increased by 30.5 percent; those in service jobs rose by 23.4 percent; while the number in blue-collar occupations declined by 11.5 percent.

Black employment in a variety of nonmanufacturing industries rose sharply during the Hudnut years, with gains of 66 percent in retail sales; 73 percent in health services; 73 percent in finance, insurance, and real estate; 86 percent in business and repair services; 41 percent in transportation; and 28 percent in construction.

A hearty employment picture among blacks led to the corollary: low unemployment. In 1990, black unemployment in Indianapolis was just 12.1 percent, the seventh-lowest black unemployment rate of any major U.S. city. Today, with overall unemployment at 4.6 percent, black unemployment is estimated at 11.2 percent (ACB Data Consulting estimate).

This has resulted in a vibrant income picture for blacks in Indianapolis. While declining slightly in actual terms during the '80s, black income in Indianapolis was higher than that for blacks in the state, the nation, and most major cities. The 1990 census reported that the black median household income in Indianapolis was $19,928, compared with $29,152 for all households. That was the 12th highest among the nation's top 25 cities and 10th highest among the 35 largest black communities, according to ACB Data Consulting.

In spite of this good news, there are some dark sides to the story of Indianapolis, in terms of its minority community. The progress of the Hudnut years missed many persons living in the "inner city," Center Township. Even though the township contains the city's downtown gentrified neighborhoods, Center Township is the city's poorest area. Forty-five percent of the city's households earning less that $10,000 are there.

For blacks in Center Township, the figure is bleaker. Blacks there are older, far poorer, and less educated than those living in the rest of Indianapolis, especially on the city's north, northwest, and northeast sides. Median black income in the inner city is just $13,800. Sixty-five percent of blacks earning less than $10,000 live in Center Township. Of the township's 56 census tracts, 17 have black median incomes of less than $10,000.

Not only did more and more members of the black middle class leave the inner city; they were joined by the black working class. Of blacks earning between $10,000 and $25,000 yearly, only 44 percent live in Center Township. In the inner city, slightly more than a third of blacks, 36.5 percent, live below the poverty level. Slightly more than half, 52.9 percent, graduated from high school and just 4.6 percent graduated from college.

One of the bright spots for the Indianapolis African-American community has been home ownership. Some 43 percent of blacks own their own homes, the seventh-highest percentage among major cities, and nearly 60 percent of blacks live in a single-family home. But in the inner city, black home ownership has become a problem because of high tax rates on low-valued property. During the Hudnut years, the number of black home owners declined 7 percent in inner-city areas. The average value of the homes of those remaining is slightly under $30,000.

Contrasting with this bleak picture for blacks in the inner city is the bright picture for blacks in the rest of Indianapolis, especially those living in the northern third of the city, the areas north of 38th Street. This part of the city, home to 36 percent of the city's population, is home to 40 percent of its black population.

Blacks in the northern third of the city not only live more often in an integrated area but also have far higher income and education levels than blacks in the rest of the city. The median black household income in the northern third of the city ranges from $25,332 to $29,457, more than double the inner-city black median income. Black poverty rates in this area range from 10 percent to 16 percent. High school graduation rates range from 77 percent to 85 percent, with college graduation rates ranging from 13 percent to 20 percent. Black unemployment there is between 6 percent and 10 percent, lower than for blacks citywide.

During the Hudnut years, black home ownership in the northern third of the city increased from 40 percent to 60 percent. The area is home to 38 percent of the black working class (those earning from $10,000 to $25,000), 46 percent of the black middle class (those earning from $25,000 to $50,000), and 61 percent of the city's black upper class (those making more than $50,000).

This dichotomy between African-Americans in the northern third of the city and the inner city—the division of blacks into two communities, the haves and the have nots—is one of the most troubling aspects of today's Indianapolis.

Another problem area is education. In my opinion, one of the failures of the Hudnut years was the noninvolvement by Hudnut's vaunted public-private partnership in improving our city's schools, especially the Indianapolis Public Schools. Indianapolis is plagued with a high dropout rate. One of every six persons aged 16 to 19 in Indianapolis is not in school and never graduated. Indianapolis's overall dropout rate is ninth highest of any major city; among blacks it's the 11th highest of any major city. The black dropout rate is highest in Center Township (22 percent), but surprisingly, it is also high in the northern third of the city, 18.5 percent in Pike Township and 16.5 percent in Lawrence Township.

Among blacks there is high dissatisfaction with the educational system. It is fueled in part by a widely held perception that racial busing helped to destroy the value of black neighborhood schools. The prevailing feeling among Indianapolis's blacks is that integrated schools are not receiving the type of support and nurturing they would have received in schools in their neighborhoods, with African-Americans bearing the brunt.

Education is a problem in Indianapolis that requires an entrepreneurial solution, a solution of the public-private partnership. However, the community's will to treat education the way we treated the building of the Hoosier Dome or obtaining the United Airlines project is lacking.

Compounding the other problems is race relations. The attitudes that I recounted at the start of this critique still exist in Indianapolis. Almost daily I hear of stories of mistreatment of blacks at the hands of nonblacks. These stories, some true, some embellished, unfortunately help fuel a prevailing attitude of benign neglect and callousness by whites toward blacks.

The general laissez-faire nature of this city's African-American community is an important factor. We can come together across ideological, economic, and political lines to create positive events such as Indiana Black Expo, the largest exposition of its kind in the nation, and the Circle City Classic, the nation's second-largest black sporting event. We can come together to raise hundreds of thousands of dollars for organizations such as the United Negro College Fund. Yet we can't seem to harness those same entrepreneurial and volunteer energies to create a similar spirit among whites (and blacks) to confront the basic, difficult problems facing the races in Indianapolis.

And hanging over the black community, like a queasy feeling in one's stomach, is the Michael Taylor case. One of the contradictions in this city is that for our size, we're not a very violent community. In spite of the frightening images on the local evening news, for the size of this city (812,000) our homicide rate is relatively low. And for the size of the black community, it is very low. Black homicides ranged from 71 in 1991, to 86 in 1992, to 63 in 1993. The relatively low level of violence, even though crime gangs are growing in our city, means it's still possible to build bridges between the community and law enforcement. Our moderate crime level means we can still effect cooperation between citizens and their police. But blocking that cooperation, within the black community, is the lingering aftertaste of the Michael Taylor killing, a watershed in the black community's relations with its city.

The problem of police fatal shootings of black suspects began in the mid-1970s, reaching a peak with the Taylor case. In the black community, this case has taken on some of the tragicomic aspects of the JFK assassination case: numerous conspiracy theories; advocates, both credible and incredible, offer "evidence" of plots and conspiracies. The net result is a continuing climate of distrust and disbelief in the good will of whites and the continued slow erosion of race relations and tolerance in this city.

Contradictions. That's what the Hudnut years mean to me. Dizzying heights of great accomplishment. Growth and development that translated into progress in incomes, employment, education levels, home ownership, residential integration for many African-Americans. But for other African-Americans, mainly those living in the inner city, the Hudnut years meant a deteriorating public school system, increased poverty, and hopelessness. And for the whole African-American community, lingering distrust of whites and of law enforcement, and a judicial system that they perceive as unfair.

If we as a city, black and white, don't come to grips with these ills and repair them, then the massive investments and progress made during the Hudnut years will have been for naught.

Dennis J. West

I am a lifelong resident of Indianapolis. My parents bought their first and only home on what was in 1953 the easternmost edge of the city. I grew up in Irvington, while my grandparents both lived on the west side, in Haughville. This physical relationship helped me to be an observer of the city and its development during our weekly travels east to west and back again.

I am also a part of the baby boom, a generation which has bridged significant transformations. Although we had parents who were factory workers and union members, many of us have never been in a factory, having been the beneficiaries of higher education which has carried us beyond our parent's standard of living. We are also part of the generation which bridged between segregation to fair housing, discrimination to equal opportunity, and from centralized to the launch of many self-help and community-directed activities.

The years during which Bill Hudnut served as mayor of the city (1976–91) spanned some significant transitions. Some of these transitions included economic restructuring, leadership transitions, governance, suburbanization, the effects of urban renewal, the maturing of the baby-boom generation, and the evolution of a transportation system. These issues were not necessarily ones which promoted cohe-

---

Dennis J. West has served as President of Eastside Community Investments since 1984. ECI serves the near east side of Indianapolis supporting a mission aimed at creating wealth and building community. He became a resident of the Highland-Brookside community in 1980 and became involved with ECI in 1981 as a member of its Board of Directors. Dennis continues to reside in the Highland-Brookside area with his wife, daughter, and son.

sion. In fact, as I will describe them, they were the sources of significant disruption. Yet through this period Hudnut helped lead a city, and in some important ways, manage people through these changes.

Economic Factors

In 1969, one out of every 4.5 nonfarm workers in the United States worked in Fortune 500 companies. There was a significant presence of manufacturing and factory jobs. For my peers who were not going to college, Indianapolis appeared to be ringed with opportunity. My friends had a clear expectation that their high school diplomas would land them in a factory if that was their choice. Such an opportunity would probably mean a job of at least $10 per hour plus overtime plus benefits. All the factories had personnel offices, and all were accepting applications. We had Ford, Chrysler, RCA, International Harvester, Schwitzer, Allison, Jenn-Air, Chevrolet, Insley, Western Electric, and Mallory—factories where the prospect of lifetime employment with benefits seemed likely. Many I knew were on the same course as their fathers.

The world has changed greatly since 1969. We have been on a straight line of decline with respect to jobs in the Fortune 500s. By the end of Mayor Hudnut's tenure the ratio of employees in Fortune 500 companies to other companies had declined to fewer than one in ten nonfarm workers.

An illustration of the change is the evolution of RCA. In the 1960s it employed 15,000 persons in Indianapolis. Today, after two acquisitions, Thomson Consumer Electronics employs 1,800 workers, 1,100 of whom are white-collar employees. This same story played out several times through our city's recent history. As Hudnut pointed out, by 1980 Indianapolis had two times as many jobs in the service sector of our economy as in the manufacturing sector—a complete reverse from the period following World War II. The economy which had mass produced products had mass created opportunity and had brought economic progress for many families. But suddenly that economy was passing away before many others were able to enjoy the same economic strides. Minorities and women, who in many cases had been victims of discrimination, never achieved the job security, the high wages and benefits, which characterized this period.

What was confounding about these changes was that at first it seemed that they were caused by economic recession. But as time went along, the words "structural change" floated into our city vocabulary. We were one generation removed from lifetime employment; the average job tenure by the end of the 1980s was under 4.5 years.

Leadership Transitions

The changes affecting our economy also affected city leadership. Corporate restructuring meant new leaders coming to town while others disappeared. Institutions such as Western Electric—which had seemed so new, large, modern and permanent when I was a child—were part of an unimaginable era, one in which a major employer could simply close and call it quits. The 1980s also brought deregulation and waves of acquisitions and mergers. Those who were less familiar with the city were suddenly part of its corporate leadership. Indianapolis was often described as a community of "good old boys." The very familiar names continued to be part of the visible leadership scene, but new names were beginning to appear.

Beginning with Mayor Barton, Indianapolis had created a forum, the Greater Indianapolis Progress Committee, where civic leaders and citizens could debate and formulate issues of civic import for the mayor. Mayor Hudnut used GIPC to broaden the debate by including neighborhood leaders and even some whose views might be controversial. This transition has, I think, continued to evolve and Indianapolis continues to greatly value its diversity of leadership.

Unigov has generally been discussed in the context of its effect on the political landscape, through the consolidation of government which supported a larger tax base. Suddenly a bunch of folks were now citizens who had heretofore been part of a town, community, or subdivision which was outside of Indianapolis. All of a sudden small towns and subdivisions were referred to as neighborhoods. The mayor's office sought to catalogue these "neighborhoods" and quickly built a list of over 100 neighborhoods with whom it would regularly communicate.

This extension of nomenclature was important to the incorporation of these new pieces of the city, which otherwise would have lost their identities. It was, however, painful to those of us who had consciously chosen to live in an "urban neighborhood." Our badge of uniqueness, the name which said that we had chosen a different lifestyle, was given over to . . . subdivisions. The good for the city was a descriptor of uniformity, the harm is that funding streams designated for urban neighborhoods seemed to now inevitably lead to editorials which question "why money is wasted in 'urban neighborhoods or targeted neighborhoods' because our neighborhood has needs too."

Urban Renewal

Urban renewal coupled with the development of the interstate system created one of the most dramatic transformations in our city. I remember my first exposure to urban renewal, which was probably project A or B at the intersection of New York Street and White River Parkway. Along the south side of New York Street there were several homes belonging to families who would sit on their porches throughout the hot summer. I remember them vividly; one part of the ritual on our return home from my grandparents' house was to wave to those families. One day, large signs were posted and shortly thereafter the families and then their houses were gone. Urban renewal and development of the interstate system greatly changed the feeling and function of neighborhoods in Indianapolis for decades. It was the source for enormous mistrust by citizens of their government. It disrupted the patterns of neighborhood commerce and markets, often with fatal effects. My father would take us to a cafeteria called Zaph's located at 1000 East Market. This became a ritual on his pay days. The interstate took Zaph's parking lot and made the business virtually inaccessible. First the business went out and now the building has been vacant for nearly a decade.

The urban renewal initiative had nearly dissipated by the time Mayor Hudnut took office. However, its effects on residents of Center Township were significant, causing many, particularly African-Americans whose communities were most often eradicated or disrupted, to have lasting distrust for government and its intentions. After college I spent four and one half years working in city government during Mayor Hudnut's tenure. There were times when we tried to promote low-cost or deferred-payment rehabilitation loans to residents of Center Township. Among elderly African-Americans we were often confronted with a widely held theory that this was just another way for the city to "get the land." As a result, we found it hard to promote many programs.

Model Cities

On the heels of urban renewal and the interstate's development came the Model Cities program, probably the first significant effort by government, federal and local, to invest in targeted urban neighborhoods. Model Cities seemed to have had two deleterious effects. First, the seemingly omnipotent government, which had taken land for highways and urban-renewal developments, was exposed as impotent when it came to community revitalization. Second, many city officials never understood that dynamic. Even now there are many former city employees who continue to believe that they were victims of the lack of community cooperation. They believed that the plan which they had developed was good and that the seeds of revitalization would have been sown and that dramatic improvement would have followed quickly, if only the people would have cooperated. They did not understand enough about their own history and the calluses of distrust which had built up because of the highways and urban renewal. They did not understand that markets evolve and can be built but they are not simply placed in neighborhoods. My contemporaries in city government were often facing neighborhood meetings in which a citizen would say, "The city promised us a shopping center, how is it coming?" Model Cities was long on maps and short on market reality. They also did not understand that their plans had precluded the "ownership" of those intended to be beneficiaries. Model Cities had the effect of making distrust mutual; government officials in many cases were as mistrusting of residents of urban neighborhoods as the citizens had become of their government.

Model Cities set the stage for the development of community-based institutions, and in particular community development corporations. CDCs came out of their communities, most often led by community residents. Indianapolis was one of the early supporters of this movement.

Demographics

A few weeks ago, my daughter and I were having breakfast at a McDonalds at Tenth and Bosart. There was a group of men who appeared to be in their sixties and who also appeared to have a regular

Saturday morning breakfast appointment. The focus of their conversation was World War II. I have often marveled at what a cohesive force the war was for our parent's generation. The conflict meant that a significant segment of our society was trained together and thrust into a common cause. When they triumphantly returned home, they entered a workforce which was also dominated by large institutions, factories, and unions. By the same token their social institutions were also large. Mainline denominations dominated the religious landscape, large institutions dominated social services, and political parties had large cohesive networks—precincts, wards, and committee workers all had roles, responsibilities and status.

In contrast, the baby boom had its war, but it was not a force in training as many of us were hopeful of avoiding the conflict in Vietnam. Our war did not provide a training point for my generation and clearly it was not a point for social cohesion. In fact our war ripped our society and families apart. We were raised in periods of strong examination where right and wrong were being reshaped before our eyes and with many of us active in the marches and means which shaped and reshaped the values of the nation. We hit our adult ages when questioning had become a norm, public discourse a gift, and social progress a cause.

This seems to me to be another significant transformation about our city and society. We were brought into this world under a far different set of experiences than our parents. Many of the large institutions which were of our parent's generation were not relevant to us. In fact, most were in decline as the boomers moved into decision making positions. This state of transition has been particularly relevant as we have moved from the end of Mayor Hudnut's tenure.

Desegregation

Indianapolis was a segregated city. Indianapolis's schools were segregated. Federal courts pushed Indianapolis to remedy the situation, and this was done with a one-way busing order. One-way busing had a significant and deleterious effect on major parts of Center Township. Good-paying jobs, interstate access, and housing policy which promoted new suburban development pushed the city toward urban sprawl. This was further exacerbated by the one-way busing order. We knew friends who had lived in Woodruff Place in Center Township. Their children went to three different schools in the first three years of court-ordered busing. By the fourth year, they too had moved to the suburbs, where they possessed some choice over the schools their children attended.

Large parts of Center Township saw housing markets stall or erode. Areas which were largely single family in character became difficult areas in which to move property. The population losses were only compounded by lending institutions that would not lend money. When I bought my first house on the near east side of Indianapolis it was generally acknowledged that only First Federal Savings and Loan, now First Indiana Bank, would make mortgages in the community.

Hudnut's Style

All of these issues speak to an unsettled time of transition. But in the early days Mayor Hudnut was a different type of leader. He was unusually accessible and listening. He regularly went on radio call-in shows and listened to citizens about the performance of city government. He brought aides with him who took down information, and he promised immediate response and action. This style was not always the easiest style if one was a bureaucrat. The day's schedule was totally disrupted if your project or program was the source of a dissatisfied phone caller, for radio phone programs are not about due process. The point remains that the mayor stood for the opportunity to allow citizens to sound off about their government with the promise of results to address the issue.

As the mayor ran the city, he paid great attention to details which frustrated the common person. Chuckholes, snow removal, street repair, and trash removal seemed to be at the heart of what concerned people. As a result, that was very much a part of what the city did well. Hudnut seemed to be able to use his base of popular good will to build an agenda of development projects which were acceptable to the public. I think that the acceptability could be characterized as the quid pro quo for listening to people and attending to their basic concerns first. By being accessible and listening to citizens and providing regular venues to listen but then responding with a sense of urgency and conviction, Hudnut built a mandate to develop a major agenda for downtown development and amateur athletics. In a time when so much was unsettled, Hudnut represented himself and his administration as one which could be trusted. He listened to the stories and struggles of the common man and woman, and they at least respected him and many of them loved him.

This was a terribly unsettling problem for would-be neighborhood activists. The man's commitment to access put him in a position where he was absolved from nearly any confrontation. For the past 14 years I have been involved in different aspects of neighborhood development. There were many times when people were fed up with some aspect of the city's response to an issue affecting their community. Hudnut would come out and be totally disarming. He would shake everyone's hand, pat people on the back, inquire about them personally, and diffuse the energy of confrontation.

Hudnut's leadership style bound much of Indianapolis in support for his agenda. His popularity spoke for itself in terms of his popular vote achievements. His ability to energize a room is legend. On many occasions he would appear at our ribbon cuttings or groundbreakings and his effect alone would shift the mood of everyone present into a true celebration. In completing a project you would naturally feel good about what had been accomplished, but Hudnut had a gift to imbue the same joy of accomplishment to all who were assembled. The transfer of energy was awesome and inspiring.

Hudnut and the Economy

The Hudnut Administrations oversaw one of the greatest structural changes that we may see in our lifetime. Through the Hudnut years the communications era advanced. The ability to process information expanded exponentially. The United States economy changed rapidly, too. We moved from a society of producers to a society of processors. We saw many large factories close. In the near east side where I live and work, Schwitzer, Insley, Mallory, A&P, Pepsi, Thomson Consumer Electronics, and Nabisco all left facilities standing vacant. Millions of square feet of factory space sits as a reminder of a time when blue-collar work and lifetime employment seemed to be an opportunity for many. Unfortunately, this only represents a small piece of the issues which the city was to face, as large companies down-sized, restructured, consolidated, or went offshore.

Indianapolis as part of the Rust Belt generally managed through this period. The city set up an Indianapolis Economic Development

Corporation (IEDC) which has served as ombudsman, packager of incentives, and promoter of the city. IEDC showed that the city was not paralyzed in the face of economic restructuring; in fact it was proactive. A product of this period, as we emerged out of the recession of the late '70s, was to begin to express every economic activity in terms of jobs created. It was important to create jobs, but the quality of jobs and thus the quality of the investment was not always part of the equation. We had developed economic tools which primed the economic pump, but the tools assumed that the well had not gone dry. In very real terms the structural nature of the changes of our economy caused us to lose valuable time with respect to education, skill development for workers and venture and seed capital for entrepreneurs because our tools were aimed at what had been and not what could be. The counting methods used to gauge economic success can mask real economic activity. Recently the *Economist* reported that "America's economy has one and a half times more janitors than investment bankers, stockbrokers, lawyers, accountants, and computer programmers put together."

Hudnut and Neighborhood Development

Through this period, neighborhoods generally did well. Indianapolis was one of the first cities to consistently contract with community development corporations to do housing and commercial development activities for the areas which they served. The city helped to spark the development of several community development corporations by opening access to its Community Development Block Grant Program via third-party contracts. As a result there was support for a service delivery vehicle in the community and resources being provided by the city in support of its operations. This was a significant development in light of Model Cities. I think that it is fair to say that during their infancy the expectations surrounding the viability or likely success of the community based organizations was not great. Yet the city responded to this new movement of institutions which were being formed in the late seventies with a consistent commitment of financial support.

The efforts of the city and the community development corporations made possible a number of significant projects. Fountain Square did significant commercial and facade improvements, as well as several housing projects. Business Opportunities Systems (BOS) completed dramatic and significant developments along Indiana Avenue. Most notably, it was responsible for the restoration of the Madame C. J. Walker Building and at least three other commercial and office developments along Indiana Avenue. BOS has supported the development of newly constructed houses which fit into its community and has made its mark through conducting significant housing rehabilitation work. BOS was also a partner in the redevelopment of Lockefield Gardens. Serving the area focused around Methodist Hospital, Near North Development Corporation was able to develop an industrial park in partnership with the city. It has worked to stabilize and encourage investment along the Meridian Street Corridor. It has generated a significant number of units in support of the elderly and handicapped through their Kenwood Place developments. It has also created a Science and Technology Park along the canal. ECI also developed an in-city industrial park, the Larry R. Smith Industrial Park. The city helped ECI to capitalize a small business investment company which has been one of a handful of sources for venture capital during the past decade. ECI developed ten limited partnerships, which included the conversion of a school into apartments and a parish house into apartments, and had a significant effect in reusing many of the properties which had been boarded and vacant. ECI also began what is now a series of programs which invest in people. These include the establishment of family day care homes, a microenterprise program, and Basta, a transitional housing program for families who had been victims of domestic violence.

In other parts of the city there were major restoration efforts at the Devington Shopping Center, another adaptive reuse school conversion project, Coburn Place, and the significant revitalization of Massachusetts Avenue, which features new lighting and landscaping along this commercial strip.

During his closing years, Mayor Hudnut engaged corporate leadership to join with the city and community groups to create the Indianapolis Neighborhood Housing Partnership. The partnership was intended to help address the more than 30,000 substandard housing units which exist in Indianapolis. The creation of this intermediary came about to focus corporate, philanthropic, and governmental resources to finance and invest in better quality housing.

The Hudnut administrations had the ability to mobilize creativity and major resources for downtown development and economic development projects. The same kind of creativity and leadership did not transfer as easily to a social agenda. There was an all-out assault to revitalize the downtown and to improve the quality of life as measured in cultural and sports amenities, but the same energy and concern did not transfer to ensuring a minimum quality of life standard for all citizens. This is not to say that Indianapolis lacked innovations. The Hudnut Administration did contract with community development corporations, it did help initiate the Indianapolis Neighborhood Housing Partnership and it established an environmental court which in part expedited orders and hearings for cases of unsafe and unsanitary housing. But in contrast, the downtown required a massive mobilization of capital, both public and private. It required on many occasions for the mayor to challenge the banks to take second looks at projects or make a judgment for the civic good. In neighborhoods there was not the same push to mobilize massive amounts of capital. To those in inner-city communities it appeared that not only public dollars but political capital was being used in the development of downtown, and it was hard not to draw contrasts. Neighborhoods would hear about the kind of resources being put into projects which the city deemed to be key for downtown revitalization and wonder how monies could be mobilized for some things but not others.

I experienced Mayor Hudnut as a compassionate leader who would offer his energy and attention to social issues when he understood the circumstances and plight of citizens. I saw the mayor quickly study and appear before congressional staffers to appeal for an extension of the low-income-housing tax credit. When the mayor understood the issues he was a brilliant spokesperson. He was captivating and persuasive. In 1986, ECI began an event, "Caulk of the Town," where over 1,000 volunteers have annually participated in the weatherization of 100 homes. During that first event we found 13 families who were approaching winter without furnaces. Upon learning this fact Hudnut used many public forums where he would speak about what we had learned. In learning about the issues, Hudnut became an advocate. I think that becoming aware firsthand of issues helped the mayor muster forces toward solving problems. I think that was part of where the drive to establish the Indianapolis Neighborhood Housing Partnership came. The challenge was getting the mayor to own the issue, to cause an unleashing of the energy, enthusiasm, and leadership that would craft a solution.

Hudnut and the Social Fabric

As has been suggested, global changes and local changes through the period of Mayor Hudnut's reign were significant. These changes were substantive and life altering for many families. Hudnut managed through these times and in fact led. Unigov moved Indianapolis from a modest city to the 12th largest in the nation. It also brought about the reality of people being literally subscribed into citizenship. To his credit, Hudnut gained and maintained a strong political mandate. All of the changes and transitions which we were facing gave him a stage upon which he could excel, he could speak, he could persuade, he could energize, and he could lead. The mayor could calm us through a blizzard and mobilize us through the Pan Am Games. He could persuade us to believe that there was still a pulse in our downtown which could be revived, and achieve full recovery.

The times were perfect for the mayor, and in many respects the mayor was perfect for the times. It was a time in which so many transitions challenged a sense of social cohesion, yet Mayor Hudnut, whether you supported his priorities or not, seemed to be able to bind this city and engage people to be supportive and involved.

Fay H. Williams

I ndianapolis, my chosen hometown, is a good place to live and work. It has strong cultural institutions, low unemployment, reasonable living costs, and a friendly atmosphere. The past 20 years have seen it transformed from a rather slow-paced, somewhat isolated city into a town with a renewed civic vitality that is the envy of many communities.

Much of this change is due to the many projects initiated during the years Bill Hudnut was mayor. Those years were characterized by a continuous and sustained effort to move the city in a particular direction, and the administration was able to develop and articulate a clear vision for the city which people understood and many could support, identify opportunities and move quickly to take advantage of the movement, gather allies who controlled the resources necessary to make things happen, and stifle and/or ignore criticism and opposition.

I was surprised to be invited to write my observations of the Hudnut years—surprised because the mayor has expressed displeasure at some of my public comments that indicated my disapproval of the process by which many decisions were made, namely the absence of women and minority participation and the limited opportunity for public discourse. I also happen to be a registered voter of the other party. I am also not an insider to community politics or decision making, but have been an

---

Fay H. Williams is an attorney who has been in private practice in India-napolis for over 20 years and is currently Chairman of the Board of the Union Institute. She has served on the national boards of the League of Women Voters of the United States, the National Civic League, and Common Cause. In India-napolis she has been President of the Board of the Community Service Council and volunteers her time to many civic and cultural institutions.

active citizen mainly in the social-service and civil rights arena since moving to the city the late 1950s. My views are those of a person on the sidelines who occasionally gets close enough to the action to be heard by the major players.

The Mayor as a Personality

I first met Bill Hudnut in the late 1960s when we both served on the board of the Mental Health Association. He became president of the board and even then his leadership style was impressive, but very autocratic. I had no contact with him from that time until he became mayor in the late '70s. It would seem that he had undergone a change of personality from this stiff, formal person to a friendly, outgoing one.

Bill Hudnut is one of the few white males over age 50 that I know who is truly a "boundary crosser." He seems to be genuinely comfortable in all settings and with all people. He is at home preaching, singing, and clapping his hands in the pulpit of Mount Vernon Baptist Church in the inner city as well as marching as a leprechaun in the downtown Saint Patrick's Day parade. He is one of the few white politicians who came to events in the African-American community and stayed after he had spoken. This personality endeared him to lots of people, and even when we disagreed, we respected this trait.

I also know, however, that he can be thin-skinned and can retaliate against those who have disagreed with his programs. But nobody's perfect, and this personality, this "civic entrepreneur" and boundary crosser, gave our city a renewed spirit. The mayor could bring out the best in those areas that he chose, and during his years in City Hall we saw massive capital improvements using both public and private money. The nature of the projects meant that it was a game only a very few could play—and the rest of us had to watch.

Assessing the Administration

I have given considerable thought to how this critique could be structured so that there would be some context to my observations. The National Civic League's Civic Index for measuring city hall performance appeared to be the most appropriate tool to use for this purpose. This index assists communities in developing their problem-solving capacity and helps in evaluating candidates for the All-American City awards. It enables me to present some specific examples of my concerns with supporting rationale, instead of merely stating my views.

Community vision and pride. The Hudnut years represented an era when we demonstrated great pride. We constantly heard what we could be, the focus on amateur sports was developed, and considerable money, public and private, was spent on blockbuster events and encouraging the leadership of many of the sports organizations to relocate to Indianapolis. The mayor was the ever-present cheerleader.

The organizational structures for implementing this vision were created or strengthened and were not governmental entities, but were clearly aligned with city government.

This vision had no room for any other than the good times agenda—and the hard issues like the deteriorating housing stock, declining schools, and high black infant-mortality rates were largely ignored by the top leadership during the early years of the Hudnut Administration.

The middle-class, well-educated person with disposable income had many opportunities to demonstrate civic pride. There were many openings, ribbon cuttings, parades, and hosted events that received national attention. I and many of my women friends liked what was happening but knew we were excluded when the real decisions were made and the priorities determined.

Government performance. City government was at the center of all the activities. It was remarkable that a city that does not have home rule could enjoy the autonomy and freedom to accomplish so much. This required cooperation between state and local government and federal support. It was also necessary to create or strengthen several quasi-governmental organizations to implement part of the vision. The mayor used his appointment powers to place persons friendly to the vision on the boards, and money from the city budget along with private funds enabled these organizations to function. These organizations with their interlocking boards and strong relationships with city government were early examples of the public-private partnership many political figures talked about in the '70s and '80s. They also demonstrated that the old-boy network was not going to be inclusive or share decision making. These organizations could do what government could not do and we could not hold them accountable.

In "Measuring City Hall Performance," published by the National Civic League Press, the introduction states: "Very few people can say with confidence exactly what mayor and local councils do with our money once it has been transferred from our pockets to the city coffers." This is not true of Indianapolis during the Hudnut years. We watched our skyline grow, we saw the Hoosier Dome rise, and we attended events in some of the sports venues built during the period.

I was often troubled by the lack of openness and the absence of clear standards and procedures to govern decision making. I do not believe that any laws were broken, but there were many reasons to suspect conflict of interest on the part of some in leadership roles. Indiana does not require citizen endorsement of many expenditures made by local public officials; nor do we have strong ethics laws governing conflict-of-interest issues. We knew where the money was going, but we had little to say about it—we decided to have the Pan Am Games, but our public parks summer program was cut back. There are few mechanisms in our local government for citizen review of expenditures. This makes it possible for a small group to obligate all of us. We also do not have the ability to recall any official; we must live with them unless a crime is committed. We are fortunate that the Hudnut years made a commitment to a progressive agenda even though the process was not very open or democratic.

Intercommunity and intergovernmental cooperation. Many of the ventures would not have been possible without the cooperation of the surrounding communities and state and federal government: the expansion of the airport landing the United deal, the growth of the Indiana–Purdue campus. A number of people in key leadership roles resided outside of Marion County but had professional and business lives in the city. The mayor appeared to have a very good working relationship with the leaders of other governmental entities in the region.

Citizen participation. This city of neighborhoods has a citizen group organized and usually run by volunteers in nearly every area from the wealthiest to the poorest neighborhood. During the Hudnut years there were regular meetings at City Hall with the leaders of the neighborhood organizations. Although there was a great deal of citizen involvement in neighborhood and civic organizations, these people were not participants in real decision making. The nature of partisan patronage politics in Indianapolis meant that the real decisions about fiscal matters were often made in Republican caucus, and candidates were chosen by the screening committees or conventions of the major political parties. Voter turnout especially in the primary is low, and most issues are not the subject of a public hearing.

Community leadership. We were fortunate to have good leadership in the private and nonprofit sector at the same time. Hudnut was at the reins of the city; the board chair of GIPC led an effort to make that organization more inclusive and democratic; the leaders of the Indianapolis Chamber, United Way, and certain cultural institutes were progressive individuals committed to both the growth of their institutions and the city. They were also more committed to inclusiveness and diversity than the people at the reins of many of the Hudnut initiatives.

Intergroup relations and equal opportunity. There is a minimum of racial conflict and hostility in the city, but Indianapolis is a very segregated city. This might appear to be contradictory, but both are true.

The separation of the races means that most of us have limited contact with people unlike ourselves. Except for a few workplace contacts, there is very little social interaction. Mayor Hudnut made appointments which were firsts for this city, including the appointment of Dr. Lehman Adams, a black dentist, to the board of Citizens Gas and Coke, and the appointment of Paula Parker Sawyer, a black woman, as deputy mayor.

Wherever race was the issue the mayor was clearly on the side of equity and fair play. His very public stand on affirmative-action hiring in the Indianapolis Police Department cast him as an opponent of President Reagan. His administration clearly made many gains in this area.

Deficiencies and Shortcomings

I see several major issues as deficiencies in the Hudnut years.

Decision making was not broadly shared. The structure of our city government and the political culture tend to eliminate the need for broad-based decision making. We are not a city that enjoys home rule, and the rationale of partisan patronage politics makes it possible to bypass the public on many important decisions. The planning and implementation of major projects was achieved with a very few people. Even City-County Council decisions and strategies could be arrived at in secret because of the overwhelming Republican majority on the council. Women and minorities were conspicuous by their absence—we watched from the sidelines. There was a great deal to cheer, but we would rather have been players. As a citizen and community activist, I prefer to have some say in the efforts to improve my community. I want to feel that my voice speaking about my needs and visions is heard. The mayor himself was everywhere, talking to everybody; however, I knew that the real planning was done by men in a suite at the Columbia Club, a private club. That kind of activity should take place in a public forum in a democracy.

Community resources were not fully utilized. The spirit of giving and voluntarism were very high during these years. Many citizens of good will gave of their time and enabled the city to stage very successful events such as the Pan Am Games and the Final Four. The mayor's ability to recruit top professionals and volunteers for leadership roles made a big difference. Unfortunately, inclusiveness and diversity were not valued, and this circle of longtime friends and associates tended to close rank and exclude people they did not know. The result is that the talents of many were underutilized, and the city will suffer in the long run.

The community was not willing to confront critical local issues. The city tended to ignore critical problems as it went about image building. The city did initiate some action in certain areas—the PRIDE project, organized to implement the school desegregation order, and the Healthy Babies Campaign, to reduce the rate of black infant mortality, are commendable efforts on difficult issues. But attention was given to these issues only after they began to affect the marketing of the city. These programs were never fully integrated into the official fabric of the city and were soon eliminated as entities. Human development was never a priority, and economic development was basically capital improvements, funneling money to the wealthy and giving them tax incentives, not focusing on workforce issues or basic quality-of-life questions.

Projects did not address the community's most important needs. The projects which are the source of the greatest civic pride, in my opinion, did not address the most important needs. The Final Four basketball tournament and the addition of hotels, for example, did not enhance the quality of life for most of the residents, though they are a source of great publicity and civic pride. Many of our streets and sidewalks meanwhile were crumbling; a bridge that I drove by frequently had barricades limiting traffic to one lane for at least two years (30th Street, a major thoroughfare through the black community).

This effort to measure the Hudnut years using the civic index was a healthy exercise for me. More than two years after his departure from office, most things appear different and better. I found many more areas of agreement than I had originally thought. My greatest concern continues to be that the tax base for Indianapolis Public Schools was harmed by the tax abatement and exemptions granted to the big projects which contributed great wealth to a very few. I also believe that the city administration did not pay sufficient attention to the changing economy that resulted in the loss of a number of high-paying jobs for female and minority citizens. Perhaps Hudnut's efforts were indicative of a continued belief in the trickle-down theory.

I believe very strongly in full citizen participation and civic responsibility. This city has not developed ways to involve citizens in major decisions. During the Hudnut years we had a small group of citizens who controlled the resources and made decisions for the rest of us. Most of those decisions were good, but we need to have decision making in a forum where the people can be held accountable. We know that they cared about the city. I only wish they could care as much about the democratic process and inclusiveness.

The Hudnut years were good years for many in the city, but many were left out and left behind. I believe that putting the same energy and creativity into solving our school, housing, and crime problems would have made a great administration an even greater one, and many more people would have beaten a path to our door.

Harrison J. Ullmann

T

he hard work of mayoring involves the making of choices—choices about which problems to solve and which opportunities to seize. Most mayors in most cities never get to it. They are afraid they will choose the wrong thing to do; they are afraid they will be criticized by the press and their opponents; they are afraid they will lose the love of the electorate. So they spend their terms avoiding choices, and when they are done with their offices the opportunities often have left town but the problems have not.

Bill Hudnut made choices. He chose to favor downtown, and he chose to support the amateur athletics strategy that the coalition of downtown interests proposed to him. He might have made other choices—we needed better jobs than we got to replace the jobs we lost when plants such as Western Electric and Chrysler left our town, for one example; many of our neighborhoods needed the attention and the resources that the downtown got, for another.

But the choice Hudnut made was successful and useful to the entire city. The amateur athletics strategy was a spectacular success, and we have a better downtown than we had before Hudnut became mayor. So I will not criticize our former mayor for not choosing any of the other problems and possibilities for his agenda. Except for one . . .

Indianapolis has bad schools and weak universities. Our community suffers because we do not have a workforce with the educated talents

Harrison J. Ullmann, editor of NUVO *newsweekly and editor and publisher of* The Indiana Letter, *has been a Hoosier journalist for more than 30 years. He lives in Indianapolis with his wife, his books and files, and an indifferent cat.*

and the trained skills that attract the best investments in the best industries. Our families suffer because the city's economy cannot hold our
most talented, most educated, most ambitious sons and daughters. Our
public and private sectors suffer because neither taxpayers nor customers make enough money.

If there are serious failures in the Hudnut record, this is where they
should be entered. We needed the leadership in education that Hudnut
did not give us; our problems are worse and our opportunities fewer
because he did not.

He had his reasons for avoiding the issue of education, and they are
all good and plausible.

The laws written to break the control of the Ku Klux Klan in Indianapolis took away all of the mayors' legal authority and political responsibility for the public schools. Our community still holds men and
women who remember why those laws were written, and it holds many
more men and women who would not want Republicans and Democrats making partisan politics out of public education. If Hudnut had
proposed policies and programs for the city's public schools, he would
have been criticized for meddling in affairs that were not his proper
concern.

The laws written by the Indiana General Assembly to establish
Unigov confirmed the proposition that the city's government should
have nothing to do with the city's schools. Hudnut was a part of the
coalition that established Unigov; he and his colleagues in the coalition
had neither political nor civic interests in the schools, and they lobbied
to make sure the Indiana General Assembly gave them none.

Nor did the Republicans who then lived and voted in the suburban
townships of Unigov have any interest in solving the problems of a city
school system that no longer educated their own children. They had
moved to the suburbs to escape the ethnic and urban problems of the
city's public schools. They had voted for Unigov after they had been
assured they would have to give neither their children nor their taxes to
Indianapolis Public Schools. Most of them did not want the mayor they
elected spending his time and their money on city schools that were no
longer their schools.

The irony is that the founders of Unigov so carefully and deliberately ignored the problems of the city's public schools that they gave the
federal courts reason to hold the entire state of Indiana responsible for
both the history and the remedies of segregation in the Indianapolis
Public Schools. The judges said that in actively excluding the public

schools from Unigov's reforms, the legislative allies of Unigov's founders were guilty of the deliberate preservation of segregated public schools within the boundaries of the old city of Indianapolis. That's why there are so many school buses on Unigov's streets.

Another irony is that in keeping full authority for the racial reconstruction of IPS in the federal courts, any responsibility for the remedy was kept from Unigov and its mayors. The court gave them some of the guilt but absolved them from any political punishment. The citizens may not like the tax and social costs of a desegregated IPS, but they have forgotten whose fault it was.

As for higher education during the Hudnut Administration, the presidents and trustees of Indiana and Purdue universities believed they owed their responsibilities to the entire state, not to its separate cities, and they did not want the mayors of Indianapolis meddling in the affairs of their new campus at Indiana University–Purdue University at Indianapolis.

Nor did the presidents want the mayors of Indianapolis asking the General Assembly for academic assets that belonged in Bloomington and West Lafayette, like schools of music and schools of engineering, or research and graduate programs in the sciences and humanities, or primetime football and basketball programs. The presidents were worried then, and now, that the political, economic, and social power of Indianapolis would pull the resources of prestige and money away from their flagship campuses in Bloomington and West Lafayette if IUPUI became a fully developed university with graduate programs and research establishments in a full range of academic disciplines.

While the presidents worried, the leaders of the amateur athletic strategy in Indianapolis looked at the new IUPUI campus developing on the city's near west side and saw only a source for the sites, facilities, and borrowed money that their strategy needed. They asked the presidents not for schools of engineering and graduate programs in the sciences but for sports facilities and the bond issues to build them. The presidents of IU and Purdue were happy to cooperate in the city's athletic enterprises, particularly when they learned these did not include IUPUI football and basketball teams that would compete with the Hoosiers and Boilermakers. Hudnut would have been opposed by the universities and at odds with his own supporters if he had campaigned for an IUPUI that would become a fully developed university, with comprehensive research and graduate education, with an academic reputation and scholarly prestige that competed with Indiana University in Bloomington and Purdue University in West Lafayette.

So Hudnut had good and plausible reasons for ignoring education in the city that elected him again and again and again. The laws were in his way, powerful institutions would have opposed him, and his own people wouldn't have wanted it. But no one else could have given the city the leadership that its problems in education require. When Hudnut finally left office, the city's schools were worse than they had been and the city's colleges and universities were not as good as they could have been.

And as a result, Mayor Hudnut's successors now have other problems to solve. The city does not have the businesses and industries that make enough jobs for the highly educated, highly paid professionals who in other cities support the fine and performing arts, the upscale malls in the suburbs and gentrified neighborhoods in the central city, the great restaurants and good newspapers. The cultural assets important to the city's quality of life—the restoration of the Circle Theater or the survival of the Indianapolis Repertory Theater and the City Market, as examples—must be heavily subsidized because the population of donors and patrons is too small in Indianapolis.

The city's shortage of residents in important economic and demographic categories is demonstrable in census data. Entire urban industries—advertising and public relations, for example—are almost nonexistent in Indianapolis. And even when the urban industries are well represented—banking and insurance, for example—the jobs are concentrated in the lower-income brackets. Indianapolis is a city of branch offices, not home offices. Our city misses the inventive and entrepreneurial ferment in commerce that a major research campus would give it.

In large measure these deficiencies are the consequence of the city's bad schools and weak universities. An educated workforce is the essential resource for the most prosperous and energetic of U.S. industries. But our schools and colleges do not give our city the resources that attract the best investments in these best industries. We get backshops but not home offices in the service industries. We get assembly plants that manufacture products designed, financed, and marketed in other cities.

There is no useful purpose in criticizing a mayor for avoiding an initiative that could not succeed. Mayors are usually gone from office by the time the bills for their disasters arrive, but the citizens and the tax-payers keep their offices forever. So it may be virtuous to fail in a good though hopeless cause, but there is nothing useful in it for the people who would have to live with the failure and pay for its costs.

The obstacles to a Hudnut initiative in education were substantial, and risks of failure loom large even in hindsight. But the risks of failure were less than they seem, and I think Hudnut would have succeeded if he had taken up the cause of education in Indianapolis. Here are some of the reasons why.

Bill Hudnut is as good a politician as any that Indiana has recently raised. He has a great, energetic charm. He is articulate and persuasive. He likes people and they like him. He can fill a room and dominate a crowd with his personality. He is intelligent and well-read; he compre-hends the substance as well as the politics of the issues at hand. He is a formidable advocate for any cause he takes up.

Bill Hudnut is a mainstream Republican in a community with main-stream Republican preferences. He is fully supported by all the major Republican constituencies except those of the radical, righteous Right. His Democratic opposition never gave him an opponent in his races nor any competition in the issues. And he enjoyed friendly and cooper-ative relationships with most of the Democratic constituencies in his city, including organized labor and the black leaders.

Bill Hudnut held the only bully pulpit left in Indianapolis. Most of the leaders of the city's businesses and industries had become employees of out-of-state corporations. The city's most powerful private institutions—the Lilly Endowment, for example—had no enthusiasm for public leadership in public causes. The leaders of the city's political and social constituencies—labor unions, for example—had taken up very narrow priorities for their very narrow visions. There was no bullying that could be done from any of these little pulpits.

Bill Hudnut was mayor in a city that has no tradition or talent for public debates. Once the leaders of the community set a priority or start an initiative, the opposition is expected to retire in silence. None of the leaders of the institutions and interests that might have opposed a Hudnut initiative in education would have led any public opposition if Hudnut had ever set education as the city's priority. They would not have competed with Hudnut for the support of the citizens; they would have avoided the controversy that the competition would have required. After all, the doubters of the downtown development strategy did almost all their doubting in private. Even the Democrats had no public complaints about Circle Centre Mall or tax subsidies for the developers.

So the effective public opposition to a Hudnut education priority would likely have been negligible in practice no matter how formidable it looked in principle. If Hudnut had taken up education as the first priority of the community, then the community would have followed where he led. He could have given us better schools and universities, but he chose not to do it.

The Hudnut record is almost entirely one of success. If there is any important failure in the Hudnut record, it is not in any of the things he did. It is in the one important thing he left undone—an undone thing that may undo us all.

Afterword:
Lessons Learned

WILLIAM H. HUDNUT III

F or 16 years I enjoyed a rare privilege: being mayor of a major American city, with all the opportunities for service and leadership it brought. Like any public official, I was elected not to be somebody but to do something. At first I did not comprehend the magnitude of the job, but it soon became clear that although doing one piece at a time is not terribly difficult, "there are so many pieces that it's like eating an elephant," as Bill Frederick, former mayor of Orlando, described it to me. A mayor is a juggler, always having several projects, problems, and important decisions in the air at once. Shifting rapidly from one thing to another is part of the job. But my hope was that at the end of the day we would have helped build a city where our citizens could enjoy a good quality of life with a local government responsive to their concerns.

During my last few weeks in office, people frequently asked me: what were your biggest achievements and disappointments? How do you want to be remembered? What would you have done differently? What kept you going? And do you have a last word? Such questions might conveniently frame our final observations, so let's look at each in turn.

What were your biggest achievements and disappointments?

That's a hard one to answer, because I will sound like a braggart if I list the former and like a whiner if I talk about the latter. Things like the Hoosier Dome, United Airlines, the Pan Am Games, bringing the Colts and saving the Pacers, our triple-A bond rating, the changes in our sky-line, the bond bank and the environmental court (both national firsts) come to mind. But are they any more important than helping a senior citizen with a problem, visiting a hospitalized city employee hurt on the job, getting a stop sign at a busy intersection, reading to preschoolers at a local library? Perhaps in times to come the Hoosier Dome will be regarded as the symbol of the emergence of Indianapolis as a major American city during these years and a fitting signature on the Hudnut years. But there's lots else.

Disappointments there were, to be sure. I have a good "forgettery" when it comes to this sort of thing, my philosophy being that you do your best and leave the rest, and rise above the criticism and hurts that inevitably come. Lincoln's words always provided me with great com-fort: "If I were to try to read, much less answer, all the attacks made on me, this shop might as well be closed for any other business. I do the very best I know how, the very best I can; and I mean to keep doing so until the end. If the end brings me out all right, what is said against me won't amount to anything. If the end brings me out wrong, ten angels swearing I was right would make no difference." So what were my big-gest disappointments? Possibly, the following three things.

First, the defeat of the Pan Am bond issue in 1985. The bond issue would have brought over $40-million worth of help to 14 neighbor-hoods long after the games were history. It also would have made pos-sible construction of low-cost housing for the 6,000 Pan Am athletes at Lockefield Gardens, which could have been rolled over into permanent housing for low- and moderate-income people in our community. Its defeat was based on a narrow appeal to self-interest and a mispercep-tion of the true facts involved. I did a poor job of communicating my vision to the public in this instance. From the defeat, however, I learned the importance of having a backup plan. It involved using the proper-ties at Fort Benjamin Harrison on the northeast side of town, where dormitories were already standing, together with grounds upon which a Pan Am village could be erected. That worked, with the cooperation of the U.S. Army, and we did not have to revert to plan C, which was to use college dormitory space, if we could gain permission, in Indianapolis, Bloomington, and West Lafayette.

Second, the time in 1990 when a group of black clergymen stood on the steps of the City-County Building calling for my resignation. That hurt. I had spent years trying to improve race relations in our city, speaking in African-American churches continuously, setting aside

Martin Luther King's birthday as a city holiday before any other city (that I am aware of) did it, keeping job-training programs going, taking a strong stand for affirmative action and equal opportunity, and on and on. So it disappointed me deeply when some fellow clergymen, if I may put it that way, called for me and the police chief to resign because they were upset over a police-action shooting and were targeting their anger on the highest local officials they could find. Later I asked their chairman (for whom, incidentally, I had arranged an invitation to the U.S. Congress to open its meeting with prayer when I was a member of the House of Representatives) why they did it. His response was "You should have taken that shooting to the grand jury." Telling him that the mayor did not have the authority to do that, only the county prosecutor, failed to mollify him. In retrospect, I must add that the clergymen's protest should be understood in the larger context of black rage and not taken personally. And to understand is to forgive. The failure of an indifferent system to reduce police brutality and the number of police-action shootings, at least as perceived by some elements of the African-American community, fuels black anger and pessimism about the white majority's will to justice. African-American people feel hated in a way I and other whites who have never been victimized by slavery, lynchings, segregation, devaluation, unequal treatment, and second-class citizenship across the generations cannot comprehend. Calling for the resignation of white leaders at the pinnacle of local power must be seen as an effort to vent pent-up feelings about oppression and injustice—feelings, incidentally, that need to be taken seriously, not dismissed lightly.

Third, this is political, but I must say that the knee-jerk reaction of organized labor in favor of Democratic candidates and against Republicans was a big disappointment to me. In 1975, when I was campaigning for the office of mayor, the local UAW-CAP Council kept my opponent in front of them for ten minutes or so, then grilled me for over an hour, in my first public appearance since undergoing surgery, and voted to endorse my opponent, in spite of the fact that in his development business he used nonunion labor. After I was elected, I established the Mayor's Labor Advisory Council and worked with representatives of local unions throughout my time in office. Yet in 1990, when I ran statewide for secretary of state, labor at the state level spent over $100,000 on TV spots to denigrate me. I asked myself, is this my reward for fifteen years of bridge building? The head of the UAW regional office told me there was no point in asking his group for an endorsement, since it had voted in favor of my opponent even before a Republican candidate was announced. And the highest statewide AFL-CIO official circulated a scurrilous attack on me in his newsletter containing some outright false-hoods. I thought I might have deserved better than this, because in the life of the city where I was mayor, I had enjoyed a good positive working relationship with labor. Being in the hip pocket of one political party seems to me to be shortsighted. It reduces labor's clout and calls into question the credibility of labor leaders who almost invariably endorse any Democrat, regardless.

How do you want to be remembered?

The short answer is that I hope my epitaph will read: "He built well and he cared about people." I want to be remembered as a mayor who served and led his city during a time of positive growth and as one who tried to be responsive to the needs of people in his constituency. Another way of putting it would be "a team builder with an entrepreneurial spirit."

The accomplishments of the Hudnut years represented a team effort. I do not want to claim sole credit for everything positive that happened because many players contributed to our successes (and failures). In spite of the distasteful egocentrism that characterizes many politicians, there's really no such thing in politics as a self-made man or woman. Anyone who has been elected owes a huge debt of gratitude to those who helped finance the campaign, get out the vote, volunteer at headquarters, and so forth; and anyone who governs should remember to say thanks to workers in the city departments who help implement the plans and programs of the policymakers at the top, and to citizens in the community who work with the political leadership to accomplish the administration's goals. No one succeeds alone. An exhilarating aspect of political life is the experience of joining others in the effort. Politics is fun. It's a game, to be played enthusiastically and well. Whether one is marching in a parade or going door to door, meeting with precinct committeemen in a ward chairman's basement or attending a political convention where the red, white, and blue of the bunting, the smell of the greasepaint, and the roar of the crowd get one's adrenalin going, politics is a thrilling and satisfying experience. You are not out there alone. A team of people believe as you do, want you to win, and will work hard with you and for you to accomplish your common goal.

The team building should occur both inside and outside City Hall.

Staff makes or breaks a mayor. Sonya Margerum, mayor of West Lafayette, says that one of the most important lessons she has learned is to
"plan with your staff, set goals, and manage towards those goals. No
one knows it all, so rely on your management team of department
heads. They are doing the work and meeting the public, so give them
credit and responsibility to carry out the job." Delegating responsibilities and giving people the authority to run with the ball without being
micromanaged helps build that team spirit, as does an atmosphere of
free give-and-take in which the mayor learns "to accept some unacceptable advice," to borrow Bill Frederick's phrase. The mayor may have
the vision and be responsible for motivating the troops, but the troops
do the implementing.

Bud Clark, former mayor of Portland, Oregon, told me once, "The
single most important thing I have learned since being mayor is the
importance of having a positive vision, setting goals and objectives and
a plan of action with all of those involved to carry out the vision." That
means using staff effectively. Authoritarian management breeds fear
and resentment in lower-level workers. This in turn stifles initiative and
cripples productivity. Many other people in an organization can make
helpful contributions, and the top person should make every effort to
instill a sense of team spirit, pride, and self-worth. True leaders want
their co-workers to succeed, and help them grow through creative
meaningful partnership in the governing process. They let others know
how much they are needed, and support their employees. We are all
equal, I used to say to our city employees, all members of the same
team; we just play different positions.

I consulted with others in deciding how to handle challenges such
as those listed at the beginning of this book. "Collegiality," remarked
former deputy mayor David Frick, "was a hallmark of the Hudnut
approach." I always asked those around me for recommendations and
options when we wrestled with tough circumstances. We met together
regularly as a cabinet and individually. We created a total quality service
program and instituted a fairly comprehensive program of continuing
education. I would sign the certificates and attend the "graduation"
sessions personally. The sessions were held in the mayor's office to send
a signal to the employees: "Your progress is very important to those at
the highest level of this organization." During my remarks at these ceremonies, I would express a threefold hope: (1) that the course of
instruction you have completed has assisted you in developing your
skills so that City Hall's productivity and customer service will increase;

(2) that what you have learned will benefit your professional development by equipping you to do a better job wherever your career path takes you; and (3) that your time in this course has helped you discover more about yourself, your talents, and your strengths and weaknesses, so that you can better fulfill your potential. I wanted the employees to know that I truly believed they had a significant contribution to make to the work of our organization and that what we could accomplish for the citizens we served would happen through partnership.

Two trends in today's world militate against participatory management. First, we live in a time when ambitious political leaders can get elected by raising enough money to run negative campaign commercials. Successful politicians are not as much a product of team effort as they used to be. Indeed, some practitioners of the political arts believe "the party's over." Once in office, they become masters at manipulating the media to their advantage. As they exploit quick photo ops and self-promotion opportunities, the sense of teamwork diminishes rapidly. Second, some politicians quickly discover that bashing the bureaucracy is good politics. They score high in the polls by riding the populist wave of cynicism about government. The public disdains the process of governing (which they consider wasteful) and the people who staff the offices of government (whom they regard as slothful), so political "leaders" make themselves look good by demeaning the work of government employees, laying them off and privatizing their functions. The media and the public love to hear the word *cut*, and smart politicians know that slashing the bureaucracy and playing on the public's antigovernment feelings is a sure-fire way to increase approval ratings, even if it does nothing to enhance an employee's feeling that he or she has a worthwhile contribution to make to a team effort.

In his book *Leadership Is an Art* (which Sam Walton used to say was the best book he ever read on leadership), Max DePree, chairman of the furniture company Herman Miller, writes that he is convinced "that the best management process for today's environment is participative management based on covenantal relationships."[1] A covenantal relationship rests on a shared commitment to ideals, values, and goals as well as to ideas, issues, and management processes. It is characterized by such things as freedom, openness, equality, warmth, love, and personal chemistry. DePree asserts that an organization is ineffective without them. Managers charged with handling resources efficiently and the leader who articulates the "what" and "when" but not the "how" can do their jobs more effectively by heeding this concept, which I tried to do while in office. Not that I achieved a covenantal relationship as a reality, but it was a goal to which I aspired inside City Hall, where I believed my calling was to build a team. As Sue Myrick, former mayor of Charlotte, North Carolina, put it, "the majority of city employees are conscientious and proud of their government," and it behooved her to reinforce those feelings.

Beyond the walls of City Hall, the mayor as community leader can set a tone of inclusiveness, caring, trust, integrity, credibility, and warmth. Such an attitude supplies one important key to community building. Government cannot do it alone, nor can the business or philanthropic communities, much less the churches, community-based organizations, and public-interest groups. It takes everyone, working as partners. Newark's mayor Sharpe James, a successor of mine as president of the National League of Cities, says: "Public/private partnerships involving the community, businesses and government are essential for the survival and growth of cities. People are more than happy to volunteer and be part of the process of turning a city around and making it work."

A strong-minded businessman who ran a family-owned business and was a member of the church I had served in Indianapolis before entering politics stopped me on a street corner early in my first term to tell me that I was trying to run the city all wrong. "Too much like the church," he said. When I asked what he meant, he responded that I was too interested in building consensus. I should be more authoritative and heavy-handed, he suggested. "Just tell 'em what's to be done, and then do it!" Evidently he had never had to work with other elected officials in a legislative body or with a constituency of 800,000 people, many of whom did not vote for you. I respectfully disagreed with him and went on about the business of consulting and forging agreement as I deemed best.

To be sure, consensus negates leadership. One cannot lead if one has a "wet-finger" approach to politics, seeking to govern by polls and always doing the popular thing. But consensus building is different. "The most effective political leaders in a democracy," says Mayor Jerry Abramson of Louisville, "are those able to build consensus, where people agree with each other [and] where people work with each other." One governs more effectively by utilizing the talents, experience, and resources of others than by trying to do it singlehandedly or failing to give credit to others.

The mayor's job is to form strategic partnerships in the city that produce positive results. The easy way is to let the pursuit of self-interest run on, with the end result being fragmentation; the difficult task is to build feelings of collaboration into the sinews of relationships in the city and thereby foster a larger sense of community. A mayor can take the lead in helping people believe in themselves and their future. In an orchestra, each player and each section contributes to the larger accomplishment, and in a city, a mayor melds a community from many people and various constituencies who have diverging points of view, differing approaches to solving a problem, and sundry roles to play.

Community means "coming into unity." Unity is not uniformity; it is the capacity to remain together within diversity. More than anyone else in a city, a mayor, simply by virtue of the office, has an opportunity to create community. Political leadership that transcends narrow self-interest can forge a sense of teamwork and a desire to cooperate for the common good. This is not a job for a technocrat; it is one for a leader who cares about people, values their individuality and creativity, and is willing to work hard to bring them together. A mayor is the custodian of the spirit of a city, the one person more than any other who can either pull people together or poison the well of cooperation and good feelings. So I'd like to be remembered as a team builder. And one with an entrepreneurial spirit.

The *Washington Post* in May 1992 noted that "some critics said Hudnut focused too much attention on downtown while inner city neighborhoods were deteriorating." Without repeating the list of things our administration tried to accomplish in neighborhoods, it is fair to say that more needs to be done.

Some new strategies will help reinforce neighborhoods. Empowerment zones (enterprise zones by another name) will help if they are not micromanaged by higher levels of government. When properly crafted with a holistic approach that combines social services, bottom-up decision making, infrastructure improvements, and tax incentives, these zones can form a good cornerstone for a relatively low-cost, high-yield urban policy. In Cleveland a subsidized mortgage loan program has been established to stabilize neighborhoods by providing whites and blacks who might flee to de facto segregated enclaves to stay together, live alongside one another, and thus combat further deterioration. Again, as is being implemented in Indianapolis, local churches can be utilized as financial centers for reinvestment of capital in neighborhoods, and a neighborhood resource center can be established in cooperation with social-service agencies to provide technical assistance to those who are committed to proactive intervention to stem blight and flight.

But the best way to promote neighborhood revitalization is for City Hall to provide the basic infrastructure of streets, sidewalks, sewers, etc., upon which human ingenuity can build to promote profitable economic activity and harmonious living. No amount of government spending alone will restore the neighborhoods. It is less important to redistribute wealth than to redistribute opportunity.

In the education area, I was criticized in some quarters for what I did not do, rather than for what I did do. What we did made up a substantial list. We initiated PRIDE (Peaceful Response in Indianapolis to Desegregated Education) and followed it up with the work of the Community Desegregation Advisory Council, to try to assure peaceful compliance with court-ordered busing. We offered the services of the mayor's office twice, in 1979 and 1990, to help resolve conflicts between the Indianapolis Public Schools administration and the teachers' union. We started the Invest Indianapolis program, which eventually blossomed into CLASS (Community Leaders Allied for Superior Schools). I spoke to classes in every high school in the county and in many elementary and middle schools, both public and private. I met numerous times with school superintendents to discuss problems. We established Youth City. The city worked closely with Indiana and Purdue universities in the development of their campus and program. I provided support for innumerable programs aimed at strengthening students, all the way from anti-drug programs to reading to preschoolers in neighborhood libraries.

I declined to involve myself in a referendum battle in 1985 to raise taxes for Indianapolis Public Schools. One must learn to pick one's battles carefully. You cannot be effective if you are always fighting on all fronts. Part of wisdom lies in knowing when to stop. I did not know whether the schools needed the additional funds for buildings, and I was not comfortable injecting myself into such a controversy, which, given the mood of the moment, seemed doomed to failure. Nor did I petition the federal court to modify the judge's busing orders. Nor did I lead any effort to restructure the school system or the method by which the school board was chosen, feeling that such an attempt, at least on my initiative, would be perceived as a political power grab or as racist. I tried to support the education enterprise without interfering. I had a pretty full plate without taking on these heavy education issues. But the thought lingers and haunts: what more could we have done?

In the ebb and flow of events, different circumstances require different responses. For the most part, our country's schools were founded by religious institutions. The first reform efforts in the 19th century were aimed at making the schools public, giving them to government to run rather than organized religions, although the United States always reserved a place for parochial education. The next reform movement sought to depoliticize the schools by separating their governance from civil government. Then, after 1954 and *Brown vs. Board of Education,* the courts more or less took over the school system. That was the situation when I entered public life in the 1970s. What could I have accomplished had I called for radical reform, given the fact that the Indianapolis Public Schools system was under the jurisdiction of the federal court? I am not sure it would have been very much.

But now the times have changed. The election of school boards should be repoliticized in a nonpartisan manner so that the public becomes actively involved again in the choosing of school board members, as it has not been for many years. It is becoming clear that school systems need reforming for two reasons: they tend to be out of control concerning raising taxes and spending money, which affects a city's economic development opportunities, and they tend to be so centralized and monopolistic that classroom change comes very slowly, and people are asking, pointblank, why their youngsters are not getting a better education. Hence mayors around the country, including my successor here in Indianapolis, are beginning to speak out about school reform. Mayor Stephen Goldsmith believes that school problems are one of the most critical issues now facing the city. Privatization of certain functions, choice and more freedom, decentralization, utilization of Information Age technology, competition, performance standards, and an accounting of how tax dollars are being spent by local school boards— all must be discussed as citizens and policymakers consider a full range of possibilities for fundamental restructuring of the education establishment in today's environment.

Even more difficult than school problems are those related to race relations. Here again, I wonder whether there was more I could have or should have done. Looking over the field of broken dreams since World War II, one might ask whether, after almost 50 years of affirmative governmental efforts to improve race relations by inaugurating one program after another to achieve better housing and more jobs, equal opportunities and civil rights for all, much progress has been made. Surveying the results of program after program, all well-intentioned, since the 1950s—urban renewal, the War on Poverty, Model Cities, Community Development Action Grants, enterprise zones, CDCs, CETA, JTPA, UDAG, and on and on and on, all of which have been tried in city after city, including Indianapolis—yet being faced nevertheless with the stark reality of two Americas, one pretty much white and rich, the other pretty much black and poor, separate and unequal, where black poverty rates remain stubbornly high and injustices such as unequal pay, blocked upward mobility, discrimination, and environmental racism cause continuing festering resentments, one is prompted to conclude that nothing helps.

However, mine is not a counsel of despair. To conclude that government cannot wage an effective war on poverty does not mean that nothing can be done. Government programs that give people incentives to become more self-reliant and less dependent on government help may contribute more to revitalization than is currently visible. A national push for welfare reform is just getting under way and may produce dramatic results in the next decade. We should never stop pursuing public policies that abate discriminatory practices and ensure equal access to employment, education, housing, and affordable health care. Programs for neighborhood reinvestment, such as the ones mentioned earlier, may produce a positive lasting effect. The lesson seems to be that social services must be included with economic pump priming in a holistic approach that emphasizes a bottom-up strategy.

At its root, however, the question remains one of attitude. Human revitalization is more difficult to accomplish than the rebuilding of a brick-and-mortar structure. Race relations involve a dimension of the spirit that is just as important as any physical project or job-training program. Hearts will have to change before healing can really come. Lack of hope produces a despairing conviction that life won't change for the better. How to rebuild hope: that is the key question. A mass societal commitment to urban education is needed which will lead to wider economic opportunity. Our culture will have to delegitimize violence, illegal drug use, and "anything goes" moral relativism, and legitimize once again traditional values such as two-parent families, self-discipline, postponement of immediate gratification, and a sense of responsibility for one's neighbors. People no longer respond very positively to howls of racism and the politics of victimization; they want better governance and less rhetoric. Respect for one another will have to be built into the sinews of our communities. Cities will have to commit to interracial dialogue, like the programs sponsored in Indianapolis in 1993–94 by a local newspaper and TV station, which could be the precursor to greater understanding and cooperation. The vitality of religious institutions, schools, community-based organizations, and social-service agencies will have to be utilized in ameliorating racial discord. It is on their doorsteps, like it or not. Drug abuse will have to be fought much more extensively. Positive recreational opportunities for young people, like midnight basketball, will have to be provided.

Above all, changing the way our society thinks about race requires leadership. Testing which way the wind is blowing may be good politics, but it's bad leadership. If polarization is to be overcome and a community moved beyond the "it's not my problem" syndrome, courageous and enlightened leaders, black and white, will have to rally communities toward conflict resolution and reconciliation.

As for economic development, did we make mistakes? Two of the most complicated and controversial projects in which I was involved as mayor were the Circle Centre Mall downtown and the United Airlines maintenance center at the airport. Could we have done a better job of putting those projects together? Who knows? One makes decisions without the benefit of hindsight. Should the city have spent $150 million assembling the land and preparing the site for the downtown mall? Was that money well spent? Were we chasing after fool's gold in making a large commitment to downtown retailing when suburban shopping malls command so much consumer loyalty? Should we have joined forces with the state to put together a $300-million package of grants and incentives to attract the UAL maintenance facility? Will United be around after the turn of the century to make good on its contractual promises? Will the payroll and vendor dollars and other ancillary benefits we envisioned being generated by the project actually materialize? Time will tell.

In the short term, one can point to certain facts to justify actions taken. At Union Station, which may finally be operating in the black, some 1,500 jobs replaced empty corridors, rusty hinges, leaking roofs, and broken windows. These jobs accounted for quite a payroll, bringing life out of urban death, breathing vitality back into a moribund building. They have generated some $50-million worth of business annually. The original $60-million rehabilitation project included $17 million of public funds. Was public money wasted, even if the developer had trouble reaching a positive bottom line? I think not. Did this constitute an unfortunate example of the oft-maligned trickle-down economics theory that business growth and investment would create jobs and incomes and thereby reduce poverty and its related social problems? Perhaps, but does that make it bad? We aimed our efforts first at revitalizing downtown in partnership with the private sector, and secondarily at cutting a smart business deal. We hoped we would accomplish both aims. We believed that what we were doing was right, and we went about doing it even though some thought we were wrong.

Some criticize tax-abatement policies as giving away tax base. They fail to answer the question, however, about what the tax base would have been if the abatement had not been granted and the project had not occurred. Would the city be better off with no AUL building downtown? Definitely not. And now, after ten years, its abatement has run out and it is paying the full boatload of property taxes on its improved downtown location. In 1987, to pick a year at random, 15 tax-abatement projects were approved, representing an investment of $110,290,093 and the creation of 2,090 jobs. Would the city be better off if no such approvals had been granted? I think not. Incentives, subsidies, grants, and abatements kick-start economic development. It might be argued that our city went too far in this direction, but again, who knows? Reasonable people may disagree.

Beyond the short term, however, it is important to learn to take the long view of things and be patient. The Hoosier Dome and the Colts, the downtown mall, many of our downtown revitalization projects such as the empty buildings along Washington Street, United Airlines—projects such as these don't develop overnight. The city puts the deal together at the front end and hopes to recoup its investment over time. Predicting exactly how or when the payoff will happen is precarious at best, but we proceed with the confidence that if a sound judgment has been made, the initial payout will be justified by the payback down the road. The media are inclined to want instant results, but these big projects don't work that way.

What kept you going?

In retrospect, I would point to five things. The first is a positive, upbeat attitude. This cannot be manufactured. It's innate. Some people see the positive potential in a situation; others do not. Some mayors have vision; others do not. Some are builders, some are wreckers. Some take risks, others take refuge. Some lead, others merely manage. Some hearts tilt toward hope, others toward despair.

After I stepped down as president of the National League of Cities in 1981, I was asked who I thought were the best mayors in the country. I put William Donald Schaefer of Baltimore and Ed Koch of New York at the top of the list, because each went far beyond being a manager. Each was in love with his city, each lifted his city's spirit, each had a driving ambition for his city, each was optimistic and upbeat (except when the Colts left Baltimore), and each truly enjoyed the job. That is the way I tried to be during my 16 years as mayor of Indianapolis. Former San Antonio mayor Henry Cisneros has written me that during his time in office he "learned the value of remaining upbeat and optimistic. Not only is a positive view of life's travails essential for personal steadiness, but it is a definite leadership tool. I learned it was important for my staff, allies, and the citizens generally to see me in a frame of mind convinced that problems and challenges could be worked out. That is not to say acting pollyannish or naive, simply certain that with enough work most challenges can be met."

Of course, there will be times when goals are not achieved, mistakes are made, and criticism is leveled. The former mayor of Houston, Kathy Whitmire, remarked to me once that "politics is a great teacher. Your accomplishments may be applauded, but you can be sure your mistakes will always be published." There will be disappointments, hurt, and suffering. Reading critical articles, especially ones you consider unfair, may be part of the game, but that doesn't mean that they don't hurt. But the point is not to wallow in self-pity or retreat into bitterness. One must press on, rise above the negative things that could easily drag one's spirits down, and never give in. Staying in a positive frame of mind as one focuses on the indeterminate possibilities for achieving good things through dynamic stewardship of one's office will help keep any mayor going.

So will the conviction that one is involved in something worthwhile. This is the second thing that gives one staying power. In spite of the public's outrage about politicians, gridlock, scandal, waste, fraud, and abuse, and beyond the cynicism, I deeply believe in the worthwhileness of the political endeavor. Politics is about power—the power of votes and the power of money. But more meaningfully yet, it is about service, helping people, building a better city, state, or country, and giving to others. From a theological perspective, it constitutes a form of ministry—not in a narrow sectarian sense, of course, but in the broader sense of living a life of useful service to others. Government is where much of the action is, and the opportunity to be a player on that stage, hopefully a player for good, is immensely rewarding. I like to think that politics gives one the chance to put love of neighbor to work in concrete ways, by developing programs and providing services that make the neighborhood a better place.

To release the power of love, which I would define as good will in action, through one's involvement in politics and holding of public office represents a high calling indeed, worth doing regardless of the brickbats, hurdles, and criticism one encounters along the way. One should avoid a fatuous utopianism that naively assumes a kingdom of love can ever be fully established here on earth, or one that self-righteously equates one's own party, platform, program, policy, or project with perfection. But one should also understand that in the dialectical tension between complacent acceptance of the status quo and a desire to transform the world in the name of justice, truth, love, or what have you, the error lies more in doing nothing than in plunging in with great enthusiasm to do one's best to assault injustice, redeem the wastelands, and heal the wounds of life.

Faith that one can make a difference is a third thing that helps keep a person going in tough times. Early in my first term as mayor, my father, an inveterate reader of the *New York Times*, sent me a column by John Oakes entitled "More Than a Mayor." I still have it, yellowed with age, underlined by Dad here and there to make sure I got the point. "A mayor of character and courage can make a difference," Oakes wrote, and I have never forgotten those words.[2] I always hoped to live up to that ideal. Not that I would succeed, but that I would try. Hope is faith directed toward the future, a belief that tomorrow can be better than yesterday, and that one's efforts can make a positive difference.

My theology professor at Union Seminary in New York, Reinhold Niebuhr, taught us to accept the responsibility of living in a continuous tension between what is and what ought to be, between acquiescence in the harsh reality of the brokenness and brutality of our earthly vale of tears and the empty utopian dream that every day in every way we can make things better. An ethic of responsibility constitutes the essence of good citizenship. I think many men and women on both sides of the political aisle are trying to be good citizens by assuming responsibility for their communities.

Not everyone in politics is a thief and a crook. I remember how saddened I was once in 1973, while driving to the Indianapolis airport with my radio tuned to a talk show, around the time when Spiro Agnew was forced to resign as vice-president of the United States. The hosts were discussing this incident, and caller after caller said, "He's no different from everyone else in Washington. He just got caught." That is not true! People in politics can lead lives of integrity and dignity like anyone else. Very few of us will stride across the pages of history and leave big footprints, but each can try to have a positive impact. One of my favorite little quotations is "I'm only one, but still I am one. I cannot do everything, but I can do something. And because I cannot do everything, that does not mean I will not do the something I can do."

The fourth thing that can make a big difference in one's ability to hang in there without becoming discouraged is the loving support of family, friends, and comrades-in-arms. They provide comfort in times of need. During tough times one can draw on the reservoir of appreciation and affirmation of family and friends to nurture one's spirit and sustain one's effort. When you are tempted to question yourself and doubt your abilities, the belief and confidence of others can pull you out of the slough of despond and set your pilgrim feet on the right path again.

Finally, one needs a sense of humor. One should take criticism seriously, not personally, and retain the ability to laugh at oneself. Sometimes it's best to ignore criticism; other times one has to stand fast and make a defense; sometimes one should just accept it and learn from it; and sometimes one should deflect harsh attacks with humor. As Kurt Schmoke, the mayor of Baltimore, wrote me, "Smiling beats frowning most days on most issues."

Do you have a last word?

In the months since I left office, I have thought about what my final thought might be. I would cast it in terms of keeping the quintessential spirit of our city alive. It's a spirit of community service, which I talked about at a farewell party given for me in the Hoosier Dome in November 1991, just a month before I left office. Beware lest the fire of this spirit be extinguished by ambitious, greedy, or complacent self-interest. Tend the fire. Nurture it. Keep it alive and well.

Beyond the parapets of the downtown skyline and the rounded top of the Hoosier Dome, the bricks on the Circle and the sidewalks in the neighborhoods, the school buildings and the libraries, the velodrome, natatorium, track-and-field facility and tennis stadium, the successes of the sports strategy and the business growth, the Aaa bond rating and the annual financial reports, the mall and United Airlines, the advanced wastewater treatment plant and the Indianapolis International Airport, Park 100 and Park Fletcher, the crimes solved and the trash picked up, the letters written and the files stored on microfilm in the basement, the tot lots on inner-city corners and the broader expanses of Eagle Creek Park, the art galleries along Massachusetts Avenue and the cabarets in Broad Ripple, the assembly lines at Allison Transmission and Ford, the "edge city" developments at Castleton and Keystone at the Crossing—indeed, beyond everything physical—there abides the infrastructure of the spirit, which can deteriorate just as easily as bricks and mortar can.

It is a spirit of generosity and self-sacrifice, a willingness to go a second mile for the sake of one's community. It is a spirit of compassion, as in the Campaign for Healthy Babies. It is a competitive spirit that believes in the unlimited possibilities of human potential to achieve goals and accomplish good things against tough odds, like going after United Airlines as the 93rd city on a list of 92. It is a spirit of cooperation that creates partnerships and strategic alliances across lines that can so easily divide—racial, political, economic, social—as when so many disparate elements came together to make the Hoosier Dome happen, and when the business community rallied to save an apparently doomed mall by pledging almost $60 million of equity money to the project.

When our city faced the imminent prospect of losing the Indiana Pacers NBA franchise in 1983 because the owners had decided to sell the franchise to an investor group in Sacramento, some of us began searching for a buyer who would keep the Pacers in Indianapolis. The trail led us from trying to put together a coalition of local endeavors, to Dave Thomas of Wendy's fame, and ultimately to Herb Simon and his brother Melvin, local commercial real-estate developers with a national scope and reputation who had pockets deep enough to do the deal if they wanted to. After weeks of negotiations, I ended up one day in Herb Simon's office, accompanied by two or three civic leaders. Herb looked me in the eye and said, with that great grin of his, "Well, I've got to do it, don't I?" To which I replied, "Yes, Herb, you've got to do it . . . for civic pride." Sure, he might make a buck in the long run. Sure, he would have fun running an NBA franchise and consorting with many famous sports personalities. But at bottom he bought the distressed franchise because Indianapolis was his hometown. He loved the city. Indianapolis had been good to him, and he wanted to give something back, to help in time of need. So he and his brother saved the Pacers. For civic pride.

That's what this city of Indianapolis at its best is all about: civic pride, community service. That is the fire of which I speak. The city's most priceless asset is the caring spirit of civic leaders and unheralded citizens who want to make it a good place in which to live, work, and raise a family and who are willing to invest their money and energy into projects that will promote what the Roman orator Cicero called "partnership for the common good." Persons such as these supply the moral fiber, spiritual backbone, and generous heart of our city. They are rich, poor, black, white, male, female, public, private, Democratic, Republican, independent, blue-collar and white-collar, but they have one thing in common: they want to build a great city.

NOTES

1. Max DePree, *Leadership Is an Art* (New York: Bantam Doubleday, 1989), 61.

2. *New York Times*, November 2, 1977, A27.

Bill Hudnut served as mayor of Indianapolis for an unprecedented four terms, achieving a national reputation for spearheading a partnership of public and private sector interests that transformed his city. A congressman and Presbyterian minister prior to his election as mayor in 1975, Hudnut was president of the National League of Cities in 1981 and received such honors as "Best Mayor in America" from City & State *magazine, the Woodrow Wilson Award for Public Service from Princeton University, and the Rosa Parks Award from the American Association for Affirmative Action. In 1987 he authored* Minister/Mayor, *a book reflecting on his dual careers in politics and religion. After leaving public life in early 1992, Hudnut served as a Fellow at the Institute of Politics at Harvard's Kennedy School and the Hudson Institute in Indianapolis. He is currently president of the Civic Federation in Chicago.*